İstanbul - 1435 / 2014

© Erkam Publications 2013 / 1435 H
ISBN: 978-9944-83-584-8

Erkam Publications
Ikitelli Organize Sanayi Bölgesi Mah.
Atatürk Bulvarı, Haseyad 1. Kısım No: 60/3-C
Başakşehir, Istanbul, Turkey
Tel: (+90-212) 671-0700 pbx
Fax: (+90-212) 671-0717
E-mail: info@islamicpublishing.net
Web site: http://islamicpublishing.net

All rights reserved. No part of this publication may be reproduced, stored in a retrieval system, or transmitted in any from or by any means, electronic, mechanical, photocopying, recording or otherwise, without the prior permission of the copyright owner.

The author	: Osman Nûri Topbaş
Origina title	: «Hak Din İSLAM» (İngilizce)
Translator	: Fulya VATANSEVER
Editor	: Süleyman DERİN
Graphics	: Râsim Şakiroğlu
Printed by	: Erkam Printhouse

ISLAM
THE RELIGION OF TRUTH

Osman Nûri Topbaş

ERKAM PUBLICATIONS

CONTENTS

PREFACE 8

Part 1
WHAT IS ISLAM? / 17

1. Allah Almighty Loves His Servants 17
2. The Greatest Need of the Human Being: Security and Peace 19
3. Islam: The Source of Peace and Salvation 21
   a. Human Beings Find Peace 21
   b. Animals Find Peace 32
   c. Trees and Plants Find Peace 37
   d. Inanimate Beings Find Peace 41
4. Islam Leads to Salvation in the Hereafter 48

Part 2
ESSENTIALS OF BELIEF / 55

1. The Declaration of Faith (Kalima al-Tawhid) 57
   a. Importance of the Declaration of Faith (*Kalima al-Tawhid*) 60
   b. Virtues of the Declaration of Faith (*Kalima al-Tawhid*) 64
2. Belief in Allah 67
   a. Proofs of the Existence and Unity of Allah 80

    b. Benefits of Belief in Allah 90
3. Belief in the Angels 92
4. Belief in the Books 94
    a. The Qur'an 95
        1) Characteristics 96
        2) Content 99
        3) Miraculousness 101
    a) Eloquence and Rhetoric 104
    b) Relating the Unseen 109
    c) Illuminating Scientific Discoveries 112
5. Belief in the Prophets 122
    a. The Last Prophet: Muhammad Mustafa 126
        1) His Noble Character 137
        2) His Striving for the Salvation of Humanity 154
        3) His Miracles 158
6. Belief in the Hereafter 170
7. Belief in Divine Destiny 181

Part 3
WORSHIP / 197

1. Ablution (*Wudu'*) and Cleanliness 204
2. The Prescribed Prayer 206
3. Fasting and the Month of Ramadan 213
4. The Alms-Tax (Zakat) 222
5. Pilgrimage (Hajj) 237
6. Other Forms of Worship 241

CONTENTS

Part 4
WORLDLY TRANSACTIONS and MORALITY / 247

1. Humility 251
2. Altruism and Generosity.. 259
3. Faithfulness and Trustworthiness 267
4. Grace and Refinement 272
5. Service 279
6. *Jihad* and the Struggle against Terror 282
    a. Islam is a Divine and True Religion 282
    b. Every Life is Sacred 284
    c. Individuality of the Crime 287
    d. Islamic Jihad 289
    e. Humane Treatment of Prisoners of War 296
    f. Working for the Welfare of all Humanity 299

EPILOGUE 305

PREFACE

Endless thanks be to our Lord Who created us out of nothing, in the best form, and Who favoured us with countless blessings.

Endless salutations and blessings be upon all the great Prophets – in particular the Eternal Pride of Humanity, the Final Prophet, the Seal of the Prophets – Muhammad Mustafa, upon him be peace and blessings, his household and his Companions.

Without a doubt, the human being has been created to perfection with regard to both their material and spiritual constitution and has been equipped with many a superior attribute enabling them to be a friend of the Truth. When beheld with the eye of the heart, it is impossible not to be left in admiration of the magnificence and brilliance of the favours and capacities bestowed expressly upon human beings as distinct from all other creation.

The Most High has created the human being in the best form as a proof of His Own power and majesty. Alongside bestowing upon them reason, heart, conviction and conscience, He has supported them with Prophets and scriptures in directing them towards eternal bliss. Moreover, He has declared the reason for their coming to the world and travelling to the world of the grave, to whom this dominion belongs, that this world is a place of learning filled with Divine trial and examination in order to test whose actions will be greater in excellence, and has revealed that this journey to eternity beginning

PREFACE

with the final breath continues as either happiness or disappointment. Thus, the compendium of commandments and prohibitions that Allah, the Most High, has made known for the happiness of His servants is referred to as **'religion'**.

Allah Almighty possesses endless mercy towards His servants. For this reason, He does not will for them to remain idle or unchecked for even a single moment, and for them to be enslaved to the desires of their carnal selves.[1] Consequently, being the most natural and instinctive source of serenity and repose for the human spirit, religion started with the first human being, Prophet Adam, upon him be peace. He is the first human and the first Prophet. Thus, from their first day on earth until the last, the family of humankind has attained the knowledge necessary for happiness in the world and in the Hereafter by means of the Prophets – the Messengers of Allah – in the best possible way, seeing and learning from living examples.

At times when, throughout the centuries, this knowledge was forgotten, lost or corrupted, Allah Almighty sent yet another Messenger and revealed once again the true nature of religion and favoured His servants with the truest instruction.[2]

Humanity has never been able to remain independent from religion due to their inherent predisposition to belief. As they distanced themselves from revelation and the Messengers, they lost the truth and instead turned to falsified beliefs. Academic research has shown that a belief in Allah, in one way or another, and remnants of true religion were unfailingly present in every tribe and society.[3]

History attests to the fact that human systems promising humankind happiness only in a worldly sense have always come and gone;

---

1. See: Insan, 76:36; Mu'minun, 23:115; Inshirah, 94:7-8.
2. See: Maryam, 19:34-59.
3. See: Günay Tümer, "Din" (Religion), *TDV Encyclopaedia of Islam*, IX, 315-317.

the Prophets, however, prescribing the formula for humankind's happiness in two worlds, have continued to live in hearts even after their earthborn existence.

In no age or era being deprived of the instruction and erudition of the Prophets, humanity continued its existence with the guidance of one hundred and twenty four thousand Prophets and, in reaching the end of time, was honoured with the final religion Islam, which responded to the needs of the time in the best possible way; Allah Almighty enabled Islam to reach perfection gradually through the Prophet's twenty-three year Prophethood and, as such, completed His favour upon His servants. For a blessing greater than that of the blessing of Islam is inconceivable. Subsequently, Allah Almighty declares that He approves only of Islam as a religion for His servants and that on no account will He accept from His servants any other.[4]

Under these circumstances, Islam, from its emergence onwards, is the religion of all humanity and is again the sole true religion that is acceptable and recognised before Allah. Thus, humanity can only reach happiness and tranquillity through Islam.

Islam possesses the most perfect conception of the world. In order for a system to be considered as having a perfected worldview, it needs to be able to provide answers to every kind of question within human imagination and comprehension, and these answers need to be systematic and harmonious and to also lie within a logical continuity. These characteristics, however, exist only within the Islamic worldview. The views of other religions or philosophical systems are either deficient or are replete with contradiction; they have not been able to establish rulings pertaining to worldly transactions (*mu'amalat*) and morality (*akhlaq*) completely. For instance Judaism, which was changed over time, was restricted to the Children of

---

4. See: Ma'ida, 5:3; Al-'Imran, 3:19, 85.

PREFACE

Israel. Also altered, Christianity was imprisoned merely between the heart of the servant and Allah, and was reduced to a system without any binding sanctions, regulation and application. Even principles of belief were determined by human beings seated in councils and were changed from time to time.

Islam, however, has been sent for all humanity and has conveyed a worldview and a system of principles of dealings embracing every aspect of life. Leaving no area unaddressed, it has regulated relations between people, to the smallest detail, in light of a set of key principles.

Allah Almighty declares that He sent Islam and Prophet Muhammad, upon him be peace and blessings, to all His servants as **"an unequalled mercy for all the worlds"**.[5] In spite of this, some were not able to know Islam for various reasons, or were raised in bigotry and negative conditioning towards it. For this reason, it is essential for Muslims to convey and teach Islam to human beings at every opportunity. Not accepting Islam after learning of it has been left to the individual will of human beings. The Almighty declares that His servants are free in this regard and that they will not be subjected to any compulsion. This is due to the fact that this world is, in all its splendour, a Divine arena of examination.

Allah Almighty would have bestowed guidance upon all His servants if He had so willed. However, the Almighty has held them in esteem and willed for them to choose the true path by using their own reason and independent willpower.[6]

However, this freedom given to human beings does not mean that they will not be accountable for their own actions. The Most

---

5. See: Nisa, 4:79; A'raf, 7:158; Anbiya, 21:107; Saba, 34:28; Bukhari, Tayammum, 1.
6. See: Yunus, 10:99; Kahf, 18:29; Zumar, 39:7; Jathiyah, 45:15; M. F. 'Abd al-Baqi, *al-Mu'jam*, "r-w-d", "sh-y-' ".

High has put forth all proofs indicating that the final religion that He sent is the path of truth and has bestowed human beings a mind with which to comprehend this. That is, in order for His servants to find the true path, He has provided them with reason, the power of contemplation, Prophets and scriptures and every kind of ease and convenience. Perhaps the most magnificent miracle in all of these is His favouring humankind with the Qur'an. This favour is the most vivid manifestation of the mercy and love of the Most High towards His servants, which will continue until the Day of Judgement. If, despite this, human beings fail to follow the religion that Allah sent and instead pursue their own vain desires and passions, the Qur'an clearly reveals the kind of punishment they are to face in return.

It was my hope, in this humble work, to help those, even if ever so slightly, who are not adequately acquainted with Islam to understand it better. I endeavoured to briefly introduce it as a perfected world-view, in respect to its belief, worship, dealings and morality. This endeavour is, at the same time, a religious responsibility for every Muslim, for which they will be held to account in the Hereafter. That is, conveying the religion that our Lord sent to all humankind is the most important duty of Muslims. Those failing to fulfil this duty will be called to a difficult account before Allah, on the Day of Judgement. For this reason, every Muslim must exert proper effort to convey the message of Islam, in accordance with their ability, by feeling a sense of responsibility in the state of humankind's affairs. The responsibility after this belongs to those who hear but refuse to accept it.

On the other hand, it is also essential for every human being living in our time to research and acquaint themselves with Islam for this is the most fundamental mission that the Creator of humankind has charged them with. Preparing opportunity and facility for this is an obligation of His Muslim servants, upon whom He has bestowed guidance.

PREFACE

It is a very stark reality that happiness in the world and in the Hereafter depends on obedience to Allah and His Messenger. Those fortunate ones who have succeeded in this have been recorded in the record of the righteous and have been favoured with the love, honour and grace of the Most High. However, those who turn away despite having heard the truths of belief, have departed from this realm as those poor souls who will remain thus in the Hereafter also, and have been subjected to Divine punishment. How meaningful it is, that the world to which they have attached themselves – being deluded by its carnal charms and their thus forgetting the Hereafter – has not mourned their loss.

Former generations, the showcase of positive or negative memories, are in this sense a clear sign from which to take lessons. The firmaments above us are those same firmaments which poured affliction and disaster on those who denied Allah in the past. The sun above us is the same sun which once illuminated the manors and palaces of many an oppressor such as the Pharaoh, Haman, Qarun and Nimrod and which then rose above their ruins. The firmament that would, as always, adorn the hearts of humankind once more is the firmament of Islam, and the unique lamp to dispel the darkness of heedlessness and overwhelm it with light is the sun of belief. Hence, incumbent upon humankind is their coming to know their Lord beneath the firmament of Islam and the sun of belief and be a servant to Him.

Taking this opportunity, I would like to express my thanks to Dr. Murat Kaya and my other students, for their contributions to this work; I beseech the Almighty that this service of theirs be a 'perpetual charity' for them.

O my Lord, do not deprive us of the luminous trace of the Prophets and the spiritual blessing of Your exalted Book. Allow all humankind to practice Islam, the religion of truth, by believing in

its actual and true form in Your Supreme presence and, as such, be included among the servants with whom You are well pleased.

Amin...

Osman Nuri Topbaş
August, 2012
Üsküdar, Istanbul

Part 1

What is Islam?

A society that has been able to absorb Islam into all its particles like the fragrance of a rose, so to speak, duly perceiving it with its spirit and form, builds a 'civilisation of virtue', just as has been the case in a great many stages throughout our illustrious and noble history. Believers possessing such a quality are the fortunate ones who have attained happiness in both worlds, regardless of the time and space in which they live.

And so, the peace and happiness of the journey of life, each facet surrounded by surprises and unknowns, is contingent upon adequately acquiring a share in the spiritual fabric of Islam.

WHAT IS ISLAM?

1. Allah Almighty Loves His Servants

Allah, the Most High, has favoured humankind in ways very different to other creation for He loves His servants much and has great mercy towards them. The thousand and one masterpieces that we constantly observe around us with great awe, the Divine embroidery and manifestations of Divine power are presented to us as each a letter of love, so to speak. It is revealed in a Qur'anic verse in relation to these bounties:

"He has also made of service to you whatever is in the heavens and whatever is on the earth, all is from Him (a gift of His Grace). **Surely in this there are (clear) signs for a people who reflect."** (Jathiyah, 45:13)

Again, in Qur'anic verses, Allah Almighty declares His love for His servants as follows:

"...Allah will raise up a people whom He loves, and who love Him..." (Ma'ida, 5:54)

"Allah is All-Pitying towards His servants." (Baqara, 2:207; Al-'Imran, 3:30)

Our Lord, the Supreme, reveals His love for His servants in a great many verses, in various contexts. For instance, He declares that

He loves "who are devoted to doing good"[7], "who turn to Him in sincere repentance" and "who cleanse themselves"[8], "the God-revering, pious"[9], "the patient and steadfast"[10], "who put their trust (in Him)"[11] and "the scrupulously equitable"[12].

The Messenger of Allah, upon him be peace and blessings, also reveals that Allah Almighty loves His servants who treat others with kindness[13], are pious, God-conscious, free from want, hidden from fame, preoccupied with reforming their carnal selves[14], are modest[15], virtuous, obedient and humble[16]. Again, the Most High treats those virtuous servants of His who shun a livelihood from begging and illicit earnings[17], who work to provide for their household[18], become fatigued in pursuit of the permissible[19], practice asceticism in relation to the world[20], show tolerance when selling, buying, repaying and requesting repayment of a debt[21], draw near to Him through obligatory and supererogatory worship[22], carry out their work in the best way[23], are of benefit to others[24], are generous[25],

---

7. Baqara, 2:195.
8. Baqara, 2:222.
9. Al-'Imran, 3:76.
10. Al-'Imran, 3:146.
11. Al-'Imran, 3:159.
12. Ma'ida, 5:42.
13. Bukhari, Adab, 35.
14. Muslim, Zuhd, 11.
15. Abu Dawud, Hammam, 1:4012.
16. Ibn Maja, Fitan, 16.
17. Ibn Maja, Zuhd, 5.
18. Daylami, *Musnad*, I, 155.
19. Suyuti, *al-jami' al-saghir*, I, 65.
20. Ibn Maja, Zuhd, 1.
21. Muwatta', Buyu', 46.
22. Bukhari, Riqaq, 38; Ibn Maja, Fitan, 16.
23. Daylami, *Musnad*, I, 157.
24. Hathami, VIII, 191.
25. Suyuti, *al-jami' al-saghir*, I, 60.

persistent in supplication[26], and love, visit and get along with one another for Allah's sake[27].

This means to say, Allah Almighty has created a great many causes by way of loving His servants. He immerses them in the ocean of love and mercy in one way or another. One of His most beautiful names is the **All-Loving (al-Wadud)** – the One Who loves much and is loved much...

The Almighty's creating human beings in the best way, bestowing upon them every kind of blessing, always forgiving their sins and delaying their punishment so as to give them a chance to repent, is the most explicit proof of how much He loves them. Again as a manifestation of this love and mercy, our Exalted Lord has revealed, in detail, the things that are of benefit and those that are harmful in both this world and in the Hereafter. The greatest blessing bestowed upon human beings is this. Allah Almighty wills for His servants to become friends to Him by observing these principles, and for them to attain eternal tranquillity as a result.

For this reason, the Almighty has established human nature upon the realities of belief in His Divinity and has embellished it with sacred rapture. In the depths of the human heart there lies a sense of truth and justice, a strong need for belief and the desire to know Allah through the heart, known as *ma'rifa*, and reach Him. These manifestations have, without a doubt, become apparent throughout history with the blessing of the practice of Islam.

2. The Greatest Need of the Human Being: Security and Peace

At the fore of the worldly needs of humankind are security and peace. It is elemental for a person to be protected from all kinds of

---

26. Suyuti, *al-jami' al-saghir*, I, 65.
27. Ahmad, V, 229.

oppression and to secure their rights, hence finding felicity in this world as well as in the Hereafter. One who is not secure in the place in which they live can have no peace and comfort. The most influential power guaranteeing this security are the Divine laws that Allah, glory unto Him, has decreed – that is, Islam.

The Most High indicates this fact as follows:

"(At least) **for (Allah's constant) favor of concord and security to the Quraysh, their concord and security in their winter and summer journeys, let them worship the Lord of this House** (the Ka'ba)**, Who has provided them with food against hunger, and made them safe from fear."** (Quraish, 106:1-4)

Man-made systems and laws are far from ensuring this security and tranquillity for they have no spiritual dimension. Prior to the emergence of Islam, the world was enveloped in a deep darkness of ignorance. Enjoying their rights belonged only to those with might. The powerless had no rights and were seen as deserving of oppression. Human beings were crushed beneath an inexpressible tyranny and persecution. Famous Turkish poet **Mehmed Akif** expresses the end of this state with the advent of Islam in the following words:

Weakness, its entire lot being oppression, was revived;
Tyranny, never considering doom, died!

Allah Almighty favoured the Quraysh tribe with a unique security in such an environment, out of His Divine grace. Comfortably conducting their political, commercial and cultural undertakings within this security, they attained material and spiritual riches and repose. When the time came, the Almighty raised up from among them His Last Prophet. By means of him, the Most High taught humankind the principles of peace, felicity and security.

3. Islam: The Source of Peace and Salvation

The word 'Islam' has such meanings as security, salvation, peace, tranquillity, submission and attaining repose. This demonstrates that the religion of Islam conferred upon the entire world a complete security, salvation and peace, in every sense. That is to say, Islam grants comfort and tranquillity not only to human beings, but to animals, plants and even inanimate beings also. The twenty three years of the Prophethood of the Messenger of Allah, upon him be peace and blessings, were spent with struggle against every kind of terror; ultimately, a religion of truth serving as a source of eternal peace and security was bestowed to this world.

a. Human Beings Find Peace

Islam raises the human being out from every kind of oppression, injustice and misery, into security. Muslim scholars maintain that the objective of religion is to establish and protect the five principles known as the **essentials of religion** (*zarurat al-diniyya*):

a) The protection of religion;

b) The protection of life;

c) The protection of mental health;

d) The protection of dignity, honour and, as a result, the preservation of progeny; and

b) The protection of property.

When these five principles are protected, the human being attains a complete peace and security.

Islam has placed well-founded laws for the protection of each of these principles and has delineated the prohibited (*haram*) and the permissible (*halal*). Islam's rulings pertaining to mundane worldly matters, known as *mu'amalat*, are more so concerned with these.

Prior to the emergence of Islam, people's belief, worship, dealings and everyday lives were in a pitiful state. Just as there was no security of life, property and honour, there was also no belief, worship and morality which would exalt the human being. People would worship the idols they made out of *halva*[28] and would eat them when they became hungry. They would command their slaves to make for them idols of wood and stone and would later anticipate help from these. When travellers camped in a certain place, they would take four stones, placing three beneath their cooking pot as coal for their fire and worship the fourth as their deity.

Abu Raja' al-'Utaridi says the following in regard to this practice:

"We used to worship stones [before Islam]. But when we found a better stone than the first one, we would throw the first one and take the latter. If we could not get hold of a stone then we would collect some earth (soil), bring a sheep and milk that sheep over it, and then circumambulate it." (Bukhari, Maghazi, 70)

Islam abolished such erroneous beliefs, which reduced human dignity to nought. It brought the exalted beliefs, worship and morality that elevated the honour and integrity of the human being. It ordered every area of human life in the best possible way. Muslims tasting the sublime feelings bestowed by Islam displayed great sacrifices in order for others to benefit from this great blessing also. A noteworthy example in this regard is as follows:

When **Umm Sulaym**, may Allah be well pleased with her, was proposed marriage by **Abu Talha**, who was very eager to marry her, she based her acceptance on the condition of his abandoning idol worship and embracing Islam. Addressing him, she said:

---

28. A kind of sweet made out of sugar and flour.

"Consider the stones that you worship. They can neither benefit not harm you. And consider the idols you make from trees. Someone comes, cuts down a tree and fashions it and then you worship it as a god. If you throw it into the fire, it will turn to ashes. Are you not ashamed to worship wood that grows out the earth and is fashioned by an Abyssinian slave? If you pronounce the Declaration of Faith and declare your allegiance to the Messenger of Allah, I will marry you and ask nothing of you [in way of bridal due]."

The words that he had heard countless times prior to this moment finally affected Abu Talha and became a means for him to be honoured with belief. Overjoyed by this, Umm Sulaym, may Allah be well pleased with her, accepted Abu Talha's acceptance of Islam as her dowry and married him without asking for anything, when she was in actual face in a position to demand as much worldly wealth as she wished. In other words, her marriage dovry was **Islam**.[29]

The Messenger of Allah, upon him be peace and blessings, vividly expresses the principle that is to ensure the security and peace of all humanity:

"No one is fully a believer until he wishes for his brother what he wishes for himself." (Bukhari, Iman, 7; Muslim, Iman, 71-72)

Sure enough, when human beings practise this altruism mentioned in the Prophetic Tradition, problems in society would be minimised and injustice would come to an end.

Islam: The Religion of Truth and Justice

The following Divine commandment prescribes a remedy for the greatest cause of unrest between human beings:

---

29. See: Nasa'i, Nikah, 63:3340-1; Ibn Sa'd, Tabaqat, VIII:426-427; Ibn al-Athir, Usd al-Ghaba, VII:333.

"**And do not consume your wealth among yourselves in false ways** (in vanities, sins and crimes such as theft, usurpation, bribery, usury, and gambling); **nor proffer it to those in authority so that you may sinfully consume a portion of other people's goods, and that knowingly.**" (Baqara, 2:188)

The Messenger of Allah, upon him be peace and blessings, once asked his Companions:

"Do you know who the bankrupt person is?" They replied:

"A bankrupt person amongst us is the one who has neither money nor property." Allah's Messenger, upon him be peace and blessings, said:

"The bankrupt person of my community is he who will come on the Day of Judgement with prayer and fast and giving great amounts in charity. And at the same time, he will come having insulted this one, and slandered that one, and unlawfully consumed the wealth of the other, and shed the blood of yet others and having beaten others still. Then any person whom he has wronged will be given from his good deeds on that Day. And if his good deeds are exhausted until he clears the account concerning all of the people he has oppressed, the sins of those people whom he has wronged will be transferred to his account and thereafter, he will be thrown into Hellfire." (Muslim, Birr, 59; Tirmidhi, Qiyama, 2; Ahmad, II:303, 324, 372)

A person who has wholeheartedly submitted to Islam, in consideration of such Qur'anic verses and Prophetic Traditions, cannot even think of causing even the slightest harm to anyone.

The understanding of **justice** that Islam brought is above every other conception. An example of such examples is as follows:

On the day of Badr, the Messenger of Allah, upon him be peace and blessings, straightened the ranks of his Companions using an arrow that was in his hand. As he passed by **Sawad ibn Ghaziya**, who was standing out of line, he pricked him in his belly with the arrow, saying,

"Stand in line, O Sawad!" Sawad, may Allah be well pleased with him, responded saying,

"You have hurt me, O Messenger of Allah. Allah has sent you with truth and justice, so allow me to retaliate". The Messenger then uncovered his belly and said,

"Go ahead, retaliate." Becoming anxious, the Ansar exclaimed,

"O Sawad! He is the Messenger of Allah!" in an attempt to bring him to his senses. Sawad, may Allah be well pleased with him, replied,

"No human being has superiority over another when it comes to justice." The Messenger of Allah, upon him be peace and blessings, repeated:

"Have your retaliation." Sawad embraced him and kissed his stomach. Allah's Messenger, upon him be peace and blessings, asked:

"What induced you to do that, Sawad?"

"O Messenger of Allah," he replied, "You see the situation we are in. I was not sure that I would not be killed, and I wanted my last recollection of you to be that my skin had touched yours."

The Messenger of Allah, upon him be peace and blessings, prayed for his welfare and heartened him.[30]

Showing painstaking attention to the rights of all creation throughout his life, the Messenger of Allah, upon him be peace and blessings, was even concerned for the rights of others while on his

---

30. Ibn Hisham, II:266-267; Waqidi, I:57; Ibn Sa'd, III:516. Cf. Abu Dawud, Adab, 148-149:5224; Diyat, 14:4536.

deathbed and, despite his weakened state, mounted the pulpit and declared:

"My Companions! If I have dispossessed anyone of any wealth, let him come forth and seize his from me." If I have (unwittingly) lashed the back of anyone, let him come forward and lash my back in return. If there be any such men as these, let them come forth without fear of retaliation or hatred, for neither of these become of me." [31]

Islam: The Religion of Grace and Kindness

Islam teaches Muslims to live their lives in consideration of the Day of Judgement and not to violate the rights of anyone else. The Messenger of Allah, upon him be peace and blessings, has succinctly described the perfected believer in the following way:

"The Muslims are those from whose tongues and hands other Muslims are safe and sound." (Bukhari, Iman, 4-5.)

Indeed, throughout their education and worship a Muslim receives training in **'harmlessness'**. They then reach such a point that no one ever thinks that any harm can come from them. Such a believer always infuses peace and trust to their surroundings.

The Messenger of Allah, upon him be peace and blessings, states:

*"The believer is comparable to the **honeybee** which eats that which is pure and wholesome and produces that which is pure and wholesome. When it lands on something it does not break or ruin it."*[32]

The honeybee is a creature that is extremely proficient, skilled, clever, useful and humble. It even works during the night. It always eats of clean and pleasant things. It gathers its provisions from flow-

---

31. See: Ibn Sa'd, II:255; Tabari, Tarih, III:190; Ahmad, III:400.
32. See: Ahmad, II:199; Hakim, I:147; Bayhaqi, *Shu'ab al-Iman*, V:58; Suyuti, *al-Jami'*, 8147.

ers. It follows and obeys its leader. Its nuisance and harm is very slight. It steers clear of things that are unclean and does not consume the earnings of another.

In exactly the same way as the honeybee, the believer earns a licit livelihood, eats of the licit and is present in places that are pure. They exude mercy in every place they are present. They hurt no one and are not hurt by anyone. When they err, they immediately redress their error and constantly maintain their character and dignity. They are humble and strive for the welfare of all people. They shun oppression, heedlessness, dissension, wrongdoing and the vain desires and whims of the carnal self.

A society with individuals like honeybees will of course attain the peak of peace and security. The Messenger of Allah, upon him be peace and blessings, gave the glad tidings of this in the early years of Islam:

Khabbab ibn Arat, may Allah be well pleased with him, explains:

One day the Messenger of Allah, upon him be peace and blessings, was sitting in the shadow of the Ka'ba, leaning against his cloak. We complained to him (about our state) and said,

"O Messenger of Allah, will you pray to Allah (for our relief)?"

The Messenger of Allah, upon him be peace and blessings, was greatly moved and, with his colour altered, he straightened himself up and said,

"Among those who were before you a (believer) used to be seized and a pit used to be dug for him and then he used to be placed in it. Their bones were scraped with combs of iron and their bodies were sawn into two from head to toe, yet, all this did not cause them to abandon their religion. By Allah! Allah will assuredly complete this religion and make it triumphant, till a rider (traveller) goes from Sana' (the capital of Yemen) to Hadramut fearing nothing save Allah and the wolf lest it should attack his sheep, but you are impatient." (Bukhari, Manaqib, 25; Isti'zan, 35; Manaqib al-Ansar, 29; Abu Dawud, Jihad, 97:2649.)

Again, Allah's Messenger, upon him be peace and blessings, said to **'Adiyy ibn Hatim**, who was hesitant about becoming a Muslim:

"Perhaps, O Adiyy, the only reason that prevents you from entering this religion is what you see of the destitution of the Muslims and their poverty. Do you know Al-Hirah?" He said,

"I do not know it, but I have heard of it." The Messenger of Allah, upon him be peace and blessings, said:

"I swear by Him in whose hand is my soul, Allah will assuredly perfect this religion **such that a woman will come out from Hiram until she circumambulates the Ka'ba without her being given protection by any person,** *and the treasures of Chosroes the son of Hormuz will be opened."* He said,

"The treasures of Chosroes the son of Hormuz?"' Allah's Messenger, upon him be peace and blessings, said,

"Yes, the treasures of Chosroes the son of Hormuz, and wealth will be given until there will be no one who will accept it."

Adiyy, may Allah be well pleased with him, later said:

"I (lived long enough and) saw a woman travel and circumambulate the Ka'ba without any fear except that of Allah and I was among those who opened the treasure of Chosroes the son of Hormuz. By the One in Whose Hand is my soul, the third thing will also come to pass, because the Messenger of Allah, upon him be peace and blessings, said it."[33]

---

33. See: Bukhari, Manaqib, 25; Ahmad, IV:257, 377-379; Ibn Hisham, IV:246; Ibn Kathir, *Al-Bidaya*, V:62.

Indeed, Islam aims to ensure that human beings live in a privileged environment of peace in which they fear none but Allah. Financial prosperity is also engendered as a result. Indeed, in the era of 'Umar ibn 'Abd al-'Aziz, the Muslims had appealed to the Caliph to ask him what they were to do with their prescribed annual alms (*zakat*), as they could not find any needy person to which they could offer them.[34]

Islam: The Religion of Magnanimity

The Messenger of Allah, upon him be peace and blessings, had granted written amnesty to a great number of people. In his work on the Prophet's letters of diplomacy, Professor Muhammad Hamidullah states that he has seen a great many copies of the Messenger's **declarations of amnesty** in various countries. The following recollection in regard to one of these arrests the attention:

When Istanbul was conquered, many delegations of neighbouring rulers came with offers of congratulations for the conquest. Among these was the Greek Patriarch of Jerusalem, Athanasios IV. Entering the presence of Sultan Mehmed II, the Patriarch showed him the declaration of amnesty that the Messenger of Allah signed with his fingerprint as well as documents from the time of Caliph 'Umar written in the Kufi calligraphic script. He requested that the places of worship in Jerusalem remain as they were. Affirming the rights that were bestowed by the Messenger of Allah to the letter, Sultan Mehmet II penned a royal decree and added the stipulation, "Damned by the curse of Allah be the one who overrules this Imperial Edict!" This decree is currently held in the Prime Ministry Ottoman Archives, *Kilise Defteri*, no. 8.[35]

---

34. See: Bayhaqi, *Dala'il al-Nubuwwa*, VI:493; Muhammad Sa'id Ramadan al-Buti, *Fiqh al-Sirah*, 434.
35. Ziya Demirel, Avni Arslan, *Osmanlı'da Peygamber Sevgisi*, Ankara 2009, 63; http://www.turkislamtarihi.nl/makaleler/kudus.php

By virtue of the principles of Islam, the Muslim community had reached such a point that those living under their administration, whether Christian or Jew, lived in affluence and were contented with their lives. They even rejected the rule of their coreligionists and invited the Muslims to their lands, to administer them with justice.

Bernard Lewis says:

"The Ottoman Empire affected Europe in a number of ways... For merchants, manufacturers, and later financiers, it was a rich and increasingly open market, and for many also it exercised a powerful fascination. The disaffected and the ambitious were attracted by Ottoman opportunity... Downtrodden peasants looked hopefully to the enemies of their masters. **Martin Luther** in his 'Admonition to prayer against the Turk', published in 1541, gave warning that the poor, oppressed by greedy princes, landlords and burghers, might well prefer to live under the Turks rather than under Christians such as these."[36]

Islam: The Religion of Compassion

Islam is a religion of compassion. Compassion is one of the most important tenets of the religion of Islam, so much so that the heading of the Book of Allah, the *'Basmala'*, mentions the names the **All-Merciful** and the **All-Compassionate** in juxtaposition to the name Allah. In the first chapter immediately following the *Basmala*, the same names have been repeated in the second verse of the Opening chapter entitled *al-Fatiha*. Allah Almighty has revealed the attribute **All-Merciful** as the first word in a later chapter, and this Divine attribute has also become the eponym for the chapter.

---

36. Bernard Lewis, *The Middle East: A Brief History of the Last 2,000 Years*, New York: Scribner, 1995, 128.

Stating herein, **"The All-Merciful He has taught the Qur'an,"** it is indicated that the Qur'an has been presented to humankind as a requirement of Divine mercy. That the Qur'an is **"a healing and a mercy"** is explicitly mentioned in the Qur'anic chapter Isra'. (Isra', 17:82)

In the other chapters of the Qur'an, compassion and mercy are repeated and encouraged hundreds of times.

One of the most exalted characteristics that Allah Almighty has bestowed upon His Prophets is mercy.

Most particularly, according to the declaration, **"We have not sent you (O Muhammad) but as an unequalled mercy for all the worlds,"**[37] this characteristic constitutes a pinnacle in the Messenger of Allah, upon him be peace and blessings, to which no one else is able to attain. An example of his unparalleled mercy is as follows:

When the armies met during the Battle of Badr, the Messenger of Allah, upon him be peace and blessings, sent envoys to the Makkan polytheists for conciliation. During this time, the enemy faced a drought. A group of Makkan polytheists, among them **Hakim ibn Hizam**, came to drink water from the well of the Muslims. When the Muslims wanted to prevent them, Allah's Messenger, upon him be peace and blessings, said,

"Allow them to drink!" They then came and drank. (Ibn Hisham, II:261)

It can be said that in Islam the first fruit of belief is mercy. The friends of Allah, who spend their lives along such a course, have described servanthood briefly through these two dimensions:

a. Fulfilling the commandments of Allah in due reverence;

---

37. Anbiya 21:107.

b. Showing mercy and compassion to the created by virtue of the Creator.

Islam is a religion of mercy. While humankind, which has stumbled into many a pit of sin and heedlessness, has become deserving of ruin and disappointment as a result of their doings, Allah Almighty wills to draw them into a climate of felicity by forever enveloping them with wings of mercy and forgiveness. His declaring, *"My mercy takes precedence over My wrath,"*[38] is a vivid demonstration of this.

Thus, it can be said that a society that duly practises Islam becomes a society of peace. Its citizens both live therein in security in terms of their worldly life and at the same time look to their continued existence in the Hereafter with hope. The Messenger of Allah, upon him be peace and blessings, states:

"He is successful who has accepted Islam, who has been bestowed with sufficient provision and has been made contented by Allah with what He has given him." (Muslim, Zakat, 125. Also refer to: Tirmidhi, Zuhd, 35:2348.)

b. Animals Find Peace

Prior to the Messenger of Allah, upon him be peace and blessings, being sent to humankind, those who were weak as well as women were not even valued. It is self-evident, then, that animals would not be regarded in such a society. Animals, in a pitiable state, would both serve human beings and would live in suffering and anguish, one on top of the other. When Allah's Messenger, upon him be peace and blessings, arrived, they were saved from oppression and were now at ease.

Abu Waqid, may Allah be well pleased with him, explains:

---

38. Bukhari, Tawhid, 15, 22; Muslim, Tawba, 14-16.

"When the Prophet, upon him be peace and blessings, came to Madina, the people used to like [eating] the humps of camels and would cut off the fat tails of sheep. He said:

"Whatever is cut off from an animal while it is alive is carrion and cannot be eaten." (Tirmidhi, Sayd, 12:1480)

In so doing, he rescued animals from this agonising and brutal torment.

The Messenger, may Allah bless him and grant him peace, cursed those who tied animals up and shot at them from a distance and who used any living thing as a target. (Bukhari, Zaba'ih, 25)

Similarly, he forbade the killing of animals in vain and leisure. He states in a narration:

"If someone kills a sparrow for sport, the sparrow will cry out on the Day of Judgement,

"O Lord! That person killed me for nothing! He did not kill me for any useful purpose!" (Nasa'i, Dahaya, 42)

Islam commands human beings to treat animals with mercy and to shun behaviour that causes them pain and suffering.

"A man said, 'O Messenger of Allah, I was going to slaughter a sheep and then I felt sorry for it (or 'sorry for the sheep I was going to slaughter')'. He said twice,

'Since you showed mercy to the sheep, Allah will show mercy to you.'" (Ahmad, III:436; Hakim, IV:257)

Again, Allah's Messenger, upon him be peace and blessings, states:

"Whoever shows mercy even when slaughtering a bird (for food), Allah will have mercy on him on the Day of Judgement." (Tabarani, Kabir, VIII:234:7915; Bayhaqi, Shu'ab, VII:482.)

The Messenger of Allah, upon him be peace and blessings, entered an orchard belonging to one of the Madinan natives (Ansar) and there saw a camel. When the camel saw him, it began to groan and its eyes shed tears. The Messenger of Allah, upon him be peace and blessings, approached it and patted it on the hump and behind its ears until it quieted down. Then he asked,

"Who is the owner of this camel?" An Ansari youth stepped forward and said:

"It is mine, O Messenger of Allah!" The Pride of Humanity said,

"Do you not fear Allah concerning this beast which Allah has placed in your possession? This camel is complaining to me that you give it too little to eat and overburden it with work." (Abu Dawud, Jihad, 44:2549.)

Sawad ibn Rabi', may Allah be well pleased with him, relates the following extraordinary example of such refinement and mercy:

"I came before the Messenger of Allah, upon him be peace and blessings, and requested something from him. He instructed that a few (between three to five) camels be given to me and then he advised:

"When you return home, tell the members of your household that they should take very good care of the animals and feed them well. Instruct them to clip their nails before milking the camels so as to avoid hurting them." (Ahmad, III:484; Haythami, V:168, 259, VIII:196)

Again, Allah's Messenger, upon him be peace and blessings, had encountered a man milking his sheep and said to him,

"O So-and-so, leave some milk for its young when you milk an animal!" (Hathami, VIII:196).

One of the Companions, **Abu al-Darda'**, may Allah be well pleased with him, once came across some people who had overburdened their camels. The camels were unable to stand to the weight they carried on their backs. After immediately relieving the camel of its excess load, Abu al-Darda', may Allah be well pleased with him, said to its owners,

"If Allah, the Most High, forgives you of this torture that you have inflicted on these animals, then He would have shown you a great forgiveness indeed, for I once heard the Messenger of Allah, upon him be peace and blessings, say:

"Fear Allah in your treatment of these mute animals. When you are journeying through a fertile land, go slowly so that your camels graze. And when you pass through a barren and dry land, go quickly so that your animals don't get hungry and weak." (Ibn Hajar, Matalib al-'Aliya, IX:346:1978)

As a result of these injunctions of Allah's Messenger, Muslims showed the kindness and courtesy which even human beings were not deemed worthy of prior to the emergence Islam, to animals. On one occasion, the Messenger of Allah, upon him be peace and blessings, had set off from Madina for Makka dressed in pilgrim garb (*ihram*). He travelled until he reached the well of al-Uthaba, located between ar-Ruwaytha and al-'Arj (between Makka and Madina), where he unexpectedly came upon a **gazelle** which was curled up asleep in some shade. The master of creation, may Allah bless him and grant him peace, ordered someone to stand watch by its side to ensure that no one disturbed it until everyone had passed by. (Muwatta, Hajj, 79; Nasa'i, Hajj, 78)

The Prophet and his Companions displayed yet another remarkable example of the way animals ought to be treated when heading towards Makka for its conquest. This attitude was also an expression of the manner of looking at creation through the eyes of the Creator. When the master of creation set off from al-'Arj in the direction of Talub, with a magnificent army of ten thousand men, he saw a dog stretched over its puppies and feeding them. Immediately summoning **Ju'ayl ibn Suraqa** to his presence, he instructed him to stand guard over the animals, cautioning him to take due care that the dog and her young were not startled by the Muslim forces. (Waqidi, II:804)

It can be understood from this that Allah Almighty does not will for even a single ant to be disturbed. In point of fact, it is indicated in the Qur'an that the stupendous army of **Prophet Solomon**, upon him be peace, were most careful with respect to not trampling upon ants unwittingly. (See, Naml, 27:18)

Another noteworthy example of such an attitude is related by **Bayazid al-Bistami**. Returning from Makka, he once stopped over in Hamadan and purchased from there some black cumin. When he returned to his homeland Bistam, he saw a few ants in the black cumin that he had purchased.

Exclaiming, "I have deprived these ants of their homeland," he set off for Hamadan once again and returned the ants to the place from which he took them. (Farid al-Din Attar, *Tazkirat al-Awliya*, I:176)

Muslims even established charitable trusts for animals and, as such, fed hungry animals, treated those that were ill and sheltered birds that were unable to migrate. It is a reflection of this mercy that foreigners travelling to Ottoman lands relate in their memoirs that the cats and dogs living in Muslim neighbourhoods revolved around human beings, while in other neighbourhoods they fled at the sight of them.

In short, Islam has also established laws pertaining to animals. In the Age of Ignorance, people had forgotten that animals had rights also and that they needed to be treated with kindness. They certainly could not have presumed that treating animals with compassion could be meritorious. The Messenger of Allah, upon him be peace and blessings, once said:

"While a man was walking on his way he became extremely thirsty. He found a well, he went down into it to drink water. Upon leaving it, he saw a dog which was panting and lolling its tongue out of thirst. It was licking the moist earth due to its extreme thirst. The man thought to himself:

'This dog is extremely thirsty, as was I.' So he descended into the well, filled up his leather sock with water, and holding it in his teeth, climbed up and quenched the thirst of the dog. Allah Almighty was well pleased with his action and forgave his sins."

The Companions asked:

"Shall we be rewarded for showing kindness to animals also?"

The Messenger of Allah, upon him be peace and blessings, said,

"A reward is given in connection with every living creature".
(Bukhari, Shurb, 9; Muslim, Salam, 153)

c. Trees and Plants Find Peace

The germination and sprouting of seeds and their developing into majestic trees, and the countless species of herbs, fruits, vegetables and flowers, in myriad colours, that grow out of the same soil are extraordinary phenomena that deserve reflection. A mind that contemplates these will ultimately reach Allah Almighty, Who creates everything in the best way, and such a mind will delve into observation of such beautiful attributes as His majesty, power, compassion and beauty.

Thus, Muslims gaze upon all living things and plants, the manifestation of Allah Almighty's matchless masterpiece, as a Divine trust. They do not pluck them unnecessarily or use them carelessly.

Islam has prohibited certain actions such as cutting down trees, plucking grass, hunting and even assisting therein, for believers who are in pilgrim dress (in a state of *ihram*) or who are in the sacred Haram region, and has established various penalties for those who violate these prohibitions. In this way, He has willed for the believers to, in time, attain such a state where they do not even commit the slightest of wrongdoing and where they do not harm any plant or living thing, a state expressing 'harmlessness' in the complete sense.

Declaring the city of Madina and the Ta'if region as a sanctuary also in addition to Makka, the Messenger of Allah, upon him be peace and blessings, has forbidden[39] destroying vegetation and hunting therein, saying,

"The leaves should not be beaten off and the trees should not be cut in the protected land of the Messenger of Allah, upon him be peace and blessings, but the leaves can be beaten off softly (out of necessity) for the fodder of one's camel." (Abu Dawud, Hajj, 95-96:2039)

Again, in reference to the grazing pasture of the **Banu Harith**, the Prophet said,

"Whoever cuts down a tree in this area must plant another in its place."[40]

Abu Du'shum al-Juhani's grandfather relates:

"The Messenger of Allah, upon him be peace and blessings, saw a Bedouin hitting the branches of a tree with the stick in his hand so that its leaves would fall and become feed for his animals. He said to those next to him,

---

39. Abu Dawud, Manasik, 96; Muhammad Hamidullah, *İslâm Peygamberi*, I:500; Muhammad Hamidullah, *al-Wasa'iq*, Beirut 1969, 236-238, 240.
40. Baladhuri, *Futuh al-Buldan*, 17; İbrahim Canan, *İslam ve Çevre Sağlığı*, Istanbul 1987, 59-60.

'Go and bring the Bedouin to me, but treat him with kindness and do not alarm him.' When the Bedouin approached, the Messenger of Allah, upon him be peace and blessings, said,

'O Bedouin, shed the tree's leaves gently and with kindness, not by beating and hitting.'

I still remember the man with the leaves upon his head." (Ibn al-Athir, *Usd al-Ghaba*, VI:351)

While the Prophet, upon him be peace and blessings, protected existing vegetation on the one hand, he encouraged revegetation and regrowth on the other. He once said,

"Even if the end of time is upon you and you have a sapling in your hand, plant it at once!" (Ahmad, III:191, 183)

What glad tidings the following Prophetic Tradition constitutes for those who plant trees:

"There is no Muslim who plants a plant or a tree, except that whatever is eaten from it is a charity for him. Whatever is stolen from that is a charity for him. Whatever is eaten from it by an animal is a charity for him. Whatever a bird eats is a charity for him; no one suffers a loss except that it will be a charity for him till the Day of Judgement." (Muslim, Musaqat, 7)

One of the leading figures among the Companions, **Abu al-Darda'**, may Allah be well pleased with him, was once planting a tree in Damascus. A person approached him and asked, in bewilderment,

"Are you planting this even though you are one of the Companions of Allah's Messenger?" Abu al-Darda' replied,

"Do not hasten to judgement; I heard the Messenger of Allah, upon him be peace and blessings, say:

'If a person plants a tree, the fruits eaten by any person or any of Allah's creatures will be recorded as charity for the one who planted it.'
(Ahmad, VI:444. See also, Muslim, Musaqat, 7)

Even when the Muslims mobilised in great armies, they strove not to inflict damage on vegetation and trees. For instance, Caliph **Abu Bakr**, may Allah be well pleased with him, instructed his troops who were in preparation for a military expedition, as follows:

"Do not be deserters. Do not defraud, nor be guilty of treachery (by stealing the spoils of war). Do not oppress or mutilate. Do not kill women, children or the elderly. Do not injure date palms and do not cut down fruit trees. Do not slaughter any sheep or cows except for food. You will encounter people who spend their lives in monasteries; do not disturb them..."[41]

Everything that exists in the universe is in a constant state of remembrance of Allah Almighty and recitation of His names. Those who are most heedless in this regard are human beings and the jinn. Consequently, a Muslim approaches the things around them with this consciousness and Muslim students and children are raised with this consciousness:

One of the greatest spiritual masters of the Ottoman period, **Uftada**, had set out with his disciples for a discussion of a spiritual nature in the countryside. Upon his wishes, all the disciples wandered about the most beautiful areas of the countryside to bring back to their teacher a bouquet of flowers. He wanted to establish the spiritual level of each of his disciples. However, Madmud Efendi held only a wilted flower with a broken stem in his hand. After all the other students presented their bouquets in great joy to their teacher, Mahmud

---

41. Bayhaqi, *Kitab al-Sunan al-Kubra*, IX:85; 'Ali al-Muttaqi, *Kanz al-'Ummal*, no. 30268; Ibn al-Athir, *al-Kamil*, II:196.

Efendi timidly presented this broken and wilted flower to his teacher, Uftada.

Uftada asked, among the inquisitive glances of his other students,

"Mahmud, why did you bring a flower with a broken stem while all your peers brought bouquets of them?" ?????

Respectfully lowering his head, he answered,

"Respected master, no matter what I were to present to you, it could never do you justice; however, whichever flower I intended to pick, I found it in glorification of its Lord, saying, "Allah, Allah". I could not find it in my heart to prevent their invocation and remembrance. Left with no other option, I was forced to bring this flower whose invocation I found to have already ceased."

Pleased to the utmost with this extraordinary and meaningful response, Uftada said,

"My son, may your name hereafter be Hudayi![42] O Hudayi, only you have benefited from this visit to the countryside!"

In this way, Madmud became Hudayi, for he was now acquainted with the Divine secrets in the universe. It was as though the universe had become like a living book that revealed its secrets to him. Continuing his life in this way, in worship of Allah Almighty, Aziz Mahmud Hudayi served as a guide to Ottoman Sultans who shaped the world. In our day, people visit his tomb in Istanbul's Üsküdar district, in throngs, and find spiritual repose there.

d. Inanimate Beings Find Peace

When human beings receive an Islamic education and training, they learn how to treat even inanimate beings with care and kind-

---

42. The word '*hudayi*' comes to mean being rightly guided and having found the true path.

ness, for these beings are also in remembrance and glorification of the Almighty – in a manner above and beyond our comprehension – and carry within them a thousand and one wisdoms. Allah, the Most High, declares:

"The seven heavens and the earth, and whoever is therein, glorify Him. There is nothing that does not glorify Him with His praise (proclaiming that He alone is Allah, without peer or partner, and all praise belongs to Him exclusively), **but you cannot comprehend their glorification. surely He is** (despite what His servants have deserved from Him) **All-Clement, All-Forgiving."** (Isra', 17:44)

When the human being behaves selfishly, irresponsibly and is concerned only for their own self-interest, inanimate beings, like the living, are also disquieted. One day, a funeral procession passed before the Messenger of Allah. Allah's Messenger, may Allah bless him and grant him peace, said,

"Relieved or relieving." The Companions asked,

"O Messenger of Allah, what is *relieved and relieving?"* He said,

"A believer is relieved (by death) from the troubles and hardships of the world and leaves for the Mercy of Allah, while (the death of) a wicked person relieves the people, the land, the trees, (and) the animals from him." (Bukari, Riqaq, 42; Nasa'i, Jana'iz, 48; Ahmad, V:296, 302, 304)

This means to say that while the place in which we live is disturbed by certain people, it finds peace with the believing servants who pursue deeds of righteousness. When Muslims live the kind of life that is demanded of them from Allah, they realise a harmony with the earth.

'Abd Allah ibn Mas'ud, may Allah be well pleased with him, relates:

"One mountain cries out to the other by name,

"O So-and-so, did a person remembering Allah Almighty visit you today?" If it says,

"Yes, they have," the mountain is very pleased.

Narrating this incident from Ibn Mas'ud, **'Awn ibn 'Abd Allah** adds:

"How can mountains not hear words of goodness when they hear evil ones? They listen to words of goodness with greater ardour and interest. That mountains hear evil speech is revealed in a Qur'anic verse as follows:

"As it is, some say: 'The All-Merciful has taken to Himself a child.' Assuredly you have (in such an assertion) brought forth something monstrous – The heavens are all but rent, and the earth split asunder, and the mountains fall down in ruins – That they ascribe to the All-Merciful a child! It is not for the All-Merciful to take to Himself a child. There is none in the heavens and the earth but comes to the All-Merciful as a servant." (Maryam, 19:88-93) (Bayhaqi, *Shu'ab al-Iman*, I:453; Tabarani, *Kabir*, IX:103)

This means to say that the sins committed by human beings disturb both time and space. In contrast, the deeds of righteousness, worship and invocation of Allah that believers perform delight time and space.

The Messenger of Allah, upon him be peace and blessings, brought love to this world. He taught human beings to love even mountains stones and inanimate beings. He stated one day,

"Uhud loves us, and we love Uhud." (Bukhari, Jihad, 71)

It was as though Allah's Messenger, upon him be peace and blessings, accepted the mountain of Uhud as living and approached it with love. In return, mountains and stones loved him also. For Allah's Messenger, upon him be peace and blessings, states:

"I recognise a stone in Makka which used to pay me salutations before my Prophethood and I still recognise it even now." (Muslim, Fada'il, 2)

This stone is the towering stone located in the street known as Zuqaq al-Hajar or Zuqaq al-Mirfaq during the tenth century after the Hijra.[43]

'Ali, may Allah be well pleased with him, relates:

"I was with the Messenger of Allah, upon him be peace and blessings, in Makka where we went to certain places together. Every rock and tree welcomed him, saying,

'Peace be on you, O Messenger of Allah.'" (Tirmidhi, Manaqib, 6:3626)

In the same way, the **trunk of the date-palm** that he used to lean on in the Prophet's Mosque was fortunate indeed. It derived great joy in being near the Prophet and in his invoking the name of Allah by its side. When the pulpit was constructed and Allah's Messenger, upon him be peace and blessings, began delivering his sermons from upon it, the trunk of the palm tree could not bear this separation. Whereas the Messenger of Allah, upon him be peace and blessings, had not gone far at all; it could still hear his voice and still see him. However, the trunk of the date palm wanted to be as close to him as possible. For this reason, it began to weep in a manner that was audible to all those who were present. When the Messenger of Allah, upon him be peace and blessings, descended the pulpit and placed his hand on top of it, its lamentation ceased. Allah's Messenger said,

"It cried because of the remembrance of Allah that it used to hear."[44]

---

43. Ibn Hajar al-Haythami, *al-Jawhar al-Munazzam fi Ziyarat al-Qabr al-Mukarram*, Beirut 1427, 155; Halabi, *Sira*, I:486.
44. See: Bukhari, Manaqib, 25, Jumu'ah, 26; Tirmidhi, Jumu'ah, 10, Manaqib, 6; Nasa'i, Jumu'ah, 17; Ibn Maja, Iqama, 199; Darimi, Muqaddima, 6, Salat, 202; Ahmad, I:249, 267, 300, 315, 363.

The Messenger of Allah, upon him be peace and blessings, did not want for any evil word, curse or insult to be directed towards any living or non-living being. He used to advise people to beseech Allah Almighty for the good of these things and seek refuge in Him from their evil. He keenly instructed them to use all created beings for good and shun making them an instrument for evil. As he has stated in a Prophetic Tradition:

"Do not curse the night, day, sun, moon and the winds, for they are mercy for some people and (a means for) punishment for others." (Hathami, VIII:71.)

"Do not speak ill of the world, for what a beautiful mount it is for the believer. They attain goodness by mounting it and again are freed of evil by means of it." (Suyuti, *al-jami' al-saghir fi ahadith*, no: 16459)

"Do not curse the wind. If you dislike what you see of it, then say, "O Allah, we ask You for the good of this wind and the good of what is in it and the good of what it is ordered to do. We seek refuge with You from the evil of this wind and the evil of what is in it and the evil of what it is ordered to do." (Tirmidhi, Fitan, 65:2252)

Abu al-Darda', may Allah be well pleased with him, states:

"If a person curses the world, the world says to them,

'May Allah curse whichever one of us is more disobedient to Him.'" (Bayhaqi, *Shu'ab*, IV:302:5187; Hakim, IV:348:7870)

Jabir ibn Sulaym, may Allah be well pleased with him, relates:

"I saw a man whose opinion people consulted, and he did not say anything without them taking his opinion.

I said, 'Who is this?'

They said, 'The Messenger of Allah.' I said twice,

'On you be peace, Messenger of Allah'. The Messenger of Allah, upon him be peace and blessings, said,

'Do not say, "On you be peace." "On you be peace" is the greeting to the dead. Say, "Peace be upon you."' I said,

'You are the Messenger of Allah?' He said,

'I am the Messenger of Allah. If harm befalls you, my supplication will remove it from you. If a year of drought afflicts you, my supplication will make things grow for you. When you are in an empty land or wilderness and lose your mount, my supplication will return it to you.'

I said, 'Advise me.'

He said, *'Do not abuse anyone.'*

(The narrator than said, 'After that I abused neither free man or slave, nor a camel or a sheep.')

Then the Prophet continued,

'Do not disdain any act of kindness. And speaking to your brother with a cheerful face is part of being kind. *Raise your waist-wrapper to the middle of your calves. If you refuse, then to the ankles, but beware of dragging the wrapper. It is part of arrogance and Allah does not love arrogance.* **If a man insults you and criticises you for what he knows about you, do not criticise him for what you know concerning him. The bad effects of that are suffered by him.'"** (Abu Dawud, Libas, 25; Haythami, VIII:72)

Allah, the Most High, declares:

"The (true) **servants of the All-Merciful are they who move on the earth gently and humbly, and when the ignorant, foolish ones address them** (with insolence or vulgarity as befits their ignorance and foolishness), **they response with** (words of) **peace,** (without engaging in hostility with them)**."** (Furqan, 25:63.)

"Woe to every one who slanders and vilifies." (Humazah, 104:1)

Luqman Hakim was a dark-skinned individual. Criticising him, someone said,

"What an unsightly face you have, O Luqman!"

Luqman Hakim retorted,

"Is your criticism directed at the embroidery or at the Embroiderer?" (Ismail Haqqi Bursawi, *Ruh al-Bayan*, [Luqman, 12])

In other words, the Almighty has created all things and they each have much distinct wisdom. Consequently, nothing should be scorned or looked down upon.

In this way, Islam bestows peace to everything in the universe. Those holding fast to it both find peace themselves and exude peace to their surroundings. When they die, the heavens and the earth weep along with human beings. While those in the world mourn the loss of these special people, the people of the grave and the angels receive them with great jubilation and happiness. The eternal life of a person whose life in the world is thus will certainly be of even greater beauty.

In the same way that those who do not follow Islam and who pursue a selfish life in accordance with the desires of their carnal self cause discomfort to the world and its inhabitants, they will disturb those graves neighbouring them after their death. One cannot help but recall the following lines of verse when they die:

Neither did they find repose themselves, nor offer it to others,
They left this world in ruin, may those in the grave endure!

O Lord, include us among those honoured with salvation in two abodes by practising Islam in the best way. May no creature come to harm from our hand or tongue. Allow us to live a peaceful life without injuring or being injured by anyone. Enable us to use all the faculties and blessings with which You have favoured us forever in the way of goodness.

Amin...

4. Islam Leads to Salvation in the Hereafter

Upon consideration of the human being's past, we see that they were in compounds of soil as an element of nature. When the time came, they passed to plants sprouting out of the soil and from there to certain creatures, until they were eventually transferred to their father as a drop of seminal fluid and from there to their mother's womb. Humankind attained a different existence in the mother's womb. There, they lived within a sac of water and were nourished with the blood they received from their mother. They were subsequently forced to leave that life which they sustained therein and opened their eyes to a different realm or world. This new life possessed conditions that were very different to those which came before. They were no longer to maintain an existence in water or be nourished with blood.

Similarly, when a human being dies, they will again move on to a different realm. The prevailing conditions in that realm will be different to those in our current life. Allah Almighty has revealed the nature of that life and what needs to be done in preparation for it, through His Messengers. These revelations are at a level which human beings can understand with the impressions they have acquired in the world. Consequently, human beings will come to perceive a great many things when they move on to that realm, analogous to the very limited knowledge a child has of the world while in its mother's womb.

It must not be forgotten that the last garment of the marketplace of this fleeting life, the shroud, will one day most certainly envelop everyone and the reality of death will set its seal on all transient transactions, desires, attractions and deceptive glitters.

As is indicated in the Qur'an and in the Prophetic Traditions, a life in the grave will manifest itself in accordance with a person's manner of living in this world. For those living a life befitting the approval of Allah, the grave will be a garden from the gardens of Paradise;

for those who spend their lives in disobedience, it will be one of the infernal pits of the Fire. (Tirmidhi, Qiyama, 26)

For the human being, a third life will begin after the life of the grave, with the Judgement, and this will have no end. This never-ending life of the Hereafter will again be shaped in accordance with their life in this world.

On that day, Allah Almighty will produce a book in which the deeds performed in the world are recorded and declare,

"Read your book! Your own self suffices you this day as a reckoner against you." (Isra', 17:14)

Other witnesses will also be brought forth on that day to testify against the human being. It is stated in a Qur'anic verse:

"And (remind of) **the day when the enemies of Allah will be raised up** (from their graves) **and gathered for the Fire: they will be driven** (to the place of reckoning) **in arrays, Until when they reach it, their ears, and their eyes, and their skins will bear witness against them as to all that they did habitually. They will ask their skins, 'Why have you borne witness against us?' They will answer: 'Allah Who makes everything speak has made us speak.' It is He Who has created you in the first instance, and to Him you are being brought back."** (Fussilat 41:19-21. See, Nur 24:24; Yasin 36:65)

"On that day she [the earth] **will recount all its tidings, As your Lord has inspired her to do so."** (Zalzalah 99:4-5)

All people will feel regret on that day. Those who live as Muslims and die as Muslims rue that they did not perform even more deeds of righteousness. Those who live their lives in wrongdoing and unbelief grieve at their not believing and abandoning sin and are stricken with an intense sense of remorse.[45]

---

45. Tirmidhi, Zuhd, 59:2403.

Those who end up in Hellfire cry out in horror, "O our Lord! Take us out, we will do good, (righteous deeds), not (the wrong) we used to do before."

However, the Almighty will declare,

"Did We not grant you a life long enough for whoever would reflect and be mindful to reflect and be mindful? In addition, a warner came to you (to warn against this punishment). **Taste then** (the consequences of your heedlessness); **for the wrongdoers have none to help them (against it)."** (Fatir 35:37)

A person's greatest helper on such a difficult day is Islam, or the belief and deeds of righteousness described by the Messenger of Allah. On that formidable day when the world of trial comes to an end and human beings begin to be called to account and receive either reward or punishment, Islam will deliver those who surrendered to it.

That is to say, the sole religion that will enable the human being to attain salvation in the Hereafter, as in this world, is again Islam. Allah, exalted and glorified be He, declares:

"The (true) **religion with Allah is Islam..."** (Al-'Imran 3:19)

"Whoever seeks as religion other than Islam, (which is the standard religion conveyed by all the Prophets during history, and is based on complete submission to Allah,) **it will never be accepted from him, and in the Hereafter, he will be among the losers."** (Al-'Imran 3:85)

Once, the Jews said to **'Umar,**

"O leader of the believers, there is a verse in your Book, which you recite. Had it been revealed in connection with the Jews, we would have taken it as the day of rejoicing." 'Umar, may Allah be well pleased with him, said,

"Which verse do you mean?"

"**This day I have perfected for you your Religion** (with all its rules, commandments and universality)**, completed My favor upon you, and have been pleased to assign for you Islam as religion.**" (Ma'ida 5:3)

'Umar, may Allah be well pleased with him, said,

"I know the day when it was revealed and the place where it was revealed. It was revealed to Allah's Messenger, upon him be peace and blessings, at 'Arafat on a Friday." (Bukhari, Iman, 33; Maghazi, 77; Tafsir, 5:2; Muslim, Tafsir, 3-5)

Both 'Arafa and Friday are days of festivity for Muslims.

According to these Qur'anic verses, the only religion which Allah accepts from humankind from the day that Allah's Messenger Muhammad, upon him be peace and blessings, was sent as a Prophet, is Islam. No previous religion or belief will be accepted, for the era of the prior Messengers ended and that of the last Messenger of Allah, upon him be peace and blessings, began. The Prophet, upon him be peace and blessings, explains this point as follows:

"By Him in Whose hand is the life of Muhammad, he who amongst the community of Jews or Christians hears about me, but does not affirm his belief in that with which I have been sent and dies in this state (of disbelief), he shall be but one of the denizens of Hellfire." (Muslim, Iman, 240)

"I bear witness that there is no god but Allah, and I am His Messenger. One who meets Allah without entertaining any doubt about these (two fundamentals) will enter Paradise." (Muslim, Iman, 44)

Hearts Attain Rest with Remembrance of Allah

The human being, in addition to their physical constitution, has a spiritual aspect also. Unfortunately, the majority of people today strive to procure only their material needs, whereas a person's body is mortal while their spirit is eternal. When human beings neglect the needs of their spirits, that are to live eternally, they experience psychological crises and depression. There is only one way to freeing the human spirit of these crises and enable it to attain eternal bliss and that is embracing Islamic belief and worship. As stated in a Qur'anic verse:

"Be aware that it is in the remembrance and of and wholehearted devotion to Allah that hearts find rest and contentment." (Ra'd, 13:28)

The greater part of illnesses in our day are depression and stress, such that these illnesses have far exceeded and outnumbered physical ones. When the era of the Prophet is considered, it quickly becomes apparent that there was no Muslim who became afflicted with psychological illness as they lived within the spirituality, love and rapture of the Qur'an and the *Sunna*. This contented their spirits and inner worlds. In fact, Allah Almighty declares that He has revealed the Qur'an as **"a healing and a mercy"**. (See, Isra' 17:82)

In the same way, the Almighty declares that He will bestow His **Divine Mercy** upon those who follow the Qur'an and His Messenger, upon him be peace and blessings.

"...My Mercy embraces all things; and so, (although in the world every being has a share in My Mercy, in the Hereafter) **I will ordain it for those who act in reverence for Me and piety and pay their Prescribed Purifying Alms, and they are those who truly believe in all of Our revelations and signs. They follow the** (most illustrious) **Messenger, the Prophet who neither reads nor writes, whom they find described** (with all his distinguishing features) **in the Torah and the Gospel** (that are) **with them. He enjoins upon them what is right and good, and forbids them what is evil; he makes pure, wholesome things lawful for them, and bad, corrupt things unlawful. And he relieves them of their burdens** (remaining of their own

Law) **and the restraints that were upon them. So those who believe in him** (with all sincerity), honor and support him, and help him, and follow the Light (the Qur'an) **which has been sent down with him – they are those who are the prosperous."** (A'raf, 7:156-157)

Such an elixir were the Divine morality that the Prophet brought to humanity, as well as his outward training and inward influence, that they produced within a short space of time a civilisation of virtue beyond imagination, out of the society of the Age of Ignorance – half of whom were savage and the majority of whom were bereft of humanity. Ignorant and savage peoples became cultured, barbaric individuals became civilised and the criminal and corrupt became pious; in other words, they became greatly righteous people possessing tenderness of heart, who lived with love and fear of Allah.

Consider a person so savage and whose heart had become so hard that they could mercilessly rip their baby daughter from her mother's embrace and then bury her alive, and so tyrannical that they could see their slaves as an item of property and subject them to inhumane treatment...

After embracing Islam and attaining guidance, such crude and ignorant people established a civilisation of virtues in humanity by deepening in knowledge, morality, propriety and conscience. When these people, who had hit rock bottom with respect to humanity and civilisation during the Age of Ignorance, began to live in accordance with the Divine commandments and morality, they reached a peak like that of Everest, so to speak.

As can be gleaned from all these, individuals and communities which benefited from the healing and mercy of the Qur'an not only achieved happiness in this world, but will also attain eternal happiness in the Hereafter. Spirits unacquainted with belief and Islam, however, will not attain peace of mind in this world and will face the pain and anguish of life after death.

Part 2

The Essentials of Belief

Allah Almighty has created human nature of a constitution that can find peace only with belief. For this reason, no human being can be freed of spiritual unease by burying themselves in the swamp of unbelief or false belief. They carry a constant feeling of discontentment in their heart. The sole solution to being saved from this state is following in the footsteps of the Messenger of Allah, upon him be peace and blessings, the greatest blessing that Allah Almighty has bestowed upon humanity. This means finding life in the felicitous climate of a Muhammadan spring.

Maintaining the honour and dignity of being his community is where the esteem of our humanity lies.

1. The Declaration of Faith (Kalima al-Tawhid)

The Declaration of Faith (*Kalima al-Tawhid* or *Kalima al-Shahadah*) is the name given to the statement that there is no god but Allah and that Muhammad, upon him be peace and blessings, is His servant and His Messenger. It is pronounced as follows:

أَشْهَدُ أَنْ لَآ إِلٰهَ إِلَّا اللهُ وَأَشْهَدُ أَنَّ مُحَمَّدًا عَبْدُهُ وَرَسُولُهُ

Ash-hadu an la ilaha illallah wa ash-hadu anna Muhammadan 'abduhu wa rasuluhu.

"I bear witness that there is no god but Allah; I also bear witness that Muhammad, upon him be peace and blessings, is His servant and His Messenger."

One of the greatest scholars of the generation following the Companions, **Sha'bi**, relates:

When **'Adiy ibn Khatam**, may Allah be well pleased with him, came to Kufa, we went to visit him with a group of Kufa's poor and said to him,

"Can you relate some of the things that you heard from the Messenger of Allah?" 'Adiy, may Allah be well pleased with him, said:

I approached Allah's Messenger, upon him be peace and blessings, and he said to me,

"*O 'Adiy ibn Khatam, become a Muslim and be saved.*" I asked,

"What is Islam?" The Messenger of Allah, upon him be peace and blessings, said,

"*It is your declaring that there is no god but Allah and that I am His Messenger and your believing completely in Divine decree with its good and bad, bitter and sweet.*" (Ibn Maja, Muqaddima, 10)

The Messenger of Allah, upon him be peace and blessings, detailed the essentials of belief as follows:

"*Belief is that you believe in Allah, His angels, His books, His Prophets, the Resurrection, and complete belief in Divine Decree and Destiny, the good and bad of it.*" (Bukhari, Iman, 37; Muslim, Iman, 1, 5; Tirmidhi, Iman, 4; Abu Dawud, Sunna, 16; Ahmad, I:97)

The Declaration of Faith is an expression of detachment from all that separates one from Allah and not holding excessive love in the heart for any other being save the Almighty. The Declaration of Faith prevents arrogance and passions becoming idols in the heart. In this way, it enables a person to remain clear of all idols, outward and inward.

Allah, glory unto Him, admonishes His servants who do not purge their hearts of inner idols in the following manner:

"**Do you** (O Messenger) **ever consider him who has taken his lusts and fancies for his deity? Would you then be a guardian over him (and, thereby, assume responsibility for guiding him)?**" (Furqan, 25:43)

By way of concrete example, when we hold a magnifying glass under sunlight, the concentrated sun's beams turn all the cinder beneath it into ashes. Every human being must carry out such a cleansing in his or her heart with the focussed beams of the Declaration of Faith. As expressed in the Qur'anic verse, hearts find rest only through togetherness with the Almighty and attain peace through remembrance of Him and mentioning His names. That all our actions must be for Allah, with Him and in accordance with His approval and good pleasure, is indicated in the very first Qur'anic verse that was revealed:

"**Read in and with the Name of your Lord, Who has created.**"
('Alaq 96:1)

If the heart becomes as such, it begins to receive a share in the manifestations of the beauty of its Lord. It seeks its Lord at each and every time and place and meets with Him. A believer who advances with their heart beholds the Divine displays in all things and lives in love and ecstasy before the Divine power and grandeur.

A few examples of the attributes of beauty to be manifested in a perfected heart are as follows:

The manifestation of **All-Merciful** and **All-Compassionate**: When the Almighty's names All-Merciful and All-Compassionate are manifested in a heart, that believer exudes mercy to every place they can reach. They become a benevolent shelter and sanctuary for those who are forlorn. They cannot remain indifferent to the audible or silent lamentations of any creature, the human being first and foremost, for mercy is the most distinguished fruit of belief and its first product.

The manifestation of **All-Pardoning**: Allah Almighty is most forgiving. Perfected believers, in accordance with the principle, *"One who does not know how to forgive cannot be forgiven,"* are very forgiving towards the servants of Allah in order to be deserving of Divine forgiveness. Thinking nothing of the injustices done to one's person and rendering forgiveness, without feeling even the slightest anger, one's temperament, is the masterpiece of spiritual maturity. It is the greatest spiritual valour.

The manifestation of **All-Munificent**: A servant who has munificence becomes adorned with all good character traits, generosity first and foremost, and becomes a perfected believer.

Manifestation of **All-Trustworthy**: A heart favoured with the manifestation of the Almighty's attribute of the All-Trustworthy perpetually feels themselves to be under the Divine 'camera', as it were, and is becomes a fine representative of their religion with their every state. They strengthen in belief and become a trustworthy and faithful servant. They strive to imbue hearts around them with belief and, protecting themselves and their environment from all possible harm, they inspire trust and security.

The manifestation of **All-Patient**: A heart honoured with this manifestation is delivered from many difficulties by becoming a monument of patience. They become eternally joyous with the sweet fruits in the Hereafter of the patience they endured in this world.

a. Importance of the Declaration of Faith (*Kalima al-Tawhid*)

The Declaration of Faith constitutes an individual's first step when entering Islam, their first evaluation and their distinguishing identity in life from that point on. A person who utters this statement is considered to have genuinely believed in Allah and to have entered the fold of the Divine religion, Islam. For this reason, the Declaration of Faith is the foundation and stronghold of the religion.

The Declaration of Faith is so sublime a declaration that the salvation and happiness of all humanity is hidden within its endless meaning and its atmosphere of mystery.

This statement is the kernel of the kernel. The other foundations of Islam and their particulars are always contingent upon this kernel.

Consequently, the Declaration of Faith and belief are more meritorious than all the other forms of worship for worship is possible only through them. All the forms of worship are within a set period of time and are observed only at those times. Even the most sublime of worship, the Daily Prescribed Prayer, is compulsory five times a day. Belief, however, is always compulsory. It is essential to constantly protect the heart from everything other than Allah and everything that pulls one away from Allah, and to keep belief vigorous under any circumstances. This belief is such that one is never religiously excused from it. Its preservation is necessary at every moment and cannot be delayed or suspended.

A person who has heartfelt conviction of the meaning expressed in this declaration enters the sphere of belief. Upon their verbal acknowledgement, they come to be known as Muslim among the people and are treated as such in the world. If the heart does not have complete belief in the Declaration of Faith, the goodness performed will be to no avail in the Hereafter. However, our All-Just and All-Merciful Lord bestows upon them certain blessings and ease in this world in return for their goodness. (See: Muslim, Munafiqin, 57, 56)

Allah, the Most High, declares:

"**Do you not see how Allah strikes a parable of a good word:** (a good word is) **like a good tree – its roots holding firm (in the ground) and its branches in heaven, It yields its fruit in every season due by its Lord's leave. So Allah strikes parables for human beings, in order that they may reflect on them and infer the necessary lessons.**

And the parable of a corrupt word [of unbelief] **is that of a corrupt tree uprooted from upon the earth, having no constancy.**" (Ibrahim 14:24-26)

Ibn 'Abbas, may Allah be well pleased with him, says the following in interpreting this Qur'anic verse.

"A 'good word' refers to testifying, There is no god but Allah; a 'good tree', refers to the believer, and 'its roots holding firm" indicates that the statement, There is no god but Allah, is firm in the believers' heart and 'its branches in heaven' with which the believer's works ascend to heaven. 'And the parable of a corrupt word' describes the disbelief of the disbeliever, for it has no basis or stability. Surely, the works of the disbelievers will never ascend nor will any of them be accepted."

A person needs to be on the path of belief in Divine Unity at the beginning of their life, throughout it and at its end. For Allah's Messenger, upon him be peace and blessings, used to say:

"The first word to be heard by your children should be, la ilaha illalah, (There is no god but Allah)." (Bayhaqi, *Shu'ab al-Iman*, VI:398)

When a child from the Banu 'Abd al-Muttalib began to speak, he himself would teach them the Qur'anic verse, **"All praise and gratitude are for Allah, Who has neither taken to Him a child, nor has a partner in the sovereignty** (the dominion and ownership of the whole creation)**, nor** (being exalted above all want or insufficiency) **has He a guardian against neediness and weakness. And exalt Him with His immeasurable greatness,"**[46] by reciting it seven times. ('Abd al-Razzaq, IV:334; Ibn Abi Shayba, I:348)

The Companions too, when their children began to speak, deemed it favourable to repeat the statement *La ilaha illallah* seven times so that their first words would be, "There is no god but Allah." ('Abd al-Razzaq, IV:334)

---

46. Isra' 17:111.

THE ESSENTIALS OF BELIEF

Humankind must live their life along the lines of this meaning and must surrender their spirit at their last breath by repeating the Declaration of Faith.

'**Umar**, may Allah be well pleased with him, once saw **Talha** to be sorrowful. When he asked him the reason, Talha, may Allah be well pleased with him, said,

"The Messenger of Allah, upon him be peace and blessings, once stated,

'I know a word the saying of which at the time of death will assuredly be a light for their book of deeds, and with it their body and spirit will attain Divine approval, mercy and repose at the moment of their death.'

Allah's Messenger, upon him be peace and blessings, passed away before I was able to ask what this word was. This is the cause of my sorrow." Upon this, 'Umar, may Allah be well pleased with him, said,

"I know that word. It is the statement, *La ilaha illallah*, which the Messenger of Allah, upon him be peace and blessings, had desired his uncle to recite. If Allah's Messenger, upon him be peace and blessings, had known of a word that was better, he would certainly have desired for him to have said this instead." (Ibn Maja, Adab, 54. Also see, Ahmad, I:6)

Allah's Messenger, upon him be peace and blessings, has stated:

"Prompt your dying people to say: 'La ilaha illallah'." (Muslim, Jana'iz, 1, 2)

"He whose last words are, 'La ilaha illallah' will enter Paradise." (Abu Dawud, Jana'iz, 20:3116; Ahmad, V:247; Hakim, I:503)

"You will die as you live and you will be resurrected as you die." (Munawi, *Fayd al-Qadr*, V:663)

What a privilege it is to live and die upon the path of Divine Unity and attain the bliss and splendour of such belief.

b. Virtues of the Declaration of Faith (*Kalima al-Tawhid*)

Allah, the Most High, has simultaneously accepted the Declaration of Faith, the mark of entering Islam, as worship so that His servants be constantly preoccupied with it and earn abundant reward. For Allah's Messenger, upon him be peace and blessings, has stated:

"The best remembrance of Allah is to say, 'There is no god but Allah'." (Tirmidhi, Da'awat, 9:3383; Ibn Maja, Adab, 55)

"The best supplication is seeking forgiveness and the best worship is the Declaration of Faith." ('Ali al-Muttaqi, I:483/2112)

The Messenger of Allah, upon him be peace and blessings, once said,

"Renew your belief."

It was said,

"O Messenger of Allah, peace and blessings be upon him, who do we renew our belief?'" He replied, may Allah bless him and give him peace,

"By saying la ilaha illallah ('There is no god but Allah') a lot." (Ahmad, II:359; Hakim, IV, 285/7657)

Abu Talib's daughter, **Umm Hani'**, may Allah be well pleased with her, went to the Prophet, upon him be peace and blessings, and said,

"O Messenger of Allah, I have become old and weak. Advise me of worship that I can carry out while sitting." He replied, may Allah bless him and give him peace,

"Recite subhan Allah (All glory be to Allah) one hundred times, [47] *alhamdu lillah (All praise be to Allah) one hundred times and la ilaha*

---

47. All glory be to Allah: I declare Him to be above having any imperfections or deficiencies.

illallah (There is no god but Allah) one hundred times.(Ibn Maja, Adab, 56; Ahmad, VI:344)[48]

Reciting collectively the Declaration of Faith in particular, among the various utterances of remembrance, has a special place. The Prophetic narration related by **Shaddad ibn Aws**, may Allah be well pleased with him, indicates this:

"We were sitting with Allah's Messenger, upon him be peace and blessings, and he asked if there was any stranger in the gathering. (The narrator said that he had implied the People of the Book.) We said that there was none.

He said, *'Shut the door, raise up your hands and say, 'There is no god but Allah.'*

We raised our hands and recited the Declaration of Faith for some time. He then exclaimed,

'All praise be to Allah! O Lord, You have sent me with "this word" and have ordered me to teach it and have promised me Paradise for it, and You do not go back on Your promise.'

Allah's Messenger, upon him be peace and blessings, then said,

"Glad tidings to you, for assuredly Allah has forgiven you!"' (Ahmad, IV, 124.)

He states in another narration:

"The word, 'There is no god but Allah', is very valuable in the Eyes of Allah. Whoever utters this word in perfect sincerity and faithfulness, Allah will place him in Paradise. And whoever utters this word without believing it, he will protect his property and his life in this world. However, Allah will hold him to account in the Hereafter." (Haythami, I:26)

---

48. All praise be to Allah: Allah Almighty is the rightful recipient of all praise, thanks and glorification.

Belief is profession with the tongue and affirmation with the heart. If there is no affirmation with the heart, despite admission with the tongue, and if affirmation remains in the mind and is not reflected in one's actions, than it will hold no value. Allah Almighty likens those who carry spiritual knowledge merely in the mind to donkeys carrying a load of books.[49]

The Most High reveals that the inner world of those who acknowledge verbally and affirm with their heart is adorned with piety and righteousness. As declared in Chapter Fatir:

"Of all His servants, only those possessed of true knowledge stand in awe of Allah." (Fatir 35:28)

In short, the Declaration of Faith affords benefit to the extent of its being reflected in the heart. After all, those to be most joyous in the Hereafter, by virtue of the Prophet's intercession, will be those who earnestly and wholeheartedly declare, 'There is no god but Allah'. (Bukhari, 'Ilm, 33; Riqaq 51)

However, sufficing with the Declaration of Faith is not enough for complete deliverance. There are also certain obligations incumbent upon a person after entering Islam. These, in brief, are obedience to the Divine commandments and avoiding the prohibitions. The Messenger of Allah, upon him be peace and blessings, has indicated some of these in the following manner:

"Belief has over seventy branches or over sixty branches, the most excellent of which is the declaration that there is no god but Allah and the humblest of which is the removal of what is injurious from the path; and modesty is a branch of belief." (Muslim, Iman, 58. Also see, Bukhari, Iman, 3; Abu Dawud, Sunna, 14)

---

49. See, Jumu'ah, 62:5.

The Companions too, not sufficing with mere verbal avowal, put forth their deeds of righteousness in the way of belief in Divine Oneness with great fervour.

When **Wahb ibn Munabbih**, from among the Successors (the generation following the Companions of the Prophet) was asked, "Is not the declaration, 'There is none that has the right to be worshipped save Allah,' the key to Paradise?" he replied,

"Indeed, but every key most certainly has its teeth; if you bring a key that has teeth, the door shall open for you; but if not, it will not." (Bukhari, Jana'iz, 1. cf. Tirmidhi, Iman, 17:2638)

Bayazid al-Bistami was told that,

"The statement, 'There is no deity but Allah,' is the key to Paradise." He replied,

"True. However, it is a fact that a key without teeth cannot open a door. The teeth of the key of Declaration of Faith are the following:

1) A tongue purged of evil speech, such as backbiting;

2) A heart purified from deception and treachery;

3) A stomach cleansed of the prohibited and doubtful things; and

4) Deeds of righteousness freed from carnal desires (such as pride, arrogance and ostentation) and innovations in the religion."[50]

2. Belief in Allah

The human mind cannot conceive of the Almighty, Who created the heavens and the earth and everything in between from nothing, for the road of human knowledge is that of the five senses, the mind and the heart. The power of all these capacities for comprehension,

---

50. 'Abd al-Majid al-Khani, *al-Hada'iq al-Wardiyya*, Damascus 1996, 320.

however, is limited. A Being Who is Everlasting, Absolute and Eternal cannot be grasped with means that are limited in power and authority. Perception, with limited means, can only be actualised as itself limited, for it is impossible for the limited to perceive that which is unlimited. We can only take as much water from the ocean as our cup will allow. The following Prophetic Tradition is a succinct expression of this truth:

"(During the journey in which al-Khidr showed Prophet Moses, upon them both be peace, various strange incidents with hidden wisdoms) a sparrow came and perched itself over the edge of the ship onto which they embarked. It then dipped its beak in the sea. Drawing Prophet Moses' attention to this scene, al-Khidr said,

'My knowledge and your knowledge, compared to the knowledge of Allah is like what this sparrow has taken out of the sea.' (Bukhari, Tafsir 18:2-4)

For this reason, attempting to conceive of and reflect upon the Almighty in terms of His essence enables one to gain nothing more than various imaginings and baseless misgivings. The eye has a certain range of visibility and the ear, a certain earshot. Every bodily organ has a limited power and strength. Similarly, the intellect also has a limit and other realms exist beyond it. If the mind's limit were surpassed, the mind would explode and a state of insanity would ensue. Consequently, the Messenger of Allah, upon him be peace and blessings, has stated:

"*Reflect upon Allah Almighty's bounties and the works of His power, but do not try to reflect upon Allah's essence (dhat), for you will never be able to do that.*" (See, Daylami, II:56; Haythami, I:81; Bayhaqi, *Shu'ab*, I:136)

Ibn 'Arabi (638/1240) has stated:

THE ESSENTIALS OF BELIEF

"Know that whatever conception of Allah we form in our minds, He is other than it."

One of the Most High's attributes is His being unlike all creation (*mukhalafat al-hawadith*).

However, attempting to grasp the Almighty's majesty, power and mercy by moving from the quality to the thing it qualifies, the art to the artist and the cause to the creator of causes, has always been encouraged. Everything in the universe, from the microcosm to the macrocosm is a mirror or showcase of Divine majesty. If perception were able to gaze upon Allah Almighty's attributes and actions (works) with a sound will and pure reflection, it is unthinkable for it to be a denier. Denial begins where the affectivity of the heart becomes corrupt through mental and intellectual activity. Even if a person possessing good sense were to open their eyes in the realm of unbelief, the probability of their deliverance from unbelief would be rather high. The Qur'an points to Prophet Abraham as an example in this regard. Notwithstanding his being born and raised in an atmosphere of denial and unbelief, he came to perceive the existence and oneness of Allah, glory unto Him, purely with his intellectual purity and inner faculties.

In this respect, it is unthinkable for sound judgement to be a denier in the absolute sense as one cannot resolve a situation by denying a thing's existence. Convincing and accurate proof and demonstration are required. Those who try to break loose by saying 'It does not exist' when unable to solve the mystery of the universe and life beyond death resemble people whose bodily health has deteriorated and are unaware of such. Their saying that they are not hungry despite their hunger is only a demonstration of their illness. An anaesthetised patient is not aware of the scalpel that cuts away at their organs like a piece of fabric. In exactly the same way, there are many people who ail their spirit towards the exalted truths without even being aware of such. Allah Almighty says of them,

"They are utterly deaf, dumb, and blind..."[51]

The Most High has bestowed the need for belief and the capacity to recognise truth in the nature of every human being. In spite of this, separation from belief and truth is only by reason of a spiritual blindness and deafness. The spirit of a person who does not believe is also innately capable of perceiving Allah, but is unable to raise this peculiarity above their subconscious to their conscious mind, due to their spiritual blindness and deafness. This is just like dreams that are seen but cannot be recalled, or a bird born and raised in a cage, which loses its ability of flight.

If one looks closely, they can see that all human and Divine religions have within them a belief in Allah; however, over time digressing from the notion of Divine Unity, this belief now presents various falsities. Consequently, they are not accepted as acceptable in Islam. This is because their belief does not conform to the Unique Creator of Universe being above and beyond all deficiencies and imperfections and Who has all the attributes of perfection and transcendence; that is to say, it does not conform to His being perfect beyond comprehension.

Some of these fallacies are enumerated in the following *hadith qudsi*, or Divine hadith, which Allah's Messenger, upon him be peace and blessings, relates from His Lord:

"Allah Almighty has said: The children of Adam denied Me and he had no right to do so. And he insulted Me and he had no right to do so. As for his denying Me, it is his saying that I cannot recreate him as I created him before. As for his insulting Me, it is his saying: Allah has

---

51. See, Baqara 2:18.

THE ESSENTIALS OF BELIEF

taken to Himself a son, but glorified am I above taking a wife or a son."
(Bukhari, Tafsir, 2:8)

At the end of time, the single unique authentic belief pertaining to Allah Almighty can be learned only from Islam. In connection with Divine and Prophetic declaration, Islam puts forward certain attributes pertaining to Allah Almighty and does not accept any deficiency in any of these or the addition of any other not befitting these. These attributes are divided into two categories according to the general and well-known classification:

a. The Essential Attributes (*al-Sifat al-Dhatiyya*)

b. The Immutable Attributes (*al-Sifat al-Thubutiyyah*)

The Essential Attributes / The Attributes of Negation (*Sifat al-Salbiyya*)

Existence (*Wujud*): Allah exists and His existence is not contingent upon anything. As such, He is known as the Necessarily Existent One (*al-wajib al-wujud*). That is, there is no possibility of His non-existence. All beings other than the Most High, however, are those that He created and are those with the possibility of existence (*mumkin al-wujud*). That is, that may or may not exist.

Eternity (*Qidam*): It is a logical necessity that existing beings originate from an original cause, in connection to cause-effect relationships. The cause must be such that it must be beyond the need to be created and must be able to create in and of itself. This cause is Allah Almighty. Hence, there is no beginning to His Exalted Existence. He is the beginning of everything. He is eternal in the past.

Permanence/Everlastingness (*Baqa*): His existence has no end and is everlasting.

Oneness (*Wahdaniyya*): Allah Almighty is One. He has no equal, peer or partner in neither in His essence, nor in His Attributes, nor in His acts.

From the moment the universe was created, its harmonious course, its impeccable order and its inter-nested endless wisdom and secrets serve to demonstrate that everything is the handiwork of one sole power. Had this power not been one but more than one, the endless harmony, matchless order and wisdom would have become confounded due to the differences between various wills and life would have become impossible. It is stated in a Qur'anic verse:

"**Allah has never taken to Himself a child, nor is there any deity along with Him; otherwise each deity would surely have sought absolute independence with his creatures under his authority, and they would surely have tried to overpower one another. All-Glorified is Allah, in that He is far above what they attribute to Him.**" (Mu'minun 23:91)

"**But the fact is that had there been in the heavens and the earth any deities other than Allah, both** (of those realms) **would certainly have fallen into ruin. All-Glorified Allah is, the Lord of the Supreme Throne, in that He is absolutely above all that they attribute to Him.**" (Anbiya 21:22)

Upon a thorough examination of the Qur'an, it becomes evident that the most important quality with which the Almighty has made His servants morally and religiously responsible is the belief in His Being or Essence. The most delicate aspect of this belief is Oneness for belief in the Divine Unity has no room or tolerance for partnership. Consequently, associating partners with Allah takes first place in Islam with regard to calling forth Divine wrath. The Qur'an gives especial attention to those warnings and admonishments that enable protection from being dragged into this intellectual wretchedness:

"...Whoever associates partners with Allah, Allah has surely made Paradise forbidden to him, and his refuge is the Fire. And the wrongdoers will have no helpers." (Ma'ida 5:72)

"Indeed it has been revealed to you as well as to those (Messengers) sent before you: "Should you associate partners with Allah, your labor will most certainly come to nothing and you will most certainly be among the losers." (Zumar 39:65)

"Assuredly, Allah does not forgive that partners be associated with Him; less than that, He forgives to whomever He wills (whomever He has guided to repentance and righteousness, either out of His pure grace or as a result of the person's choosing repentance and righteousness by his free will). Whoever associates any partner with Allah has indeed fabricated a most heinous sin." (Nisa, 4:48)

The slightest shortcoming with regard to Divine Oneness cannot be redressed with countless deeds expressing virtue. This is akin to the following example: If a person had much good done to them, but alongside this goodness, if damage was wilfully perpetrated to their honour and dignity, then the goodness done would hold no value whatsoever. When considered from this perspective, denying Allah amounts to perpetrating an unforgivable crime towards His Divine Honour. The reason for its being unforgivable is this spiritual weight and implication that it carries. That is to say, if a person dies on the path of unbelief and associating partners with Allah, their forgiveness is not possible. If they abandon their attributing partners to Allah and unbelief, and repent, this is of course forgiven with the grace of Allah Almighty. In this respect, the first thing that the Most High demands from His servants is belief and then deeds of righteousness.

Being unlike all creation (*mukhalafat al-hawadith*): Allah, glorified and exalted be He, has no peer or partner. He bears no resemblance to the created, which were created out of nothing. Consequently, He is above and beyond characterisation with any human attribute or characteristic.

Self Subsistence (*Qiyamu bi-Nafsihi*): Allah Almighty is self-existent. He has existed and will exist eternally and is the All-Enduring in His existence. He is not in need of anyone or anything in His existence. On the contrary, everything is in need of Him for their existence.

The Immutable Attributes

Life (*Hayat*): Allah Almighty is alive and possesses a continuous and absolute life. This quality is existent through His Own Being. All other life exists as manifestations of and relative to this exalted Divine attribute.

Hayat is an eternal attribute of the Almighty which ensures the certainty of His having all the attributes of perfection such as knowledge and power. This is because knowledge can only exist in a being that possesses life. A being that does not possess the attribute of life cannot have any attributes of perfection, such as knowledge and the like.

As none of the Divine attributes resemble the characteristics of His servants, His attribute of life is also unlike the life of His creation. The Divine attribute **All-Living (*al-Hayy*)** is His attribute of perfection that cannot be separated from His Essence. The life that Allah possesses is not a life that is the opposite of death, but a life particular only to Him – one that is eternal in the past and in the future. The life of creation, however, is one a fleeting one arising from the synergy of the body and the spirit, not a true life. This is why it is taken back from the mortal when the time comes.

Knowledge (*'Ilm*): Allah Almighty possesses eternal knowledge and His knowledge encompasses all things. There is nothing that remains outside the scope of His knowledge. He is indeed All-Knowing of the states and conditions of all things. That which is hidden or secret is not in the question for his knowledge. Everything is manifest and self evident to Him. All knowledge given to humankind, however, is a minuscule part of this attribute and is relative.

Divine knowledge is above being a product of thought and conception. This order, harmony and connection that is seen in the universe, with a delicacy and precision that is beyond conception, is the most faithful proof of Allah Almighty's possessing eternal knowledge. If everything, from particles to heavenly bodies, were not completely and perfectly in the realm of Divine knowledge, this universal connection and harmony that we constantly observe could not been actualised. For creating even a tiny thing in a perfect form is most certainly dependent upon knowing both it, itself, and what kind of causes and conditions are necessary for its coming into existence.

Humankind is able to reach even the smallest discovery as a result of the cumulative experience accumulated over the centuries. Whereas these discoveries, inventions and the eternal secrets that are yet to be solved are characteristics that the Most High has placed in the order of the universe in a single moment with His Divine knowledge. In order to remind us of this truth, Allah Almighty declares,

"Is it conceivable that One Who creates should not know? He is the All-Subtle (penetrating to the most minute dimensions of all things), **the All-Aware."** (Mulk 67:14)

It is declared in another verse:

"If all the trees on the earth were pens, and all the sea (were ink), **with seven more seas added thereto, the words of Allah** (His decrees, the acts of all His Names and Attributes manifested as His commandments, and the events and creatures He creates) **would not be exhausted in the writing. Surely Allah is the All-Glorious with**

irresistible might (Whom none can frustrate and Whom nothing can tire), **the All-Wise."** (Luqman 31:27)

Hearing (*Sam'a*): Allah is the All-Hearing One. His hearing bears no semblance to ours. There is no sound that remains hidden from Him. He even hears the proverbial footsteps of an ant walking quietly upon a rock. All creatures possessing the attribute of hearing, hear by means of the manifestation of this Divine attribute. The moment this manifestation is taken from them, they can hear nothing.

Sight (*Basar*): Allah Almighty's seeing, like His other attributes, is a requirement of His Divine Essence. He is the All-Seeing. There is nothing that remains hidden from His sight. Again, with the famous expression, He sees even the footsteps of a black ant upon a black rock on a pitch-black night.

The Almighty **knows** even the most secret thoughts of His creation, **hears** all their words and perfectly **sees** all that they do. Allah Almighty reminds of these attributes frequently in the Qur'an in order that His servants become honest individuals and faithful believers by being mindful of His commandments and prohibitions.

Will (*Irada*): Allah Almighty is absolutely independent in His commands, decrees and acts. He wills what He chooses and does whatever He wills. When He wills something to be, His command consists merely of saying, "**Be!**" and that thing immediately comes into existence. (See, Baqara 2:117)

Allah Almighty is the Single Unique One Who does whatever He wills. Every existence and act is dependent upon His will. In short,

"Whatever Allah wills happens; whatever He does not will, does not."

THE ESSENTIALS OF BELIEF

In this respect, just as the actions that Allah Almighty is pleased with are realised through His will, those acts with which He is displeased are also realised again through His will, as a requirement of examination in this world.

Upon examination of the Qur'an, one sees that Allah, glory unto Him, never allows any delimitation to His absolute will. He frequently reveals that He is absolutely independent in His will and that He does whatever He chooses. It can even be said, "All the Qur'anic expressions, from beginning to end, have been built upon this principle." In fact, Allah has even left indeterminate His judgement concerning the sins and offences of His servants – with the exception of denial, the association of partners with Him and violations of the rights of others – and has declared that He will treat them as He so chooses. In other words, He will forgive or not forgive whichever servant He so chooses. The hidden facet of this affair is beyond human conception. This reality is declared in a Qur'anic verse as follows:

"To Allah belongs whatever is in the heavens and whatever is on the earth; He forgives whom He wills and punishes whom He wills. And Allah is All-Forgiving, All-Compassionate." (Al-'Imran 3:129)

Power (*Qudra*): He is the Owner of Infinite Power Who has full power over everything. There is no difficulty for Him. He does whatever He wills – no more and no less – with wisdom.

The creation of this visible realm upon an awe-inspiring order is an explicit proof of Allah Almighty's power.

We must not fall into error concerning this matter by considering the Divine Power in terms of our own weakness, for the power and strength that we possess is both limited and handicapped by their opposites, weakness and impotence. However, the infinite power of Allah Almighty is both unrestricted and is above and beyond all kinds of negative qualities such as weakness. Consequently, there is no being that is not weak before His infinite power. Our power is only as much as He has granted.

The wretched end of many heedless who defied that power has taken up the disaster-stricken pages of utter disappointment in the history of humanity. Nimrod, the Pharaoh, Qarun, Abu Jahl and many others left this world as a great nothing. The death that the Almighty has willed for them when receiving them for punishment in the eternal realm has virtually been of a derisive nature. In particular, the death of Nimrod – who claimed godhead – at the hands of a puny and feeble mosquito carries a striking message in regard to Divine Power. Again, the ruin of Abraha and his army who dared to attack the House of Allah relying on their parade of elephants, by flocks of birds is another lesson from which to take heed.

Speech (*Kalam*): Allah Almighty is the possessor of speech. He is not in need of sounds, letters, words and sentences in way of this. That is, His speech is above letters and sounds and is no way similar to the words and speech of human beings. For the speech of human beings is realised only through their being granted a share in His speech.

The Qur'an as well as other Divine scriptures came into existence through the manifestation of the Divine attribute of speech.

As the Qur'an is the Divine speech, it is essential that due reverence be shown to its blessed words. Touching it without being in a state of the ritual ablution is prohibited and is a grave sin. Allah, exalted and glorified be He, declares:

"Most certainly it is a Qur'an (recited) most honorable, In a Book well-guarded. None except the purified ones can reach it (to obtain the knowledge it contains. And none except those cleansed of material and spiritual impurities should touch it)." (Waq'iah 56:77-80)

It is stated in a Prophetic Tradition:

"None, save the pure, should touch the Qur'an." (*Muwatta'*, Qur'an, 1)

"No one should touch the Qur'an except one who is pure." (Hakim, *Mustadrak*, I, 553:1447)

Bringing into Being (*Takwin*): This is Allah Almighty's attribute of creating. This means making something exist out of nothing and is particular to Him alone. Innumerable realms are His creation.

Takwin does not denote making something with the hand or with a tool. *Takwin* is a creating that is realised through the connection between will and power and the subjugation of the universe.

Allah Almighty's attribute of bringing into being, like all His exalted attributes, are eternal in the past and in the future; however, every part of the universe, which originated with the power and manifestation of this attribute, has come into being later.

❋

The Almighty's being known by His servants is primarily possible through these attributes. These aforementioned attributes and the other infinite Divine attributes exist not in accordance with the differing conditions of time and place, but exist at every moment in the Being of Allah Almighty.

The substance of all the attributes belonging to His Exalted Essence possesses a greatness and infinitude that defy description. All of them are eternal in the past and eternal in the future. All of them are absolute in Him and possess infinite qualities. That is to say, no attribute has bounds or shores. In this respect, His knowledge, speech, power, making exist and all His other Divine attributes, with these qualities, are beyond any similitude and explanation. The characteristics pertaining to our world, and ourselves however, are both restricted as well as transient. It is of course not possible for humankind, who cannot even know themselves completely in such a state, to duly perceive the Divine attributes particular to His Being. In other words, just as we cannot perceive the truth and nature of Allah Almighty's Essence, we cannot perceive the truth and nature of His attributes in the perfect sense. That which manifests itself from His attributes to our world amounts to each a crumb.

a. Proofs of the Existence and Unity of Allah

That there is an order and harmony in this endless universe that stupefies the mind is self-evident. This order and harmony, within the perfect, delicate balance that has existed since the creation of the universe, has continued to carry on without fail.

If an owner of a fruit orchard wakes up one morning to find some of their saplings overturned in a random manner, he can accept this as being the result of a storm or a natural disaster. However, if there were an order and balance in the way these saplings were uprooted, for instance if every third or fifth sapling were affected, they could not accept this as being the outcome of a natural disaster. They would understand this to mean that a being capable of such planning was responsible for this damage. Hence, one ought consider just how absurd a heedlessness it is for minds that do not accept an incident of a mere five-ten trees being uprooted being ascribed to senseless causes, to claim that the universe despite all its delicate balance came about coincidentally or by itself.[52]

Famous poet **Necip Fazıl**, calls out to those dragged into such a heedlessness:

Embraced I have been, from all directions,
If there is one embraced, is not there one who embraces?

---

52. See: İsmail Fenni Ertuğrul, *Iman Hakikatleri Etrafında Suallere Cevaplar*, Istanbul, 1978, 21-22.

THE ESSENTIALS OF BELIEF

Who is the Craftsman, the Artist Who drew this countenance,
Can there not be one who stands before the mirror and asks?

Every sound mind that has not been corrupted would mindfully realise the chain of causes in the universe and would perceive that all of these would end in a Creator of causes, or Allah Almighty the true cause of all causes, and consciously pronounce their belief. In this regard, however, Satan has set up an intrigue and trap for humankind at every corner in order to misdirect their contemplation. Consequently, it is necessary to evade Satan's ambush through sound thought and reasonable action.

It is stated in the Qur'an:

"Of all His servants, only those possessed of true knowledge stand in awe of Allah." (Fatir 35:28)

For this reason, deservedly grasping the majesty and power of Allah is, before all else, the work of knowledge. It is due to this fact that scholars studying the subtleties of the micro and macrocosm grasp in a manner more completely than anyone else the existence and power of the Creator, by virtue of the stupendous order and laws they behold.

Indian scholar **Inayatullah Khan Mashriqi** relates a poignant example of this as follows:

"It was Sunday, the year 1909. It was raining hard. I had gone out on some errand when I saw the famous Cambridge University astronomer, **Sir James Jeans**, with a Bible clutched under his arm, on his way to Church. Coming closer I greeted him, but he did not reply. When I greeted him again, he looked at me and asked,

'What do you want?'

'Two things,' I replied. 'Firstly, the rain is pouring down, but you have not opened your umbrella.'

Sir James smiled at his own absent-mindedness and opened his umbrella. 'Secondly,' I continued,

'I would like to know that a man of universal fame such as yourself is doing—going to pray in Church?'

Sir James paused for a while, then, looking at me, he said,

'Come and have tea with me this evening.'

So I went along to his house that afternoon. At exactly 4 o'clock, Lady James appeared. 'Sir James is waiting for you,' she said. I went inside, where tea was ready on the table. Sir James was lost in thought. 'What was your question again?' he asked, and without waiting for an answer, he went off into an inspiring description of the creation of the celestial bodies and the astonishing order to which they adhere, the incredible distances over which they travel and the unfailing regularity which they maintain, their intricate journeys through space in their orbits, their mutual attraction and their never wavering from the path chosen for them, no matter how complicated it might be. His vivid account of the Power and Majesty of God made my heart begin to tremble. As for him, the hair on his head was standing up straight. He eyes were shining with awe and wonder. Trepidation at the thought of God's all-knowing and all-powerful nature made his hands tremble and his voice falter. 'You know, Inayatullah Khan,' he said,

'When I behold God's marvellous feats of creation, my whole being trembles in awe at His majesty. When I go to Church I bow my head and say, "Lord, how great You are," and not only my lips, but every particle of my body joins in uttering these words. I obtain incredible peace and joy from my prayer. Compared to others, I receive a thousand times more fulfilment from my prayer.'

'Sir,' I said, 'Your inspiring words have made a deep impression on me. I am reminded of a verse of the Qur'an which, if I may be

THE ESSENTIALS OF BELIEF

allowed, I should like to quote.' 'Of course.' Sir James replied. I then recited this verse:

'Of all His servants, only those possessed of true knowledge stand in awe of Allah.' (Fatir 35:28)

'What was that?' exclaimed Sir James.

'It is those alone who have knowledge who fear God. Wonderful! How extraordinary! It has taken me fifty years of continual study and observation to realise this fact. Who taught it to Muhammad? Is this really in the Qur'an? If so, you can record my testimony that the Qur'an's an inspired Book. Muhammad was illiterate. He could not have learnt this immensely important fact on his own. God must have taught it to him. Incredible! How extraordinary!'" (Vahiduddin Khan, *God Arises: Evidence of God in Nature and in Science*, 214-15)

There have been many non-Muslim scholars preoccupied with the positive sciences that have become Muslim and many, while not professing belief, have felt compelled to concede to the truth. This state of affairs is a miracle of the Qur'an. Allah, the Most High, declares:

"Those to whom the knowledge (of the truth) **has been granted are well aware that what is sent down to you from your Lord** (the Qur'an) **is the truth** (and what it declares of the afterlife is therefore true also)**, and that it guides to the Path of the All-Glorious with irresistible might, the All-Praiseworthy."** (Saba 34:6)

"We will show them Our manifest signs (proofs) **in the horizons of the universe and within their own selves, until it will become manifest to them that it** (the Qur'an) **is indeed the truth. Is it not sufficient** (as proof) **that your Lord is a witness over all things (just as He is witnessed to by all things)?"** (Fussilat 41:53)

Every eye that looks upon the universe with a mind to draw lesson gazes upon the innumerable scenes of the reflection of these verses:

Examples of Divine Power

If only human beings and animals had existed in the universe, they would have used up all the oxygen in the air and would have perished and become extinct with the resultant increasing levels of carbon dioxide a certain time later. However, the Power that created this universe also created plants and trees and, through giving them the ability to use up carbon dioxide and convert it into oxygen, He established a balance and continuous flow in the world.

Allah Almighty has also filled three quarters of the world with water. He has created the greater part of one quarter as barren rock faces or deserts. The remaining small part is soil. However, what an Exalted Power it is that He has made this soil, with its endless change and transformation, the source of sustenance for all beings. Consider the following example:

Let us consider a particular animal species. If all the members of this species, from those that came in the past to those to come in the future, had come to the world at once, neither the world as a habitat, nor its provisions would have been enough for them. However, Allah Almighty creates them within the law of continuity, spreading them over a more expansion stretch of time than that of space. The same is true for all living beings. Consequently, the world, with the mystery of time and space, is able to serve as a stage for trillions more times its normal capacity. That is to say, the role that living beings have in our world are dependent on a balance and limitation.

For instance, a sycamore produces millions of seeds every year. For these seeds to be dispersed, they each have a 'parachute', so to speak. By means of the wind, they reach distance lands. If the individual seeds belonging to one sycamore each became a new tree, then each quarter of the earth would have been subjected to the invasion of sycamores within a short period of time. That is, the great globe would have been much too tight for a single tree. This example can be extended to all beings. This demonstrates the presence of an unfathomable harmony and balance.

The existence of such a perfect, intricate and fine balance mechanism is a lofty sign of the existence and unity, power and majesty of its Maker. It is declared in a Qur'anic verse:

"And the heaven – He has made it high (above the earth), **and He has set up the balance."** (Rahman 55:7)

"He Who has created seven heavens in harmony. You do not see any fault or incongruity in the creation of the All-Merciful. Look yet again: can you see any rifts? Then look again and yet again (and however often you do so, with whatever instruments to aid your looking), **your sight will fall back to you dazzled** (by the splendor of Allah's creation), **and awed and weakened** (being unable to discern any flaw to support any excuse for claiming that there could be any sharing in the dominion of the universe)." (Mulk 67:3-4)

Moreover, Allah Almighty has conferred all living beings such qualities that even if they are nourished with similar nutrients, they produce different yields and these complete each other in such a way as to make life as a whole possible. For instance, while a cow or a sheep would generate meat, milk and wool if they ate a mulberry leaf, the silk worm would procure silk from the same leaf. If a particular species of deer were to eat the same thing, it would produce musk. The bee's ability to produce honey from the nectar of flowers is beyond the power of the most perfect being in creation – the human being. The colours, scents and petals that flowers produce from the soil are wondrous qualities that no chemist is capable of producing. While the animal turns grass into meat and milk, the human being does not have the power to produce a single gram of meat or milk from tonnes of grass in the laboratory.

A person possessing sound judgement would behold the existence and grandeur of Allah no matter where in the universe they turn. Such manifestations as sending Messengers, enabling humankind to reach perfection through their language, knowledge and morality and raising scholars from among them, are all the product of Divine grace. On the other hand, the result of all disciplines that serve human beings in a thousand and one ways is to ultimately illustrate the existence and majesty of Allah and make human beings taste their weakness, and to help humankind perceive their position of servanthood to Him. If a person looks at himself or herself and at the universe with a fair mind, they would immediately understand just how ridiculous and strange it would be not to believe before the unmistakable Divine power and dominion.

There are black and white holes in the firmaments. Allah Almighty swears by these holes that science has only just recently discovered in the following way:

"I swear by the locations of the stars (and their falling)**, It is indeed a very great oath, if you but knew."** (Waqi'a 56:75-76)

This reality, which present science has only just discovered, demonstrates just what an incredible magnificence we are face to face with. The term 'white hole' is given to the place where stars are born and 'black hole' to the place where they die. A small object emerges from white holes and, with a sudden expansion increasing trillions of times its size, generates an enormous star mass. There are, on the other hand, many massive stars many times the size of earth that, when the time comes, enter black holes and die. In this respect, the sun that illuminates our skies will one day also experience the reality mentioned in the verse,

"**When the sun is folded up (and darkened)...**"[53]

On that day, its life too will come to an end. That day will assuredly be the Day of Resurrection. And beyond...

Humankind cannot help but immediately fall to the ground in prostration and seek refuge in Allah.

And so, eyes that can see recognise that this world is but one speck of dust in the billions and trillions of dust particles swimming in the universe, before the Divine dominion. Mountains, plains, oceans and humankind are all within this speck. It is with this weakness and helplessness that the human being is, apart from their servanthood, but nothing.

These examples, as only a drop from the oceans, are sufficient in demonstrating the logical necessity of accepting the existence of a Being Who is All-Wise, All-Powerful, Self-Subsisting (by whom all subsist), All-Providing... However, in order to see this truth, the eye of the heart rather than the eye of the body needs to be open. It is declared in a Qur'anic verse:

"**Do they never travel about the earth** (and view all these scenes with an eye to learn lessons)**, so that they may have hearts with which to reason** (and arrive at truth)**, or ears with which to hear** (Allah's call)**? For indeed, it is not the eyes that have become blind; it is rather the hearts in the breasts that are blind.**" (Hajj 22:46)

All Things are in a State of Motion and Change

If we reflect upon this visible realm, we see that everything changes from one form into another. For instance, a fertilised ovum changes into a clot clinging, a clot clinging changes into a formless life of flesh and a formless life of flesh changes into flesh and bone.

---

53. Takwir 81:1.

Such transformation exists in stars, heavenly bodies, minerals, plants, or in everything.

There is tremendous motion within the atom. Electrons spin with extreme precision and at an unfathomable speed. As for protons and neutrons – its nucleus personnel – as they are compressed within a much smaller volume, their speeds are extraordinarily high when compared with electrons, so much so, that they spin at a rate exceeding 60,000 kilometres per second.

If we recall that there are approximately 100 trillion atoms on a pinhead that we accept to be one millimetre square in size, we would recognise the impossibility of having a complete understanding of the power of the Supreme Being Who administers the motion in the universe.

A true causer is required for all this movement and change to be realised and that is Allah Almighty, the Supreme Creator. For it is certainly not possible for these extraordinary and impenetrable states to take place without any causer or through an unconscious agent.

Upon contemplation of these, we see that even one particle is sufficient to move from the art to the Artist. How aptly a poet illustrates this:

Of what need is the world to know His existence,

When a single particle He created is sufficient demonstration.
(Şinasi)

Diverse Creations Come into Being from the Same Matter

The essence of all the different beings we see in our surroundings is always the same. All of them came into existence from matter. Different elements are always parts of the same constitution. For instance, heavenly bodies always come into existence from the same matter; however, each one of them has an identity, state, magnitude and life unique to itself. Some of them are cold while others are extremely hot.

Plants and animals originate from elements such as nitrogen, carbon, oxygen and hydrogen. Whereas there is absolutely no connection between these elements and life, much less such attributes as knowledge, will, power, hearing and sight.

All of these are marvels of Divine Art. All the diverse and perfect beings that we see in the universe are the works of an All-Powerful Craftsman. It is not possible for a Being Who brings into existence all these masterpieces to bear any resemblance to them in any way. He is the Necessarily Existent Being, **Allah Almighty**, Whose Being is absolutely essential, from Himself and eternal in the past.

Everything has been Created with a Purpose

That everything in the universe has been created with a particular wisdom and for a particular benefit is unmistakable.

The creatures on earth are illuminated and sprout and flourish with the light of the sun and moon. The earth and moon's revolving around the sun are used to measure time. The yearly cycle of seasons, the years, the changes of day and night are the result of the earth's revolving around the sun, while the moon's revolving around the sun generates the months.

- The air that we incessantly breathe goes to the lungs and cleans the blood. Due to the fact that our body needs it more than anything else, air is found most readily and abundantly.

- The winds take rain to where it is needed by propelling the clouds. Again, the winds fertilise plants and trees, regulate the heat and clean the air.

- In the same way, the benefits of the seas are countless.

The importance of all of these and innumerable other matters in human life is obvious. Consequently, a person who gazes upon these with an eye to learn lessons and reflects upon them will reach the conclusion that there is great wisdom and purpose in the creation of all things. Accepting these as coincidence, however, means the nullification of reason, conviction and fair-mindedness. These are the works of an All-Knowing, All-Wise, All-Powerful and All-Exalted Being – **Allah Almighty**, glorified and exalted be He.

In short, it is most easy for a person of sound judgement and who reflects to find their Lord and to be in awe and admiration of Him and this Divine splendour and majesty. This is the most natural result of a sound judgement and a crystal clear conscience. If a person duly reflected upon the happenings in the universe and in their own selves, they would come to belief, if unbelieving, and would increase in certainty and advance in knowledge and love of Allah if already a believer.

b. Benefits of Belief in Allah

The Almighty has placed within human nature or disposition the need to believe. For this reason, a person who does not possess authentic belief becomes ill at ease, spiritually, and lives with a deep feeling of discontent and restlessness in their heart. The sole remedy for this is to believe in the way shown by Allah Almighty.

On the other hand, a person who believes in a Lord Who constantly sees, hears and knows them, possesses good character as well as a respect for rights. Owing to this, they live a peaceful life. In the same way that they do not harm anyone, they are also not harmed by anyone. Their eternal life in the Hereafter is better than their life in this world.

A person who believes in Allah thus cannot engage in immorality even if they where out of sight to all others. This is because they know that the Most High will surely call them to account and will reward or punish them for all their actions, and they act accordingly.

A person who believes in Allah is protected from arrogance and self-conceit and possesses humility. Pride and arrogance are the worst spiritual diseases that are to be found in human beings. Underlying all disputes, quarrels and conflicts is this sense of self-conceit. Consequently, a proud person is doomed to eventually lose all their friends and to be dragged into loneliness. 'Ali, may Allah be well pleased with him, has stated:

"The greatest loneliness is self-importance."

Humility is one of the best adornments of the human being. A person who believes in Allah knows that everything they possess has been conferred upon them by Allah. Thus, they are in a constant state of humility and thankfulness. This, in turn, ensures they get on well with and are loved by other human beings.

In addition, belief is a great source of consolation in the face of tribulations and afflictions befalling a human being. A person without belief is devastated in the face of trials and difficulties and cannot easily find a means of consolation. A believer, however, after doing whatever is in their power, trusts in Allah and surrenders to Him. If they achieve a favourable outcome, they are thankful and earn the good pleasure and approval of Allah. If they are face-to-face with the undesirable, they endure it with patience and again earn Allah's good pleasure and approval. Their every state, therefore,f is good for them. (See, Muslim, Zuhd, 64)

One who believes in Allah and acts accordingly is not too afraid of **death**. An unbeliever, however, makes life unbearable for himself or herself with a fear of death. They can neither find peace in this world, nor in the Hereafter. As they fail to take into account that which is beyond death, they can commit any harm or treachery in this world, at the first opportunity. They can even consider causing the greatest damage for the slightest self-interest.

Belief in Allah and worship of Him also has certain health benefits. According to a study published by the *International Journal of Psychiatry in Medicine* in February 2002, the probability of those who frequently attend congregational worship contracting digestive diseases, excluding cancer, is reduced by half. Death due to cardiovascular diseases (heart attacks and stoke included) is reduced by twenty one percent and death due to respiratory diseases reduced by sixty six percent.

This study highlights in particular the fact that the psychological benefits of religion are becoming more and more apparent. As a person's belief and spirituality strengthens, their spirit becomes distanced from anxiety and stress. They attain heightened capacities, a strong sense of belonging, clarity in perception and an illuminated life.

3. Belief in the Angels

Angels are subtle beings created out of light. This is why we cannot see them in their own manner and form. However, Allah Almighty can show them to whosoever He wills.[54] There have been instances where they have been visible to great Prophets in their own forms. The angels do not possess such characteristics, like human beings, as eating, drinking and the like. As they have been created solely for the purpose of worship of Allah Almighty and observing His commandments, they have not been given a carnal soul. Thus, angels can never commit error, disobedience and wrongdoing. They are extremely powerful and strong.[55]

---

54. Hud 11:77-82; Hijr 15:59-69; Maryam 19:17-21; Najm 53:67, 13-17; Takwir 81:23.
55. For the attributes of angels, see Baqara 2:30-34; A'raf 7:11, 27; Hud 11:69-70; Hijr 15:28, 51-52; Isra' 17:61, 92; Kahf 18:50; Ta-Ha 20:116; Saad 38:71, 73; Najm 53:5' Tahrim 66:6; Takwir 81:20.

They are too numerous to be counted. According to narrations, every raindrop and snowflake that descends to earth is brought down by an angel, and an angel that has descended to earth once never gets another turn until the Last Day. This is the wisdom behind raindrops and snowflakes descending to the earth without ever colliding with one another. If one looks closely, it is possible to see that come down without collision even during storms. In short, everything – from the particle to the heavenly body – is a showcase of Divine majesty.

The angels are, in a sense, like the spirit that has been given to us. Consequently, in the same way that we do not deny the existence of our spirit despite our inability to see it, we cannot deny the existence of angels.

The angels of of varying degrees with regard to excellence. There are four archangels: Gabriel, Michael, Azrail and Israfil, upon them all be peace.

Archangel Gabriel, peace be upon him, is the angel charged with conveying revelation to the Prophets. Archangel Michael, peace be upon him, is authorised with monitoring natural events. Archangel Azrail, peace be upon him, (the Angel of Death) is given the duty of seizing souls. Archangel Israfil, peace be upon him, is responsible for blowing the trumpet for the Resurrection.

As can be seen, the angels also have other responsibilities outside worship of the Almighty. Some of them help human beings, upon Allah's command. Especially in times of hardship for believers, the assistance and blessing of the angels have been witnessed at many instances throughout the history of Islam.

In addition, there are also the guardian angels (*hafadha*), the noble scribes (*kiramun katibun*), the interrogating angels in the grave (*Munkar* and *Nakir*), the angels imploring Allah for the forgiveness of those who commit sin and those that pray for humankind to be guided to the straight path.

Even a person's survival in this world fraught with danger is contingent upon the protection of the angels. These angels appointed by Allah shield the human being from danger and harm until their death. When the appointed time comes, they withdraw from the scene and leave a person face-to-face with their death. As stated in a Qur'anic verse:

"(Every person advances through varying states, before and after, and) **by Allah's command attendant angels succeeding one another accompany him, before and after him, to guard him** (and record his deeds)..." (Ra'd 13:11)

It must not be forgotten that it is Allah Almighty Who bestows the power possessed by the angels.

If a person makes light of one of the angels or criticises them, this causes them to leave the folds of belief. Consequently, one must vehemently avoid such expressions or jokes involving angels.

4. Belief in the Books

Allah, the Most High, has sent His commandments and prohibitions from the time of the first human being and the first Prophet, Adam, upon him be peace, first in the form of scrolls and then as books, with the increase of social matters that came with the increase in the human population. All these scrolls and scriptures were the true and valid books for their own particular time. Consequently, belief in the Books is belief in the original forms in which they were sent from Allah.

According to narration, of the scrolls, ten were sent to Prophet Adam, fifty to Prophet Seth, thirty to Prophet Enoch (*Idris*) and the last ten to Prophet Abraham, upon them all be peace.[56] Of the great scriptures, the Torah was revealed to Prophet Moses, the Psalms to Prophet David, the Gospel to Prophet Jesus, upon them all be peace, and finally, the Qur'an was sent to the Master of creation, Prophet Muhammad, upon him be peace and blessings.

The Divine scriptures are like a letter sent by Allah Almighty to His servants. These books, which regulate the lives of human beings and prescribe the formula for eternal happiness, are the reflection of Divine attribute of speech on the speech and perception of human beings. Consequently, each of them is a distinct miracle of speech, in addition to the messages they convey.

The essence of all the scrolls and scriptures, that is the matters pertaining to belief, is identical. Rulings concerning worship and pertaining to everyday worldly matters have differed in certain ways in accordance the structure of society.

Sending scriptures [nor any other single act] is incumbent upon Allah, glorified and exalted be He. This is entirely His Divine grace and favour for His servants.

a. The Qur'an

The last of the Divine Books, the Qur'an, has abrogated all the previous Books, or has rendered their rulings null and void. Changing and developing human needs over the course of time as well as heedless human intervention and manipulation in those Books has essentially rendered this necessary.

The greatest characteristic of the Divine Books is their undisputed reliance on Divine revelation. However, this characteristic has remained a quality particular only to the Qur'an, for the other Divine Books faced immense human alteration after the Prophets through

---

56. Ibn Kathir, Tafsir, [Nisa 4:163]; Ibn al-Nadim, al-Fihrist, Tehran 1966, 24.

whom they were revealed, and have ultimately taken on the identity of books penned by human beings. This was, in fact, one of the reasons for the revelation of the Qur'an. Moreover, with **"Its seal** [being] **a fragrance of musk,"**[57] the Qur'an includes all the Divine Books and is the most perfect of them. By virtue of its being the last, it is under the protection of the Almighty Himself.

1) Characteristics

The Qur'an was revealed to the Prophet Muhammad Mustafa, upon him be peace and blessings. It is a miracle in many ways. It was immediately recorded and memorised as it was sent down in parts.

The first verses that were revealed were devoted to the praise and laudation of **"the Pen"** and **"what they write with it line by line"** and throughout the course of its revelation, great emphasis was placed on **the Book**.[58] For this reason, the Messenger of Allah, upon him be peace and blessings, gave considerable importance to the Qur'an being written as well as memorised, for its preservation.[59]

The recitation of the Qur'an in their daily-prescribed prayers has been made obligatory, as with its being recited and listened to outside the prayer and those reading it have been given the glad tidings of receiving ten rewards for every letter recited.[60] In addition, the Qur'an

---

57. Its seal is a fragrance of musk: This is an expression used in reference to those things whose completion and close is as beautiful as the fragrance of musk and whose best is saved for last. It is mentioned in the twenty-sixth verse of the Qur'anic chapter entitled Mutaffifin.
58. 'Alaq 96:1-5; Qalam 68:1; Baqara 2:2; Zukhruf 43:2; Dukhan 44:2.
59. The following works can be referred in order to see just how reliable is the methodology employed by Muslims in preserving and transmitting the Qur'an up to the present day: Muhammad Mustafa A'zami, *The History of the Qur'anic Text: From Revelation to Compilation: A Comparative Study with the Old and New Testaments*, Leicester: UK Islamic Academy, 2003; Muhammad Hamidullah, *Le Saint Coran*, "Introduction", Istanbul: Beyan, 2005.
60. Tirmidhi, Fada'il al-Qur'an, 16.

has constantly been recited in the Friday Sermons, where all Muslims gather, in discussions or gatherings of a religious nature and in one-to-one meetings.⁶¹ This has enabled it to be transmitted to us via numerous reliable channels, being preserved in the best possible way.

The recitation of the Qur'an's being a form of worship has ensured its being interwoven with the lives of Muslims and its assuming a place in every aspect and phase of life. In this way, believers have been favoured with the honour of being forever with the Divine Word. In other words, the Qur'an has always held a central position in the lives of Muslims.

In addition to **writing** and **memorisation**, a third method has been implemented for the preservation of the Qur'an:

"Receiving personal instruction by a well-trained and authorised teacher," has been laid down as a condition.⁶²

---

61. See: Muslim, Jumu'ah 49-52, Musafirin 142; Abu Dawud, Buyu', 36:3416; Ibn Maja, Salat, 178; Ahmad, III:432, IV:9' Ibn Hajar, al-Isaba, 2546 ['Rafi' ibn Malik']; Ibn Ishaq, Al-Sirat, 128.
62. Two of many proofs which demonstrate that the Qur'an has been transmitted to the present day in written form alongside its being preserved through memorisation, are the following:
1) Analysing four original manuscripts and the present-day Qur'an over a ten year study, former president of Turkey's Directorate of Religious Affairs (Diyanet) Dr. Tayyar Altıkulaç demonstrated, matching the scripts word by word and letter by letter, that there is no difference between them whatsoever. As a result of his word to word and letter to letter of analysis of the original manuscript of the Qur'an ascribed to Caliph 'Uthman which is held in Istanbul's Topkapı Museum – with an exact reproduction being prepared by the OIC Research Centre for Islamic History, Art and Culture (IRCICA) – Altıkulaç explains that it is exactly the same as the Qur'an presently read by Muslims across the world. He also notes that he conducted the same analysis of the al-Mashhad al-Husayn manuscript again belonging to Caliph 'Uthman, which is located in Cairo. Mentioning that he conducted the same study of the manuscripts in the Turkish and Islamic Arts Museum and in Tashkent, Altıkulaç said,
"These are all manuscripts written within the first Islamic century, in differing geographical regions. Just as they resemble each other perfectly, they are also

Allah, glory unto Him, declares:

"Indeed it is We, We Who send down the Reminder in parts, and it is indeed We Who are its Guardian." (Hijr 15:9)

The Qur'an was revealed in parts in connection with various events and needs. When a verse was revealed, the Messenger of Allah also used to detail where in the Qur'an it would be placed. With the approach of the Prophet's demise and the resultant end of revelation, the Qur'an was completed as a book with an imposing unity and coherence.

The arrangement of the Qur'an and the manner in which it presents its subject matter does not resemble any text penned by human beings. It has a structure entirely unique to itself. The Qur'an being divided into chapters and the chapters being separated into verses has facilitated its memorisation. The miraculous eloquence, fluency and coherence of the Qur'an are also instrumental in its being easily memorised.

The topics comprising the Qur'anic content have been spread throughout, from its beginning to the end. This style of arrangement, and with the added role of repetition, is more effective, instructive and beneficial in various ways such as the reader or listener's being able to review several topics simultaneously, their being the address-

---

exactly the same as the copies of the Qur'an that are read the world over. While there are slight, basic differences in orthography, which have no bearing on the meaning or essence, there is nothing which concerns the fundamental. Neither more nor less. I see this to be a very important outcome for Muslims." (http://www.habervaktim.com/haber/136521/kurani_kerimin_degismedigi_ispatlandi.html 14.08.2010)

2) On 5 April, 2010, "The 1400th Anniversary of the Qur'an" exhibition was held in the Turkish and Islamic Arts Museum, Istanbul. The very first manuscripts of the Qur'an written on deer hide were on display as part of the exhibition. (http://www.habervaktim.com/haber/136864/iste_kuranin_ilk_nushalari.html, 16.08.2010)

ees of both counsel and admonition and their being able to see parallels between this Qur'anic structure and their own diverse lives.

There are one hundred and fourteen chapters in the Qur'an, of varying lengths. Each chapter has a different number of verses.

2) Content

The Qur'an continues as a miracle of speech and eloquence that defies the centuries. The key issues presented therein, as a formula for deliverance, are briefly the following:

1. The essentials of belief, Divine Unity, the names and attributes of Allah, making Him known as He deserves to be known, the Hereafter...

2. Deeds of righteousness, worship, worldly transactions, morality, rulings concerning human actions – what they are commanded to do and what they must avoid...

3. With respect to the human being's physical constitution: the stages of their creation, their worldly life and ultimately their death. In terms of their inner world: the unrefined qualities of the carnal self and the perfected qualities of the spirit; the way in which training of the carnal self and purification of the heart is to be realised, in order for a person to ascend from the unrefined character to the perfected one...

4. The composition of the universe: the seven heavens, the sun, moon, stars – their creation and end – natural events, the lengthening and shortening of shadows, rain, the cycle of day and night, the creatures living between the earth and the heavens...

5. Historical facts: the positive and negative states of societies and their situations in the world and the Hereafter, manifestations of Divine reprisal, Prophets and the countless examples in their stories, lessons from the past, the causes and repercussions of events...

6. An expansive ocean of contemplation and recollection extending from the eternity without beginning to the eternity without end... Transition from contemplation to emotion...

The Qur'an is a means for the emergence of profound feelings in the heart. When the believer with a developed world of the heart looks at the Qur'anic verses, they delve so deeply, as though they were looking into a bottomless well, that they receive many boundless meanings from them.

Some scholars such as **Imam Suyuti** maintain that every kind of knowledge that the human mind can acquire is contained in the Qur'an, at the very least as a kernel or sign. For Allah, exalted and glorified be He, has declared:

"We have neglected nothing in the Book." (An'am 6:38)

"We have sent down on you the Book as an exposition of everything (that pertains to guidance and error and to the knowledge of good and evil, and to happiness and misery in both worlds), **and guidance and mercy and glad tidings for the Muslims** (those who have submitted themselves wholly to Allah).*"* (Nahl 16:89)

For this reason, the Qur'an possesses a richness that can respond to all the needs of humanity until the Last Day. **Hamidullah** says the following in relation to this point:

"The Qur'an serves practically all the needs of the Muslim community not only in our own age of political as well as material and intellectual weakness among Muslims, but served all the purposes of the powerful Muslim states, even at the height of their widest expansion from the Pacific to the Atlantic Oceans. This community has always found all the necessary knowledge pertaining to their belief, worship, social life and law, as well as all their other needs, within this book."⁶³

3) Miraculousness

Allah Almighty has rendered the Qur'an a miracle that affirms both His and His Messenger's truth. For this reason, its aspects of miraculousness are too numerous to be counted.⁶⁴ It will continue to reveal its secrets, when the time comes, until the Last Day. Some of its aspects of miraculousness which have been realised until the present day are as follows:

• The Qur'an's challenging human beings to produce something similar,

• The unbelievers' inability to produce the like thereof, despite their having much cause to oppose and compete with the Qur'an, and despite their feeling a fierce need for this,

• Its being distinct from all literary forms,⁶⁵

• Its possessing a beauty of verse, order and compilation at the pinnacle of eloquence to a degree unattainable by any being,

• Its comprising information pertaining to the Unseen, both past and present, and these coming true.⁶⁶

• The inner spiritual impression that the Qur'an engenders in hearts. No word of poetry or prose other than the Qur'an, even at times of fear and consternation, provides as much pleasure and taste to the heart when heard. When the Qur'an is listened to, hearts find

---

63. Muhammad Hamidullah, *Le Saint Coran*, "Introduction," 23.
64. For further detail, see: Osman Nuri Topbaş, *Rahmet Esintileri*, İstanbul 2010, s. 221-372.
65. Rummani, *al-Nukat fi I'jaz al-Qur'an* in *Thalath Rasail fi i'jaz al-Qur'an*, ed. Muhammad Khalaf Allah & Muhammad Zaghlul Sallam, Cairo n.d., 1968, 101.
66. Qadi 'Iyad, *al-Shifa' bi Ta'rifi Huquq al-Mustafa*, Cairo 1995, 227-247.

repose and hearts expand.[67] When people savour its spiritual taste, they are deeply shaken, are filled internally with devoted reverence, their hairs stand on end and their heart begins to pulsate with excitement. The Qur'an intervenes between their carnal self and the

---

67. Professor Sayyid Qutb relates the following anecdote in reference to the Qur'an's effect on hearts: "I am not giving any example witnessed by anyone else. I am only relating something that happened to me about 15 years ago [approximately 1948], for which I have no less than six witnesses. "We were seven Muslim passengers travelling on board an Egyptian ship across the Atlantic to New York. There were also 120 foreign passengers, none of whom was a Muslim. It occurred to us to hold Friday prayers on board, in the middle of the ocean... The Captain, an Englishman, facilitated our task and allowed any of the crew and other workers, all of whom were Nubian Muslims, to join the prayer, provided that they were not on duty at the time. They were overjoyed by this, as it was, in their experience, the first time ever that Friday prayers had been held on board. I delivered the khutbah, or sermon, and led the prayers, while many of the foreign passengers were watching nearby. When the prayer was over, many of them congratulated us on a 'successful service'. That was how they viewed our prayers. One particular lady, whom we were later informed was a Christian from Yugoslavia fleeing from the oppression of Tito's Communist regime, was particularly touched. In fact she could not control her feelings and her eyes were full of tears. She shook our hands warmly and said in broken English that she was profoundly touched by the discipline and spiritual calm of our prayers. She then asked which language the 'priest' was speaking. She simply could not imagine that prayers could be led by a layman, but we made sure to explain this point to her. She also said that although she could not understand a word of what was being said, the language had a remarkable musical rhythm. She then added something that was a great surprise to us all. She said that certain phrases or sentences which he used were different from the rest of his speech. They were more clearly musical with an even more profound rhythm. These phrases filled her with awe. It was as if the imam was deriving his speech from the Holy Spirit. We reflected on what she had said and concluded that she meant the Qur'anic verses quoted in the khutbah and recited during the prayer. The whole thing was truly remarkable as the lady did not understand a word of Arabic... This incident, and similar ones reported by different people, confirm that the Qur'an has some secret which enables certain hearts to react to it when they hear its recitation... But why do we wonder at this when we see thousands of uneducated Muslims greatly influenced by the rhythm of the Qur'an, despite their inability to understand it. In a sense, they are not much different from this Yugoslav lady. (Sayyid Qutb, *Fi Zilal al-Qur'an*, [Yunus, 10:38])

deep-seated beliefs they hide within. There are many enemies of the Prophet who came to him with the intention of assassinating him but abandoned their initial intention just as soon as they heard the Qur'an, embraced Islam and whose hostility became transformed into amity and unbelief into belief.[68]

- Its being conveyed by an unlettered individual,[69]
- The truth in its meanings,
- The coherence and fluency in its wording,[70]
- The Qur'an's unique melodic rhythm,
- Its history (revelation, compilation, etc.),
- Lack of any redundant words or expressions,
- Its containing scientific facts.[71] The Qur'an is always ahead in terms of scientific developments, with science confirming and following it. There are a great examples of this is such disciplines as astronomy, embryology and medicine.

According to **Imam Suyuti**, the miracles of the Qur'an are too numerous to be constricted. He himself makes mention of thirty five points in his three-volume work on the subject.[72]

There is no need for an extensive knowledge, culture and flair for eloquence and rhetoric in order to understand the miraculous aspects of the Qur'an. Every person who reads it with due reflection, whatever their culture or education, can easily grasp its miraculous structure.[73]

---

68. Khattabi, *Bayan I'jaz al-Qur'an*, 24, 64. Suyuti, *al-Itqan*, IV:14-16.
69. Baqillani, *I'jaz al-Qur'an*, Beirut 1988, 50-68.
70. Suyuti, *al-Itqan*, IV:9.
71. Rafi'i, *I'jaz al-Qur'an*, 131.
72. Suyuti, *Mu'tarak al-aqran fi i'jaz al-Qur'an*, I:3.
73. Buti, *Min Rawa'i' al-Qur'an*, 160.

They can immediately recognise it to be the word of an All-Powerful Creator and that it cannot be the work of a human being.

a) *Eloquence and Rhetoric*

The society in which the Qur'an was revealed was at the peak of poetry and oration. Poetry and oratory contests were publicly held at fairs. Everyone, young and old, was preoccupied with the art of rhetoric and poetry. Despite this, all oratory and poetic masters writhed with desperation before the eloquence, rhetoric and miraculous verse of the Qur'an and were buried in to the depths of silence.

The Qur'an challenged them time and time again, demanding them to gather together all their helpers and produce the like of the Qur'anic verses. Notwithstanding this explicit challenge, those Arabs who were devoted to their pride and who would sacrifice their life, possessions and their whole family for the sake of their ego, did not respond.

Walid ibn Mughira, from among the Makkan poytheists, once came to the Prophet. The Messenger of Allah, upon him be peace and blessings, recited certain sections from the Qur'an to him. Walid's heart softened slightly towards Islam. Hearing of his state, Abu Jahl approached him and said,

"O uncle, your people have mustered and are collecting money and property to give to you," for you went to Muhammad to seek something from him." To this, Walid replied,

"The Quraysh know well that I am one of the wealthiest of them." Abu Jahl said,

"Then say such a thing about Muhammad that your people should understand you to be averse to him, that you do not care for him and that you deny him." Walid said,

"What shall I say? By Allah! None of you is better conversant than I with poetry, rajaz[74] and qasida, and by Allah never did I hear anything similar to it. But, by Allah, his recitation resembles none of these. It possesses indescribable beauty, and there is an air of splendour about it, that it remains at the summit with nothing to surpass it."

Abu Jahl was adamant:

"Your people will not be appeased until you have spoken against him." He replied,

"Allow me time to think." Having done so, he said:

"This is nothing but sorcery (of a sort transmitted from sorcerers) from old times." (Wahidi, *Asbab al-Nuzul*, 468)

His situation is most vividly described in the Qur'an as follows:

"He pondered and he calculated (how he could disprove the Qur'an in people's sight). **Be away from Allah's mercy, how he calculated! Yea, be away from Allah's mercy! How he calculated! Then he looked around** (in the manner of one who will decide on a matter about which he is asked). **Then he frowned and scowled. Then he turned his back and** (despite inwardly acknowledging the Qur'an's Divine origin), **grew in arrogance, And he said: 'This is nothing but sorcery** (of a sort transmitted from sorcerers) **from old times. This is nothing but the word of a mortal.'"** (Muddathir 74:18-25)

With the rapid increase in the number of Muslims and such heroes as Hamza and 'Umar, may Allah be well pleased with them both, having become Muslim, the Makkan polytheists became even more perturbed. They held a meeting to discuss ways of preventing the advance of Islam, under the pretext that,

---

74. Rajaz is one of the poetic meters in Arabic prosody.

"Muhammad's situation has become all the more serious for he has thrown into disarray all our affairs. Let us send to him our most learned in sorcery, soothsaying and poetry to talk to him."

They decided to send **'Utba ibn Rabi'a** to Allah's Messenger, upon him be peace and blessings. 'Utba reiterated such proposals that the Makkan polytheists had made before as wealth, rank, position and women and spoke at length. The Messenger of Allah, upon him be peace and blessings, listened to him quietly until he finished speaking. Then addressing him with his title, he asked, *"Is this all you intend to say?"*

When 'Utba replied in the affirmative, Allah's Messenger, upon him be peace and blessings, said,

"Now you listen to me."

Reciting the *Basmala*, he began reciting the Qur'anic chapter Fussilat. After reading the thirty seventh verse and performing the prescribed prostration, he said,

"O father of Walid, you have heard what I have recited. This is my reply to your proposition, now you may act as you see fit."

Makkan polytheists seeing 'Utba from afar when on his way back to the Qurayshi leaders, said,

"By Allah, 'Utba returns with a face much altered. He is not the same man as when he left." The leaders of the Quraysh were waiting for him in great anxiousness. When he reached them, they asked,

"What happened? Tell us all that you heard." 'Utba replied,

"By Allah! I have heard something the likes of which I have never heard before. It is neither poetry, nor sorcery, nor do they resemble the words of a soothsayer. When he said,

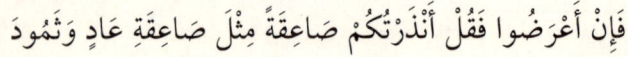

"If they turn away in aversion, say (to them): **'I have warned you of a punishment striking like the lightning** (that struck the tribes of) **Ad and Thamud,'**[75] I had to hold my hand over his mouth so that he would not continue and swore an oath on the basis of our kinship. Due to my knowing that everything that he has transpired exactly as he said it would, I feared that what happened to 'Ad and Thamud might happen to us.

O people of the Quraysh, listen to my words. Leave him alone to his own devices, for if he is not successful the others will deal with him and you will be saved from him, but if he is successful, his victory will be your victory, his strength and honour will be your strength and honour. In this way, you will be the happiest of people by virtue of Muhammad."

When, upon hearing this, the Qurayshi leaders said,

"O 'Utba, you too have been bewitched!"

He replied, "This is my view. You may do what you please." (Ibn Hisham, I:313-314; Ibn Kathir, *al-Bidaya*, III:111-112)

During the ninth year after the Emigration, delegations began to visit Madina from different places. During this period, **Abu Harb ibn Khuwaylid** from the 'Ukayl tribe also came to visit the Messenger. The Messenger of Allah, upon him be peace and blessings, recited the Qur'an to him and communicated to him the message of Islam. In awe before the Qur'an and Islam, Abu Harb said,

"By Allah! You have either met Allah or you have met one who has met Him, for we have heard nothing the likes of it."[76]

Before the revelation of the Qur'an, many poetry and oratory contests were held at fairs. In spite of this, no one could say, "Let us

---

75. Fussilat 41:13.
76. Ibn Sa'd, I:302-303; Ibn al-Athir, Kamil, II:286; Ibn al-Khaldun, Tarikh, II:2, 51.

produce something similar to the Qur'an and contend with it." These famous poets and orators rejected the Qur'an despite accepting its Divine origin in their conscience, purely because of their ego. They accepted that the Qur'an was the word of Allah, but – Allah forbid the thought! – ascribed error to His will and discretion. To their minds, obscured with carnality, the Qur'an should not have been revealed to a poor orphan, but to either **Walid ibn Mughira** from Makka's wealthy, or **'Amr ibn 'Umayr** from among the wealthy elite of Ta'if. Sure enough, Walid ibn Mughira had said,

"Is the Qur'an to be revealed to Muhammad instead of me, the greatest chief of the Quraysh, or 'Amr ibn 'Umayr, the leader of the Thaqif, as the two leading figures of Makka and Ta'if?" (Ibn Hisham, I:385. cf. Zukhruf 43:31)

Whereas, the value of servants in the eyes of Allah is by virtue of neither wealth nor nobility, but only through piety and God consciousness. Moreover, the Prophet Muhammad Mustafa, upon him be peace and blessings, was the most honoured of them with respect to nobility.

Famous Arab poet and orator **Abu al-A'la al-Ma'arri**, says the following in relation to the miraculousness of the Qur'an:

"Those lead astray, those guided, those deviating from the middle way and those finding the true path, all of them have been united in the fact that the miraculous **Book** brought by Muhammad, upon him be peace and blessings, reigns triumphant... *Whenever a single Divinely-revealed Qur'anic verse or a part of it is placed among the word most superior in eloquence, this verse stands out like a star shining resplendently in the middle of the darkness...*"

In seeking proof of the Qur'an's being a miraculous book passed down to the present day without losing anything of its influence, it is not possible to find proof more explicit and binding than experience

THE ESSENTIALS OF BELIEF

and observation. For from the time in which its revelation first began until the present day, there has been no one who has been able to challenge it. Those aiming to attempt such a task, falling into disgrace before all humanity, have brought upon themselves a humiliation which will follow them until the Day of Judgement.[77]

b) Relating the Unseen

The Qur'an encompasses a great deal of information and signs pertaining to the Unseen. Contained within it are signs, details and references to the past, the present and the future.[78]

The first scene of the creation of the human being, the events unfolding here (embryology), former societies and their life stories, the Prophets sent to them and the connection they had with these are all included in information relating to the past.

The Divine Being of Allah Almighty, His attributes, acts, the angels and jinn, the world of the grave, knowledge about Paradise and Hellfire, and especially the verses describing the intrigues and deceptions occurring to the hearts and minds of the People of the Book, hypocrites and unbelievers, as well detailing as their mindsets, comprise the information about the Unseen in relation to the time of revelation.

The most important of news pertaining to the Unseen are those relating to the events which will unfold in the future. When history too affirmed that these predictions transpired exactly as revealed in the Qur'an, there was no doubt remaining regarding the Qur'an's

---

77. See: Buti, Min Rawa'i' al-Qur'an, 126, 129, 130; Karaçam, Ismail, *Sonsuz Mu'cize Kur'an*, 159-175; Hacımüftüoğlu, Nasrullah, *Kur'ân'ın Belâğati ve İ'câzı Üzerine*, 58-62, 90.
78. Salah 'Abd al-Fattah Khalidi, *al-Bayan fi I'jaz al-Qur'an*, Amman 1991, 234; Yavuz, "İ'câzü'l-Kur'ân", *TDV Encyclopaedia of Islam*, XXI:405.

being sent from the **Knower of the Unseen**, Allah Almighty. Some of the predictions concerning the future are outlined below:

The Pharaoh's Body

When the Pharaoh and his army pursued **Prophet Moses**, the sea had split into two, Moses, peace be upon him, and those with him safely crossed to the other side and the Pharaoh and his men drowned. **Just as the Pharaoh** was about to drown in the whirlpools of the Rea Sea, he wanted to profess his belief, having been compelled to do so. Allah, the Most High, declared to Him:

"**Now?** – (You surrender now) **when before this you always rebelled and were of those engaged in causing disorder and corruption? So this day** (as a recompense for your belief in the state of despair which will be of no avail to you in the Hereafter), **We will save only your body, that you may be a sign for those to come after you. Surely, a good many people among humankind are heedless of Our signs (full of clear warning and lessons).**" (Yunus 10:91-92)

Not long ago, the Pharaoh's body was found during research. At the present time, this body is exhibited in London's British Museum, in room 94. Despite the thousands of years that have passed by, Allah Almighty has preserved it in order for people to draw lessons from it.

Victory of the Romans

In a war that had broken out between the Christian Romans and the Zoroastrian Persians the latter were triumphant. Makkan polytheists wanting to take advantage of this taunted the Muslims saying,

"You thought that you would be victorious due to a Divine Book. Look at the Zoroastrians; they defeated the People of the Book – the Romans." They thus tried to demoralise and discourage them. Upon this, Allah Almighty revealed the following Qur'anic verses which would give joy in the believers:

"**Alif. Lam. Mim. The Byzantine Romans have been defeated, In the lands close-by, but they, after their defeat, will be victorious within a few years – to Allah belongs the command** (the absolute judgment and authority) **both before and after** (any event) **– and at the time (when the Romans are victorious), the believers will rejoice, Because of Allah's help leading them to victory. He helps whom He wills to victory. He is the All-Glorious with irresistible might, the All-Compassionate** (especially towards His believing servants)." (Rum 30:1-5)

At that point, the Romans had languished to such an extent that no one considered the possibility of their becoming victorious once again after this devastating defeat. However, the Qur'an strongly reinforced this, declaring:

"(This is) **Allah's promise. Allah never fails His promise, but most people do not know this** (as they have no true knowledge about Allah)." (Rum 30:6)

Allah Almighty ultimately fulfilled His promise. Upon the consensus of historians, the Romans defeated the Sassanids in less than nine years. On the same day, the Muslims had overcome the Makkan polytheists at Badr and thus rejoiced.[79] This was the second miracle foretold in the fourth and fifth verses.

Again, the Qur'an indicated that the enemy forces would be defeated at the Battle of Badr[80], and that a short time later the Muslims would be victorious and conquer Makka.[81] These came about exactly as indicated. Many other similar examples can be provided.[82]

---

79. See: Tirmidhi, Tafsir, 30:3191-3194; Ahmad, I:276; Qurtubi, *al-Jami'*, XIV:3.
80. Qamar 54:45.
81. Fath 43:16, 27. For examples, refer to: Yusuf al-Hajj Ahmad, *Mawsu'at al-i'jaz al-'ilmi fi al-Qur'an al-karim wa-al-sunna al-mutahhara*, Damascus 2003, 20-24.
82. For further detail, see: Osman Nuri Topbaş, *Rahmet Esintileri*, İstanbul 2010, 279-293.

It was not possible for the Messenger of Allah to predict such events concerning the Unseen without reliance upon revelation. Hence, the Qur'an is the word of Allah and all its statements are most true.

c) Illuminating Scientific Discoveries

The Qur'an, whose actual purpose is to guide the human being, provides compendious information in the field of the natural sciences in particular, when drawing attention to belief in Divine Unity; modern science's later discovery of these truths constitutes another facet of its miraculousness. That is to say, the Qur'an is perpetually ahead of its time while the sciences follow in its tracks.

It is stated in a Qur'anic verse that scholars conducting scientific research and attempting to unearth the unchanging laws that Allah has placed in nature and society will eventually come to see that the Qur'an is a book that is the product of Divine revelation.[83] According to another verse,[84] the Qur'an indicates certain facts that will come to light in the future. The unbelievers, however, blindly attempt to refute and contradict it without having first examined its method and without waiting for the actualisation of its predictions.[85]

The Qur'an's shedding light on scientific discoveries is one of its distinct miracles that will continue until the Last Day, across all time and space. The Qur'an continues to demonstrate its resplendence anew each and every time. For ever-increasing scientific advancements confirm and corroborate this knowledge. The following can be offered by way of example:

The Fingerprint

The discipline that studies fingerprints (dactyloscopy), has pro-

---

83. See: Saba, 34:6.
84. See: Yunus, 10:39.
85. Alusi, *Ruh al-Ma'ani*, XI:119-120, (Yunus 10:39)

pounded that fingerprints remain the same throughout one's lifetime without undergoing any alteration and that no two fingerprints are alike. Consequently, the most reliable identification in the security forces as well as the judicial system is conducted with the use of fingerprints. This fact was discovered and began to be utilised at the end of the nineteenth century whereas the Qur'an has drawn attention to this characteristic of fingerprints centuries prior, as follows:

"**Does human think that we will never assemble his bones** (to resurrect him)**? Yes, indeed, We are able to make whole his very fingertips** [*bananahu*]**. But human** (by willful choice) **denies what lies ahead of him** (the other life, because he desires to live only as he pleases)." (Qiyama 75:3-4)

It is the Skin that Feels Pain

Chairman of the Department of Anatomy and former Dean of the faculty of Medicine, University of Chiang Mai, Thailand, **Professor Tejatat Tejasen** conducted a study on pain and obtained the following results:

In order for pain to continue for extended periods of time after skin has been burned and sensation lost, the sensitivity of the skin needs to be restored. This is because pain and all other sensations are initially received at the level of the skin, by means of nerve endings; as skin tissue is burnt, these nerve fibres are debilitated and pain is no longer felt, for the brain realises its primary function in sensation by means of the skin.

Having obtained such scientific results, Tejasen was shown the Qur'anic verse:

"**Those who** (knowingly) **conceal and reject Our revelations, We will land them in a Fire to roast there. Everytime their skins are burnt off, We will replace them with other skins, that they may** taste the punishment. Assuredly, Allah is All-Glorious with irresistible might, All-wise." (Nisa 4:56)

The Qur'anic verse astounded Tejasen and he stated that the Qur'an could not possibly be the work of any human being. When he retuned to his country, five of his students embraced Islam during the first of his several lectures on his discoveries. Attending the Eighth Saudi Medical Conference held in Riyadh, he himself pronounced the Declaration of Faith and then exclaimed in jubilation, *"The most precious thing that I have gained by coming to this conference is to have become a Muslim."* He thereafter devoted the remainder of his life to the Qur'an.

Atomic Fission

Fourteen centuries ago, the Qur'an declared:

"...Not an atom's weight of whatever there is in the earth or in the heaven escapes your Lord, nor is there anything smaller than that, or greater, but it is (recorded) **in a Manifest Book."** (Yunus 10:61)

The Qur'anic verse refers to beings which are smaller than atoms. Whereas, the fact that the atom could be divided has only been recently discovered. Previously, it was thought that the atom was the smallest, indivisible component of matter.

Great Muslim thinker **Mawlana Jalal al-Din al-Rumi** (1207 – 1273) referred to this truth centuries earlier:

"If you split a particle (atom), you will find within it a sun and heavenly bodies revolving around it."

Eva de Vitray-Meyerovitch, the translator of Rumi's *Majalis al-Sab'a*, *Fihi Ma Fih* and *Mathnawi* into French, is one of the rare personalities who was able to decode Rumi's profound messages. She says:

"I am proud to say that the last work of Rumi that I translated took me ten years. This is an extraordinarily beautiful and great work...

Consider that **Rumi** says that if one cut an atom, one would find a core with planets revolving around it. But he states the need for caution regarding the extraordinary energy these *atoms contain, saying that these could reduce the world to ashes. As is evident, he refers to the dangers of the atom bomb in the thirteenth century. He says that there are nine planets. Whereas science propounded this in only 1930.* Previously, it was thought that there were seven planets. When it was asserted in the West that the sun revolved around the earth, **Rumi** said that the earth, like the other planets, was a small planet. Even more extraordinarily is that he said, 'On this little planet Earth, a small part of the universe, every human beings are subject to the influence of the stars. The moon affects women's fertility, the tides whereas the sun affects vegetation and animals...'"[86]

Rumi received all his knowledge, wisdom and spiritual blessing from the Qur'an and the Prophetic Traditions of Allah's Messenger.

Things Created in Pairs

Allah Almighty declares in the Qur'an as follows:

"And all things We have created in pairs, so that you may reflect and be mindful." (Dhariyat 51:49)

"All-Glorified is He (in that He is absolutely exalted above having any peer or partner), **Who has created the pairs all together out of what the earth produces, as well as out of themselves, and out of what they do not know."** (Yasin 36:36. See also Ra'd 13:3)

---

86. http://www.medyapazari.com/turkiye/atom-bombasinin-tehlikelerinden-haberdar.html

Scientists have discovered in recent times that plants and other beings were also created in pairs, like human beings and animals. Even atoms are in pairs. Some of them are positively charged and some negatively charged. For instance, positive electricity flows to negative electricity and the light goes on; the positive cloud flows towards the negative cloud and it begins to rain. This Divine law prevails in all creation.

The Expansion of the Universe

It was discovered recently that the universe is expanding and the galaxies are moving apart from each other at enormous speed. According to this law, colossal galaxies are pulling away from each other in manner directly proportional with the distance in between them. For instance, while a galaxy ten million light years away from us is moving away from us at a speed of 250 kilometres per second, the speed at which a galaxy ten billion light years away pulls away is 250,000 kilometres per second.[87]

This phenomenon is indicated in the Qur'an as follows:

And the heaven, We have constructed it mightily; and it is surely We Who have vast power, and keep expanding it." (Dhariyat 51:47)

Protected Canopy

Meteorites, remains of dying and exploding stars, are dispersed to all parts of the firmaments. Allah Almighty protects the earth from these. **Jupiter** and **Saturn**, with its incredible gravity, hold many objects that pose danger for earth. Meteorites that escape these two planets from time to time and approach earth and attracted by the **moon**. Due to the fact that it has no atmosphere, every meteorite that

---

87. Osman Çakmak, *Bir Çekirdekti Kâinat*, Istanbul 2005, 28.

descends on the moon strikes its surface. The craters generated on the moon by these collisions can even be seen with a small telescope.

The meteorites overcoming the moon barrier, if not too big in size, begin to burn due to friction upon entering the earth's atmosphere. **By virtue of this phenomenon referred to as 'shooting stars',** meteorites become scattered in the form of small dust particles in the mesosphere before reaching the earth's surface. Each of these dust particles then become a seed for a raindrop.[88]

Moreover, the magnetic field and various layers of the atmosphere, which come about from the earth's movement and encompass, it protect the earth from harmful rays coming from space as well as from solar flares.

The atmosphere also protects us from the incredible cold in space, which reaches minus 270 degrees. For instance, temperatures on the moon, which is without an atmosphere, are minus 150 degrees at night and approximately 100 degrees during the day. As it does not have a "protected canopy", all the heat and light coming from the sun reach the moon's surface as is.

These realities are indicated in the Qur'an as follows:

"And We have established the heaven as a canopy well-secured (against collapse and the ascension of devils). **Yet they turn away from all such signs** (of truth manifested) **in the universe."** (Anbiya 21:32)

The Seas that do not Mix

It is declared in the nineteenth and twentieth verses of the Qur'anic chapter Rahman:

---

88. Çakmak, *Bir Çekirdekti Kâinat*, 94, 127.

"He has let flow forth the two large bodies of water, they meet together (But) **between them is a barrier, which they do not transgress** (and so they do not merge)." The same matter is indicated in the sixty-first verse of Chapter Naml.

The truth revealed in these verses is a miracle of the Qur'an that became understood in our century. In the most recent discoveries, it was ascertained that there is a veil of water located at the **Gibraltar Strait** at the point of intersection between the Mediterranean Sea and the Atlantic Ocean, preventing the two bodies of water from mixing. In this way, the two seas do not merge with each preserving their essential characteristics. The same kind of invisible water barrier was discovered in the 1960's at the point of intersection of the Gulf of Aden and the Red Sea, in the **Mandab Strait**. According to scientific explanation, these two bodies of water with differing levels of salt and densities did not mix by virtue of the phenomenon known as **"surface tension"**.

The greatest benefit of this miracle of creation is its allowing an environment for the subsistence of diverse species in different waters.

Rivers and Seas

The barrier of water mentioned above is observed in inlets and river deltas where fresh water rivers open to the sea. While the merging of rivers with one another seems exceedingly easy with both their surface currents and undercurrents, on no account do they mix with salt water at the points at which they meet with the sea. Had Allah Almighty not placed this law between these two seas, which prevent their merging, the fresh water rivers of the world would have merged with salty sea water and would have become annihilated along with the all the different species living within them.

This is indicated in a Qur'anic verse as follows:

"And He it is who has let flow forth the two large bodies of water, one sweet and palatable, and the other salty and bitter; and He has set a barrier and an insurmountable, forbidding ban that keeps them apart." (Furqan 25:53.)

Billow Upon Billow, Darkness Upon Darkness

Diving to the depths of the oceans is virtually as difficult a matter as going to space. Human beings can only dive to depths of about seventy metres without special devices for this task alone; beyond this is the impossible. For this reason, two hundred metres below the seas is almost darkness and beyond one thousand metres is a complete, absolute darkness.

Allah Almighty made known to us, more than 1400 years ago, that the depths of the seas are as dark as to prevent our seeing even our own hand:

"Or their [the unbelievers'] deeds are like veils of darkness covering up an abysmal sea down into its depths, covered up by a billow, above which is a billow, above which is a cloud: veils of darkness piled one upon another, so that when he stretches out his hand, he can hardly see it. For whomever Allah has appointed no light, no light has he." (Nur 24:40)

The expression, **"like veils of darkness covering up an abysmal sea down into its depths"** at the beginning of the verse reveals a quite different scientific truth discovered again in recent times: **Internal waves...**

The oceans, as one moves deeper and deeper, are made up of layers of different densities. These layers are formed in exactly the same way as the waves on the surface of the ocean. These are referred to as 'internal waves' and cannot be seen with the naked eye. They can, however, be perceived through the differences in heat and salt levels between the layers of a body of water.

All these new discoveries serve as confirmation of the Qur'an.

Just as the Messenger of Allah, upon him be peace and blessings, was not a seaman, he also never travelled by sea. However, there are such verses in the Qur'an which pertain to the seas. Upon reflection, we reach the conclusion that the Qur'an could not have come to the Prophet via any way other than through Divine revelation. A person who describes a certain landscape can only use the elements in the environs in which they live or in places to which they have travelled, in doing so. Despite the Qur'an being revealed in a region covered in desert, in it, mention is made of rivers gushing forth, lush green scenery, rain-laden clouds giving life to the earth, vineyards and orchards, and mountains and seas.

Atmospheric Pressure

The Qur'an likens the state of the unbeliever to the situation of a person whose chest tightens and contracts as they ascend towards the heavens.[89]

Scientific discoveries at present have posited that air density decreases, pressure drops and oxygen levels decrease as one ascends. Thus, as a person rises, they experience difficulty breathing and their chest becomes tight and constricted.

The pronunciation and musical quality of the word in the Qur'anic verse which expresses this meaning enables a person to practically experience, as it were, the same meaning.

Just as there was no means or device in the Prophet's time allowing one to ascend to great heights, there were also not even very high mountains within the geographical region in which he lived. In that case, such a similitude and expression could only belong to Allah Almighty, the All-Knowing.

---

89. See, An'am 6:125.

Fertilising Winds

More than fourteen centuries ago, it was stated in the Qur'an:

"And We send the winds to fertilize, and so We send down water from the sky, and give it to you to drink (and use in other ways)..." (Hijr 15:22)

Centuries after the revelation of this Qur'anic verse, it was discovered that the winds fertilise plants and clouds.

The winds have been given the important duty of carrying the particles known as the **'Condensation Nucleus'**. The small particles of liquid rising from above the seas, the dust particles raised from the deserts and the ashes sprayed from volcanoes are carried to the highest strata of the atmosphere be means of the wind. With these, the water vapour in the air is fertilised and condensation of water vapour begins. Without these, the condensation of water vapour and the formation of clouds in the atmosphere would not be possible and human beings would, therefore, be deprived of rain.

The pollen and seeds belonging to the countless species of plants on earth are carried from one to the other via the winds. In this way, the reproduction and propagation of plants, the continuation of their species and their producing yield such as flowers, fruits and vegetables is ensured.

Allah, glorified be He, declares that clouds are heavy.[90] Scientists calculating the rain coming from the clouds determined, for example, the weight of rain covering a land of fifty kilometres square at a thickness of one centimetre, to be half a million tonnes. They have asserted that a single rain cloud can weigh around 300,000 tonnes.

Hail and lightning, and the relationship between these are indicated in the forty-third verse of Chapter Nur.

---

90. A'raf 7:57.

The Qur'an has indicated a great many scientific truths like these, such that some of these have been discovered while the remainder await discovery.[91]

5. Belief in the Prophets

The Prophets are the guides to the truth.

As humankind is prone to showing weakness when it comes to walking in straightforwardness on the true path, and stumbling into a great many transgressions, Allah Almighty has supported them with Prophets out of His pure grace. In this way, Allah Almighty, after making known the limits of accountability through His Books and Prophets, has held the human being morally and religiously responsible. He has not deprived any community from such a favour. It is declared in a Qur'anic verse:

"Surely We have sent you as Messenger with the truth, as a bearer of glad tidings (of prosperity in return for faith and righteousness) **and a warner** (against the consequences of misguidance); **and there has never been a community but a warner lived among them."** (Fatir 35:24)

The aim of religion is to reduce the carnal inclinations in the human being to the absolute bare minimum, to the point of anni-

---

91. For a detailed discussion on the Qur'an and science, see: Osman Nuri Topbaş, *Rahmet Esintileri*, Istanbul 2010, 293-372; Maurice Bucaille, *La Bible le Coran et la science: les ecritures saintes examinees a la lumiere des connaissances modernes*, Paris: Seghers, 1980 (*The Bible, The Qur'an and Science*, Translated by Alastair D. Pannell and Maurice Bucaille, New York: TTQ, Inc. 2003.); Afzalur Rahman, *Quranic Sciences*, London 1981; Ömer Çelik, *Tek Kaynak İki Irmak: Kur'ân'dan Teknolojik Yansımalar*, Istanbul 2009; Imaduddin Khalil,"The Qur'an and Modern Science: Observations on Methodology", *The American Journal of Islamic Social Sciences*, 1991, Vol. 8, No. 1, 1-13; Vahiduddin Khan, *God Arises: Evidence of God in Nature and in Science*, Islamic Books, 2003; M. Sinan Adalı, *Kur'an Mucizeleri*, Istanbul 2010.

THE ESSENTIALS OF BELIEF

hilation so to speak, and to bring to the maximum of development spiritual characteristics. However, in order for this aim to be realised, the human being is in need of a tangible example. One of the wisdoms behind Prophets being sent is their being a perfect exemplar for human beings to follow.

Allah Almighty declares:

"Assuredly you have in Allah's Messenger an excellent example to follow for whoever looks forward to Allah and the Last day, and remembers and mentions Allah much." (Ahzab 33:21.)

The Prophets are not restricted to only those mentioned in the Qur'an.[92] According to narrations, 124,000 or 224,000 Prophets were sent. Some of them were given an independent law, while others continued the law brought by previous Prophets.

The Prophets have been charged not through merit but through Divine appointment. Consequently, they possess certain distinct qualities bestowed to them by Allah. Belief in the Prophets becomes complete within the framework of the following characteristics:

Truthfulness: The Prophets are always truthful in their words and their actions. Their words and actions are mirrors to one another. Their speaking falsehood is impossible. Their truthfulness is of a greatness such that even those who do not believe in them confirmed.

Trustworthiness: The Prophets are the trustworthiest individuals among humankind. Even those who were not believers held infinite trust towards them. The title used for the Messenger of Allah, upon him be peace and blessings, **Muhammad the Truthful**, was constantly used by the Makkan polytheists and they would entrust their own prized belongings not to their associates, but to Allah's Messenger, upon him be peace and blessings, for safekeeping. Even

---

92. See, Nisa 4:164.

when the Prophet was to emigrate to Madina, he held in his possession belongings of the Makkan polytheists that they had entrusted with him. And despite the threat of death, he had left 'Ali in Makka to give them back to their rightful owners.

Intellect: The Prophets were of the highest degree among human beings in every way, especially in regard to reason and intellect. They possessed a strong memory, superior reason and power of persuasion. The Prophet's life, for instance, is replete with manifestations of this.

Communication of the Divine message: They convey the message of Allah perfectly and as commanded to humankind. There was neither addition, nor anything amiss in their communication of the message.

Infallibility: They are removed from committing any kind of sin and wrongdoing, in secret or overtly. However, there were sometimes occasions of involuntary lapse, in order for them also to feel their weakness and to avoid people's forgetting that they too are human and as a result ascribing godhead to them. They must display behaviour that enables others to take example from them. Otherwise, saying, "The things that the Prophets enjoin are beyond our capacity," human beings would have found an excuse for not observing the Divine commandments and prohibitions.

Apart from these five characteristics of the Prophets, there are also the following three characteristics, which pertain solely to the Messenger of Allah, upon him be peace and blessings:

1. Allah's Messenger, upon him be peace and blessings, is the **Beloved of Allah**, is superior to all the other Prophets and is the most honoured of humankind.[93]

---

93. See: Tirmidhi, Manaqib, 1:3616; Darimi, Muqaddima, 8; Ahmad, VI:241; Haythami, IX:29.

2. The Messenger of Allah, upon him be peace and blessings, has been sent to all humanity and to the jinn. That is, he is the **Prophet of Humankind and the jinn**. The religion that he conveyed will endure until the Last Day. The other Prophets, however, were sent for a limited period of time and some of them where sent exclusively to a particular community or people. In this respect, while the miracle of every Prophet was exclusively for their time, the miracles of the Messenger of Allah, upon him be peace and blessings, encompass all time. The Qur'an in particular, as the greatest miracle given to him, will remain everlasting and protected from manipulation and corruption until the Day of Judgement.[94]

3. **The Seal of the Prophets (*khatam al-anbiya'*)**, that is the last of the Prophets.[95]

4. Allah's Messenger, upon him be peace and blessings, has been assigned the praised position or rank of intercessor on the Day of Judgement (***Maqam al-Mahmud***). For this reason, he, as the Prophet of mercy, will intercede on the Day of Judgement on behalf of those of his community who have sinned.[96]

5. He has been granted to ability to inculcate fear in the hearts of his enemy from a distance of one month's journey.

6. The entire earth has been ordained pure and made a place of worship for him and his community. Accordingly, any believer from among his community can pray wherever they are, when the time for the prescribed prayer sets in.

7. Spoils of war, not permissible for any Prophet before him, were deemed permissible for him.

---

94. See: Bukhari, Tayammum, 1.
95. See: Muslim, Masajid, 5, 6.
96. See: Bukhari, Tawhid, 36; Bukhari, Tayammum, 1.

8. The quality of comprehensive, or succinct, speech (*jawami' al-kalim*) has been bestowed to him.

9. The keys to the treasures of the world have been placed before him.[97]

In short, all the Prophets are blessed individuals who have guided humanity upon the principle of Divine Unity. Denial of the Prophethood of anyone of them whose existence has been affirmed with the Qur'an causes a person to leave the circle of faith. For instance, if a person denies the Prophethood of Prophet Jesus, they cannot be a Muslim for all the Prophets communicated the same principles and, as a result, the religion finding expression in their conveyance was perpetually Islam.

"And peace be upon the Messengers. And all praise and gratitude are for Allah, the Lord of the worlds." (Saffaat 37:181-182)

a. The Last Prophet: Muhammad Mustafa

Allah Almighty declares regarding the People of the Book:

"O you who believe! Keep from disobedience to Allah in reverence for Him and piety, and truly believe in His Messenger (Muhammad). He will grant you twofold of His mercy (one for your believing in all the previous Prophets, and one for the Last Prophet)**, and He will appoint for you a light to move** (on the straight Path in this world, leading to Paradise in the Hereafter)**, and He will forgive you. God is All-Forgiving, All-Compassionate."** (Hadid 57:28)

Ibn 'Abbas, may Allah be well-pleased with him, interprets this Qur'anic verse in the following way:

"One of the two portions of His mercy that are mentioned in this verse is by virtue of their belief in Prophet 'Isa (Jesus), peace be

---

97. See: Muslim, Masajid, 5, 6.

upon him, the Gospel and the Torah. The other is due to their belief in and affirmation of Prophet Muhammad, upon him be peace and blessings.

Implied in the light mentioned in the Qur'anic verse is their following the Qur'an and the Messenger of Allah, upon him be peace and blessings..." (Nasa'i, Qada, 12)

The Messenger of Allah, upon him be peace and blessings, has also stated that Allah Almighty will grant a twofold reward to those from the People of the Book who believe in their own Prophet as well as in the Prophet Muhammad, upon him be peace and blessings. (See: Bukhari, 'Ilm, 31)

In order to be among the believers at the present time, belief in the Prophet Muhammad Mustafa, upon him be peace and blessings, alongside belief in Allah Almighty is pivotal. Belief becomes realised as a result of these two facets becoming completely established in the heart. In this respect, neither belief in Allah Almighty only is sufficient, nor belief only in His Messenger.

It is stated in a Qur'anic verse:

"Obey Allah and obey the Messenger." (Ma'ida 5:92; Nur 24:54, 56; Muhammad 47:33; Taghabun 64:12)

"He who obeys the Messenger (thereby) **obeys Allah."** (Nisa 4:80)

"Whoever obeys Allah and His Messenger has surely attained to a mighty triumph." (Ahzab 33:71.)

It is for this reason that the Declaration of faith – or the proclamation of Allah's Unity and that Muhammad, upon him be peace and blessings, is His servant and His Messenger – is the first pillar of Islam.

Belief in the Messenger of Allah necessitates acceptance of, obedience to and love towards him.

Great Muslim scholar **Ahmad ibn Hanbal** has said:

"I looked to the Qur'an and saw obedience to the Messenger of Allah, upon him be peace and blessings, being commanded in thirty-three places."

He then recited the following verse:

فَلْيَحْذَرِ الَّذِينَ يُخَالِفُونَ عَنْ اَمْرِهٖ اَنْ تُصِيبَهُمْ فِتْنَةٌ اَوْ يُصِيبَهُمْ عَذَابٌ اَلِيمٌ

"**...So, let those who go against the Messenger's order beware, lest a bitter trial befall them or a painful punishment afflict them.**" (Nur 24:63.)

He then repeated this verse over and over and said:

"What is the bitter trial that the verse reveals will befall one? It is disbelief and associating partners with Allah. This trial perhaps befalls a person thus: When a person rejects one of the Messenger's words, upon him be peace and blessings, a deviousness occurs to their heart and their heart begins to swerve. Eventually, that person's heart completely pulls away from guidance and drives its owner to ruin."

Ahmad ibn Hanbal subsequently recited this verse:

"**But no! By your Lord, they do not** (truly) **believe unless they make you the judge regarding any dispute between them, and then find not the least vexation within themselves over what you have decided, and surrender in full submission.**" (Nisa 4:65)[98]

❊

The Messenger of Allah, upon him be peace and blessings, honoured this world with his presence on Monday, 12 Rabi' al-Awwal,

---

98. Ibn Batta al-'Ukbari, *al-Ibana al-Kubra*, No: 99; Ibn Taymiyya, *al-Sarim al-Maslul*, Beirut: 1417, I:59.

571 – corresponding to 20 April – just before sunrise, in the city of Makka. His blessed lineage can be traced back to Adnan, the noblest of the progeny of Prophet Ishmael's son Kedar (Qaydar).[99] A member of the Quraysh tribe, Allah's Messenger, upon him be peace and blessings, is of noble descent in terms of both his paternal and maternal lineage.

His father died two months prior to his birth, while his mother died when he was six years of age. His orphaned childhood and youth was spent in a great purity and nobility under the care of his uncle. He spent some time working as a shepherd[100] and was later preoccupied with trade.[101] He became widely known for his honesty and fairness in trade and, gaining repute and respect, took on the title, **al-Amin: the Trustworthy**. Trustworthiness became his second name, as it were. When he reached the age of twenty-five, he began to be called only with the name **al-Amin**.[102] The Makkan polytheists trusted not their own associates, but the Messenger of Allah, who they referred to as **Muhammad the Trustworthy** and entrusted their valuable posses-

---

99. See: Bukhari, Manaqib al-Ansar, 28; Ibn Hisham, I:1-3; Ibn Sa'd, I:55-56.
100. All Prophets worked as shepherds. (Bukhari, Ijara, 2, Anbiya, 29) In this way, before charging them with the duty of communication His message, Allah Almighty enabled them to acquire certain aptitudes that were necessary in administration. The scope for reflection, solemnity and a sense of compassion develops in people who work as shepherds. They increase their patience and feelings of acceptance and protection by herding and managing sheep and in attempting to protect them from vicious animals. Being compassionate to every created being and enduring patiently all their coarse and inconsiderate states is ultimately among the most important qualities that Prophets must possess. A shepherd protects their flock from wild beasts, monitors those that go ahead and those that lag behind and enables remaining ill and feeble sheep to catch up with the rest of the flock by carrying them in their arms. The shepherd puts out to pasture their animals in fertile lands and does not destroy them in barren places. The Messenger of Allah, upon him be peace and blessings, says: *"Each of you is a shepherd, and each of you is responsible for your flock."* (Bukhari, Wasaya, 9) This comes to mean that it is essential for all Muslims to live with such a sense of responsibility.
101. See: Bukhari, Ijara, 2; Abu Dawud, Adab, 17, 82; Hakim, III:200.
102. See: Ibn Sa'd, I:121, 156.

sions to him for safekeeping. When dispute arose among them during the repairs of the Ka'ba, with respect to reinserting the Black Stone, all of them submitted without hesitation to the arbitration of Allah's Messenger and he, in turn, prevented potential warfare with a single stroke of genius.[103]

The Messenger of Allah, upon him be peace and blessings, was the most superior among his tribe in terms of nobility, the most esteemed in terms of lineage and the best with respect to morality. It was he who was most meticulous in observing the rights of neighbours, the most outstanding in gentleness and the most removed from doing harm to and oppressing others. His reproaching and condemning others and his arguing with anyone was unheard of.[104] He distinguished himself among all human beings with his elevated morality. Everyone knew and respected him by virtue of his moral excellence and good character.

Duty of Prophethood

The Messenger of Allah was conferred the duty of Prophethood when he reached the age of forty. He had not expected such a thing; however, Allah Almighty again fulfilled His will, in the usual manner.

The Messenger of Allah, upon him be peace and blessings, began his mission of Messengership under very difficult conditions. He patiently endured many hardships in order to lead people to the straight path and strove to establish belief, justice, mercy and love on earth. He showed extraordinary effort, at the expense of putting his own life in jeopardy, to save the lives of human beings in both this world and the Hereafter. Saying,

---

103. Ibn Hisham, I:209-214; 'Abd al-Razzaq, V:319.
104. See: Ibn Hisham, I:191; Ibn Sa'd, I:121.

"**I ask of you no wage for this** (conveying the Qur'an to you),"[105] he communicated the message solely for the sake of Allah. The obstinate unbelievers, however, were resistant.

The Messenger of Allah, upon him be peace and blessings, was illiterate. Like many others of the time, he did not know how to read and write. Allah, exalted and glorified be He, declares:

"**You did not** (O Messenger) **read of any book before it** (the revelation of this Qur'an), **nor did you write one with your right** (or left) **hand. For then those who have ever sought to disprove the truth might have a reason to doubt** (it)." (Ankabut 29:48)

For this reason, it was not possible for the Prophet to have relayed what he conveyed to the people from any other book or person. An illiterate person's at once beginning to reveal very important knowledge after the age of forty, with the highest degree of eloquence and rhetoric, could only have been possible with Divine revelation. This was something that all his enemies at the time knew and acknowledged.

The Makkan polytheists strove to make Allah's Messenger, upon him be peace and blessings, abandon his cause. They used his beloved uncle as a mediator. They told the Prophet that they would make him their king, give him riches and make him the wealthiest among them, marry him to the most beautiful of women and that they were prepared to do whatever he wanted. Leaving no room for any doubt, the Messenger of Allah, upon him be peace and blessings, responded with the following words:

"*I do not want anything from you. Neither money, nor wealth, nor leadership! The only thing I want is this: That you abandon the*

---

105. Saad 38:86.

worship of idols and worship the One God, Allah." (Ibn Kathir, *al-Bidaya*, III:99-100)

Unable to take any concessions from the Prophet, the Makkan polytheists resorted to intimidation. They increased the torment and torture they exacted against the Muslims with every passing day. Some of the Muslims immigrated to **Abyssinia**, where justice prevailed at the time.

The Makkan polytheists severed all possible connections with the Muslims and their defenders, the Banu Hashim, including trade, marriage and all human interaction. Writing this up as pact, they hung it up on the wall of the Ka'ba. This **boycott** and **embargo** continued, with all its severity, for three years. The Muslims endured great deprivation and hardship. They were forced to eat the bark and leaves of trees due to their hunger and the wailing of children could be heard from afar.

O Lord! Forgive My People for they Do Not Know!

The boycott ended after three years. However, during precisely this time, the Prophet's uncle Abu Talib died. Before long, the Prophet's wife Khadija also passed away. With this, hostile assaults reached the level of savageness. The Messenger of Allah, upon him be peace and blessings, went to the city of Ta'if, 160 kilometres distance from Makka, taking Zayd ibn Harith with him. He stayed in the city, where some of his relatives also resided, for ten days. The townsfolk first ridiculed them. Then they began their insults and subsequently they lined both sides of the streets where Allah's Messenger passed and had the youth stone him on top of that. Even in the face of this heinous treatment and while covered in blood, that source of compassion and Prophet of mercy, not to speak of cursing, made the following entreaty concerned that anything might taint his mission:

"O Allah! To You I complain of my weakness and lack of ability, my being scorned by others. O Most Merciful of the merciful, if You are not angry with me, I mind not. O Lord! Guide my people, for they know not. O Allah! Your pardon is the greatest thing I desire..." (Ibn Hisham, II:29-30; Haythami, VI:35)

As can be understood from his supplication, the sole aim of Messenger of Allah, upon him be peace and blessings, was to earn the good pleasure of Allah Almighty and to fulfil the mission conferred by Him in the best possible way. Even the greatest torture and hardship he faced were of no consequence to him, for he was the **Prophet of Mercy**.

Allah's Messenger, upon him be peace and blessings, relates his return from Ta'if as follows:

"...I departed in deep distress. I did not recover until I arrived at Qarn al-Tha'alib. There, I raised my head and saw a cloud which had cast its shadow on me. I saw in it Jibril (Gabriel), peace be upon him, who called me and said,

'Indeed, Allah, the Exalted, has heard what your people have said to you and the response they made to you. And He has sent you the angel in charge of the mountains in order for you to command him to do whatever you wish to them.' Then the Angel of the Mountains called me, greeted me and then said,

'O Muhammad, Allah listened to what your people had said to you. I am the Angel of the Mountains, and my Lord has sent me to you so that I may carry out all your orders. If you wish I will bring together these two mountains and crush them in between.' But the Messenger of Allah, upon him be peace and blessings, said,

'I rather hope that Allah will raise from among their descendants people as will worship Allah the One, and will not ascribe

partners to Him (in worship).'" (Bukhari, Bad'u al-Khalq, 7; Muslim, Jihad, 111)

When the Messenger of Allah, upon him be peace and blessings, was reciting the Qur'an at the place where he camped overnight on the return from Ta'if, a group of jinn listened to him. All of them recognised the truth and believed in the Messenger, upon him be peace and blessings. After conversing for some time, they returned to their communities with the mission of communicating the message.[106]

After these hardships, Allah Almighty favoured His Messenger with the Ascension. The Almighty took His servant for a journey by night from the sacred Mosque to the al-Aqsa Mosque, the environs of which He has blessed, so that He might show him some of His signs. Allah then raised him to the heavens and a particular meeting, the exact nature of which is unknown to us, was actualised.[107]

The Prophet's Emigration

During those days, a group of people coming from Madina embraced Islam. They then began to convey Islam in **Madina**. They requested a teacher from the Prophet, to teach them Islam. **Mus'ab ibn 'Umayr** and **'Abd Allah ibn Umm Maktum**, may Allah be well pleased with them both, were appointed for this task. As a result of their efforts, within a short time there remained no house in Madina in which Islam had not entered. Eventually, the Muslims invited the Messenger of Allah, upon him be peace and blessings, to Madina, pledging to protect him.

---

106. See: Ahqaf 46:29-32; Jinn 72:1-10; Bukhari, Tafsir 72, Adhan 105; Muslim, Salat 149; Tirmidhi, Tafsir 72:3324; Ibn Sa'd, I:212.
107. See: Isra' 17:1; Najm 53:1-18; Bukhari, Bad'u al-Khalq 6, Anbiya 21:22, 43, Manaqib al-Ansar 42, Tafsir 17:3, Ashriba 1, 12; Muslim, Iman 264, 272, Ashriba 92; Tirmidhi, Tafsir 94, Da'awat 58; Nasa'i, Salat 1, Ashriba 41; Ahmad, V:418; Ibn Sa'd, I:214.

THE ESSENTIALS OF BELIEF

Bara ibn 'Adhib, may Allah be well pleased with him, relates:

"The first people to come to us in Madina from the Companions of the Prophet were Mus'ab ibn 'Umayr and Ibn Umm Maktum, may Allah be well pleased with them both, who taught us the Qur'an. Then 'Ammar ibn Yasir, Bilal and Sa'd ibn Abi Waqqas, may Allah be well pleased with them all, came. Then 'Umar ibn al-Khattab, may Allah be well pleased with him, came with a group of twenty people, after which the Prophet, upon him be peace and blessings, came. I have not seen the people of Madina happier with anything more than their happiness with the Prophet's coming to Madina. This reached such an extent that I even saw the children and little ones saying,

'The Messenger of Allah, upon him be peace and blessings, has come to our city.'

Thus he came, but he did not come until after I had already memorised the Chapter of A'la and other similar Chapters to it." (Bukhari, Tafsir, 87:1)

Thus, his three year Makka struggle ended and his ten year life in Madina began.

An agreement was made between neighbouring Jewish tribes in Madina. Known as the **'Madina Constitution'**, this document was the first written constitution in human history.[108]

Subsequently, battles were fought in defending Madina from foreign threats and enemies. Eight years later, Makka was conquered without bloodshed, while in the tenth year, the entire Arabian Peninsula had surrendered to Allah's Messenger.

---

108. Muhammad Hamidullah, *The First Written Constitution in the World: An Important Document of the Time of the Holy Prophet*, Lahore: Kazi Publications, 1986.

Sent as a mercy to the worlds, the Messenger of Allah, upon him be peace and blessings, pursued such a policy of compassion in military expeditions that, despite taking the entire Arabian Peninsula under his administration in a short time, he did not allow for heavy bloodshed on both sides. He opted to resolve all problems, in the main, with conciliation.

The Prophet, upon him be peace and blessings, personally participated in twenty-nine military expeditions. In sixteen of these, no effective conflict ensued and agreements were made with the opposing side. In thirteen military expeditions, however, he was forced to engage in active conflict and in all of these the total number of Muslims martyred was approximately 140, while a total 335 enemy fighters were killed.[109]

In Islam, the real objective of war is not to kill, obtain spoils of war, annex land, water the soil with blood, destroy the earth, self-interest, procure financial gain or to seek revenge. On the contrary, it is to abolish oppression, ensure freedom of belief, guide human beings and to remove all kinds of injustice.

Desire for Union with Allah

Freedman of the Messenger of Allah, upon him be peace and blessings, **Abu Muwayhiba**, may Allah be well pleased with him, relates:

"Allah's Messenger, upon him be peace and blessings, once said to me,

'*I have been commanded to implore the blessing of Allah for those at rest in the Baqi' cemetery. Will you not come with me.*' I accompanied him. He stood beside those buried there and said,

---

109. See: Muhammad Hamidullah, *Hz.Peygamber'in Savaşları*, Istanbul 1991; Elşad Mahmudov, *Sebepleri ve Sonuçları açısından Hazret-i Peygamber'in Savaşları*, Istanbul 2010.

'Peace be upon you, O dwellers of this abode! May the situation you are in be more pleasing to you than the situation the people are in, for tribulations have approached like dark patches of night, one following the other, with each being worse than those that came before.'

The Messenger of Allah, upon him be peace and blessings, turned toward me and said,

'O Abu Muwayhiba, I have been given the keys to the treasures of this world and to lasting life in it, and now I am being offered Paradise, and meeting with my Lord. I am asked to choose between them.'

I then said,

'What would I not give for your sake, O Messenger of Allah! Is it not possible to have both? Do take the keys of this world, eternity in it, as well as Paradise.' Allah's Messenger, upon him be peace and blessings, said,

'No, by Allah, O Abu Muwayhiba. I have chosen Paradise and meeting with my Lord.'

Subsequently, he asked forgiveness for those buried in the Baqi' cemetery and returned home. The illness which gave rise to the Prophet's demise then ensued." (Darimi, Muqaddima, 14; Ahmad, III:489, 488; Hakim, III:57:4383)

The Messenger of Allah, upon him be peace and blessings, passed away to his Lord in Madina, in the year 632, the tenth year of Emigration.

1) His Noble Character

Allah's Messenger, upon him be peace and blessings, bears the best of character among all human beings. For Allah, exalted and glorified be He, has declared:

"And yours for sure is a reward constant and beyond measure. You are surely of a sublime character, and do act by a sublime pattern of conduct." (Qalam 68:3-4)

He is the most distinguished Prophet who established the best of character on earth and taught it to humanity.

Abu Dharr, may Allah be well pleased with him, from the tribe of Ghifar, had learned of the Prophet's beginning his mission of Prophethood in Makka. Addressing his brother Unays, an intelligent man and proficient poet, he said,

"Ride to the valley of Makka and listen to what he says."

When **Unays** returned from Makka, he said,

"I saw him calling people to noble character." (Bukhari, Adab, 39)

Allah's Messenger, upon him be peace and blessings, himself stating, *"I have not been sent but to perfect good character,"*[110] expresses the chief wisdom behind his mission and emphasises the importance of good moral conduct.

Some examples from his lofty character are provided below:

Righteousness

The Messenger of Allah, upon him be peace and blessings, had brought the truth. He had been sent for the reformation of human beings and to teach them righteousness. Consequently, no vain or futile word or action ever issued from him let alone words of untruth.

'Abd Allah ibn 'Amr, may Allah be well pleased with him, relates:

---

110. Muwatta', Husn al-Khuluq, 8; Ahmad, II:381; Bayhaqi, *Kitab al-Sunan al-Kubra*, X:192.

"I used to write down everything that I heard from the Prophet, upon him be peace and blessings, wanting to preserve it. Some Muslims from the Quraysh prohibited me from doing so, saying,

'Do you write down everything you hear from the Prophet? He, too, is a human being who speaks while both angry and pleased?'

So I refrained from writing and then mentioned this situation to the Prophet, upon him be peace and blessings. He gestured to his mouth and said,

'Write, by the One in Whose hand is my soul! Nothing emanates from this except the truth.' (Abu Dawud, 'Ilm, 3:3646; Darimi, Muqaddima, 43:490; Ahmad, II:162; Hakim, I:187)

Every word of the Messenger of Allah is testament to the religious commandments. His states of anger and joy could not affect his blessed heart which was perpetually connected to Allah Almighty and receiving Divine revelation, and could not cloud the springs of wisdom flowing forth from his blessed tongue.

His truthfulness was acknowledged by all, friend and foe alike. Two of the innumerable examples demonstrating this are provided below:

Even the Makkan polytheists recognised the elevated character of the Prophet and believed wholeheartedly that he could never lie. However, they did not wish to abandon certain worldly gains that they procured unjustly as well as their carnal pleasures. The Messenger of Allah, upon him be peace and blessings, once called upon Abu Jahl and his associates, who were his bitterest enemies. They said to him,

"O Muhammad! By Allah it is not you that we deny for you are a person of utmost truthfulness in our eyes. However, we deny the verses that you have brought..."

Allah Almighty revealed the following verse in relation to this matter:

"**...yet, it is not you that they deny and give the lie to** (they cannot very well call you a liar, since they themselves have called you 'the trustworthy one'); **rather, it is the signs and revelations of Allah that the wrongdoers obstinately reject.**" (An'am 6:33. Tirmidhi, Tafsir, 6:3064; Wahidi, *Asbab*, 219)

That is to say, they accepted in their conscience the Prophethood of Allah's Messenger, upon him be peace and blessings, but because they were slaves to their carnal desires, they opposed him.

Another narration in this regard is as follows:

"Madinan **Sa'd bin Mu'adh**, may Allah be well pleased with him, went to Makka with the intention of performing 'Umra, and stayed at the house of Umayya ibn Khalaf, for Umayya himself used to stay at Sa'd's house when he passed by Madina on his way to Damascus for purposes of trade. (There were bonds of friendship between them.) Umayya said to Sa'd,

'Will you wait until midday when the people withdraw to their homes, before you go to circumambulate the Ka'ba?'

When Sa'd, may Allah be well pleased with him, was circumambulating the Ka'ba, Abu Jahl came and asked,

'Who is that who is performing *tawaf* (circumambulation)?' Sa'd, may Allah be well pleased with him, replied,

'I am Sa'd.' Abu Jahl said,

'Are you circumambulating the Ka'ba in safety while you have given refuge to Muhammad and his Companions?' Sa'd, may Allah be well pleased with him, said,

'Indeed,' and they started quarrelling. Upon this, Umayya said to Sa'd,

'Do not raise your voice at Abu-l Hakam (i.e. Abu Jahl), for he is chief of this valley (of Makka).' Sa'd, may Allah be well pleased with him, then said to Abu Jahl,

'By Allah, if you prevent me from circumambulating the Ka'ba, I will sever your ties of trade with Damascus.' Umayya repeated to Sa'd,

'Do not raise your voice," and began holding him back.' With this, Sa'd became furious and said, (to Umayya),

'Leave us alone, for I have heard Muhammad, upon him be peace blessings, say that he will kill you.'

(As Umayya had threatened Allah's Messenger with death, as though the severe torture that he exacted against him was not enough. The Messenger of Allah, upon him be peace and blessings, had said that he would kill him in response.)

Umayya said,

'Will he kill me?' Sa'd, may Allah be well pleased with him, said,

'Yes, you.' In response, **Umayya ibn Khalaf** said,

'By Allah! When Muhammad says a thing, he never tells a lie.' Umayya went to his wife, in fear, and said to her,

'Do you know what my brother from Yathrib (i.e. Madina) has said to me?' She said,

'What has he said?' Umayya said,

'He claims that he has heard Muhammad saying that he will kill me.' His wife said,

'By Allah! Muhammad never tells a lie,' and in so doing confirmed Sa'd's news.

Some time later, when the Makkan polytheists set out for Badr and declared war against the Muslims, Umayya was also called up. His wife said to him,

'Have you forgotten what your brother from Yathrib had told you?' Umayya initially did not want to go to Badr, but Abu Jahl said to him,

'You are from among the nobles of this valley (of Makka), so it does not befit you to remain behind. You ought to at least accompany us for a day or two.' Umayya accompanied them for two days, but he could not return. For Allah had him killed. (Bukhari, Manaqib, 25, IV:184-185)

Humility

In spite of his being the most exalted of human beings, the Messenger of Allah, upon him be peace and blessings, was at the same time the most humble of them. The day in which he conquered Makka without bloodshed was the moment at which he appeared at his most powerful in the eyes of the people. He had the clear opportunity for retaliation for all the years of oppression and torture that both he and the Muslims had endured. He, however, was the **Prophet of Mercy and Forgiveness**. He entered Makka on that day in a state of prostration upon his camel. To a person who came to him and who began to tremble in fear while talking to him, he inspired repose, referring to an example of the time at which he was most helpless:

"'Be at ease. Do not be afraid. I am neither a king, nor a ruler. I am only the son of a woman of the Quraysh who used to eat meat dried in the sun." (Ibn Maja, At'ima, 30; Hakim, III:50/4366)

Allah's Messenger, upon him be peace and blessings, did not allow people to go to extremes with regard to his own person, instructing, *"Say, (of me) 'The servant of Allah and His Messenger.'"* (Bukhari, Anbiya, 48)

That which elevates a person and brings them nearest to truth is humility.

Adding the term, **Allah's servant** (*'abduhu*) to the beginning of the statement of affirmation of his Prophethood, Allah's Messenger, upon him be peace and blessings, has protected his community from deifying human beings, as was the case for former peoples.

Similarly, he has stated,

"Do not elevate me above the rank which Allah, the Exalted, has determined for me, for He has made me a servant before making me a Messenger." (Haythami, IX:21)

Allah's Messenger, upon him be peace and blessings, would visit the ill, attend funeral prayers, accept the invitation of slaves and mount a mule. He would seat people on the pillion of his mount and would eat on the floor. He would wear garments of coarse wool, milk his own sheep and entertain and honour his guests. He would not shy away from walking alongside the downtrodden, the widow, the poor and the helpless until their needs were met, and would not display haughtiness.[111]

The Prophet, upon him be peace and blessings, would sit among his Companions. For this reason, when a foreigner came, they would not know which was the Messenger of Allah without asking. (Nasa'i, Iman, 6)

Simplicity

The Messenger of Allah, upon him be peace and blessings, lived a most simple and humble life. His wife **'A'isha**, may Allah be well pleased with her, narrates:

---

111. See: Tirmidhi, Jana'iz, 32:1017; Ibn Maja, Zuhd, 16; Nasa'i, Jumu'ah, 31; Hakim, I:129/205; II:506/3734; IV:132/7128; Haythami, IX:20.

"A cup was brought to the Messenger of Allah, upon him be peace and blessings, containing milk and honey. Allah's Messenger, upon him be peace and blessings, said,

"Two blessings in one drink, two additives in one cup! I have no need for this; however, I do not deem these to be prohibited. I only fear that Allah Almighty will call me to account on the Day of Judgement for excesses in the world. I display humility for the sake of Allah. Whosoever is humble for the sake of Allah, Allah will elevate him, while whosoever is arrogant, Allah will debase him. Whosoever is frugal, Allah will make him wealthy; whosoever remembers death often, Allah will love him." (Haythami, X:325)

'A'isha, may Allah be well pleased with her, relates:

The Messenger of Allah, upon him be peace and blessings, never kept food remaining from breakfast for dinner and food remaining from dinner for the morning. He never had two of any garment. Neither did he own two shirts, nor two body wraps, nor two pairs of shoes. He was never seen to be idle while at home. He would either repair the shoes of one in need or mend the clothing of the forlorn."
(Ibn al-Jawzi, *Sifat al-Safwa*, I:200)

Mercy and Compassion

The Messenger of Allah, upon him be peace and blessings, was filled with endless mercy and compassion towards all humanity. Allah, exalted and glorified be He, declares:

"There has come to you (O people) **a Messenger from among yourselves; extremely grievous to him is your suffering, full of concern for you is he, and for the believers full of pity and compassion."** (Tauba 9:128)

The Qur'an also declares that his community is compassionate to all humanity, and even to their enemies. (Al-'Imran 3:119)

THE ESSENTIALS OF BELIEF

'Abd Allah ibn 'Ubayd, may Allah be well pleased with him, narrates:

The blessed tooth of Allah's Messenger, upon him be peace and blessings, was broken at Uhud, he was wounded and blood streamed down towards his face. Some of the Companions said,

"O Messenger of Allah, will you not curse them?"

Allah's Messenger, upon him be peace and blessings, said:

"Allah, glorified be He, did not send me as one who condemns and curses others. I was sent as a summoner and a mercy to humankind. O Allah! Forgive my people, for they do not know." (Bayhaqi, *Shu'ab*, II:164/1447)

Allah's Messenger, upon him be peace and blessings, was compassionate not only towards human beings, but to animals and even trees and plants. Once passing by a camel on the road, whose belly had shrunk so much because of extreme hunger that it had become one with its back, he said,

"Fear Allah in your treatment of these animals that cannot speak. Ride them in good condition and eat them in good condition." (Abu Dawud, Jihad, 44:2548)

Generosity

The Messenger of Allah, upon him be peace and blessings, was the most generous of people. One of the leaders of the Makkan polytheists, **Safwan ibn Umayya**, had accompanied the Prophet during the military expeditions to Hunayn and Ta'if, despite not being a Muslim. As the Prophet, upon him be peace and blessings, inspected the war spoils collected at Jir'ana, he noticed Safwan gazing upon the animals that were crowding around him in great wonderment and asked him,

"Are you pleased with what you see?" When he received a reply in the affirmative, he said,

"Then they are all yours." Unable to contain himself, he exclaimed,

"The heart of none other than a Prophet can be so generous," and declared his acceptance of Islam. Upon returning to his tribe, he said,

"O people, embrace Islam! Muhammad is so generous that he gives with no fear of poverty." (See, Muslim, Fada'il, 57-58; Ahmad, III:107-108; Waqidi, II:854-855)

Sufyan ibn 'Uyayna said:

"When he held nothing in his possession (that he could give), he would vow (to give when he obtained something)." (Darimi, Muqaddima, 12)

And furthermore...

When an impoverished person came to the Prophet and requested something from him, the Messenger of Allah, upon him be peace and blessings, said:

"I do not have anything, but buy something on my account and I will pay for it when I obtain some money." Not content with the Prophet's having to face such difficulty, **'Umar**, may Allah be well pleased with him, said,

"O Messenger of Allah! Allah has not held you responsible for what is beyond your means."

The displeasure of the Messenger of Allah, upon him be peace and blessings, being visible on his face, one of the Ansar said,

"O Messenger of Allah, spend! Do not fear decrease from the Owner of the Throne!"

The words of this Companion greatly pleased the Prophet, peace and blessings be upon him, he smiled, and then said,

"This is what I have been commanded." (Haythami, X:242)

As narrated by **Jabir**,

"The Prophet, may Allah bless him and grant him peace, was never asked for anything to which he said, 'No.'" (Muslim, Fada'il, 56)

His generosity rested on a very strong, unshakeable foundation, for in Islam the true wealth of humankind is the material and spiritual means they spend in the way in the way of earning His approval, in the manner He has ordained.[112] Otherwise, not those they use and consume in the world...

Forgiveness

The Messenger of Allah, upon him be peace and blessings, would always prefer forgiveness and would not tend to punishment unless it was absolutely necessary. For he always forgave those who perpetrated great hostility towards him, despite having the power to punish them and even forbid his Companions from reminding such individuals of their offences whether verbally or through implication. This is because the Prophet, upon him be peace and blessings, never wished evil upon anyone, Muslim or not, and would treat everyone with great propriety and character. When he conquered Makka without giving rise to warfare, those who perpetrated every kind of aggression and enmity towards him and the Muslims had gathered before him and awaited his judgement. He asked them,

"O people of the Quraysh! How do you expect me to treat you?" The Quraysh replied,

---

112. See: (Tirmidhi, Qiyama, 33:2470)

"We would expect nothing but goodness from you. You are a noble man, the son of a noble man." The Messenger, upon him be peace and blessings, thereupon said,

"I say as Joseph said to his brothers: **'No reproach this day shall be on you. May Allah forgive you; indeed, He is the Most Merciful of the merciful.' Go on your way for you are free!"** (Ibn Hisham, IV:32; Waqidi, II:835; Ibn Sa'd, II:142-143)[113]

And he called that day, the **'Day of Mercy'**.[114]

On that day, he forgave **Wahshi**, who killed his uncle Hamza at the Battle of Uhud, and **Hind**, who voraciously chewed on the liver of that 'master of martyrs'.[115] Even **Habbar ibn Aswad**, who pushed his daughter off her camel and thus caused her death, benefited from this great amnesty. The Messenger of Allah, upon him be peace and blessings, displayed such kindness that not only did he forgive Habbar, but he also forbade Habbar's being insulted and reproached for what he had done in the past. (Waqidi, II:857-858)

When Makka was conquered, Abu Jahl's son **Ikrima** had fled. Putting all the heinousness he had formerly perpetrated, Allah's Messenger, upon him be peace and blessings, gave him amnesty and summoned him to his presence. Travelling vast distances in pursuit of him, Ikrima's wife conveyed the Messenger's invitation to him and convinced him to go back with her to Makka. When they drew near to Makka, the Messenger of Allah, upon him be peace and blessings, miraculously and displaying great kindness, said to his Companions,

"Ikrima ibn Abu Jahl shall come to you as a believer and as an emigrant. Do not insult his father, for insulting the dead causes grief to

---

113. Yusuf 12:92.
114. Waqidi, III:352; 'Ali al-Muttaqi, *Kanz*, no. 30173.
115. Bukhari, Maghazi, 23; Muslim, Aqdiya, 9.

the living and does not reach the dead." (Hakim, III:269/5055; Waqidi, II:851)

When Allah's Messenger, upon him be peace and blessings, saw Ikrima upon his arrival, he stood up with jubilation to greet him and repeated three times,

"Welcome, O emigrant rider!" Ikrima, may Allah be well pleased with him, exclaimed,

"By God, O Messenger of Allah! I vow that whatever I have spent fighting Islam, I shall spend twice as much in Allah's path." (Hakim, III:271/5059; Waqidi, II:851-853; Tirmidhi, Isti'zan, 34:2735)

The Messenger of Allah, upon him be peace and blessings, forgave many more the likes of him, for he was not sent to destroy but reform and conquer hearts. He was sent as a mercy to all the worlds.

Cleanliness and Grace

Islam has established cleanliness as half of belief and the beginning of all worship. Thus, instructing garments to be in good order and disapproving of scruffiness in dress, the Prophet, upon him be peace and blessings, also did not approve of untidiness in one's hair and beard. He himself extremely careful with regard to cleanliness and was impeccable. **Abu Hurayra**, may Allah be well pleased with him, said,

"I have never seen a person with a countenance more beautiful than that of the Prophet, peace and blessings be upon him, such that it was though he had all the radiance of the sun..." (Ahmad, II:380, 350)

Islam has placed great importance on grace, which springs from purity and beauty of heart. Allah's Messenger, upon him be peace and blessings, never uttered any crude and coarse word and used to say:

"Nothing is heavier upon the scale of the believer on the Day of Judgement than good character; and verily, Allah abhors the shameless person who utters foul or coarse language." (Tirmidhi, Birr, 62:2002)

When the Prophet, upon him be peace and blessings, was informed of anything of a certain person, he would not say: 'What is the matter with so and so that he says such-and-such?' But he would say: *'What is the matter with the people that they say such and such?'* (Abu Dawud, Adab, 5:4788)

In a Tradition where he draws attention to both cleanliness as well as refinement, the Messenger of Allah, upon him be peace and blessings, states:

"Be on your guard against three things which provoke cursing: easing in the watering places and on the thoroughfares, and in the shade (of the tree)." (Abu Dawud, Tahara, 14:26; Ibn Maja, Tahara, 21; Ahmad, I:299; Hakim, I:273/594)

The Value Placed Upon Women

With the emergence of Islam, a legal framework pertaining to women was established. Women became the symbol of modesty and virtue in society. The institution of motherhood was awarded honour. With the Prophet's tradition, *"Paradise lies under the feet of the mother,"*[116] the woman attained her rightful place and worth. The Messenger of Allah, upon him be peace and blessings, never raised his hand towards anyone of his wives and never struck anyone.[117] For Allah Almighty has decreed, **"Consort with them in a good manner."**[118]

The Messenger, upon him be peace and blessings, has stated:

---

116. Nasa'i, Jihad, 6; Ahmad, III:429; Suyuti, I:125.
117. Ibn Maja, Nikah, 51.
118. See: Nisa 4:19.

THE ESSENTIALS OF BELIEF

"The best of you are those who are the best to their wives." (Tirmidhi, Rada', 11:1162)

"A person must not dislike his wife; if he becomes displeased with one bad quality in her, then let him be pleased with another quality which is good." (Muslim, Rada', 61)

"The world and all things in the world are precious but the most precious thing in the world is a virtuous woman." (Muslim, Rada', 64; Nasa'i, Nikah, 15; Ibn Maja, Nikah, 5)[119]

---

119. In this context, I would like to briefly touch upon a few matters pertaining to women:
1) Plural Marriage: Islam did not introduce polygamy, but legalised the existing system within certain norms. Prior to Islam, there were no restrictions placed on marriage. Islam limited the number of marriages to an absolute maximum of four. Another important issue is that more that one marriage is not a **'command'** for believers, but a **'sanction'** in the face of certain compelling conditions. This is practised to avoid the break-up of families and for women not to be left without protection in such cases as war, illness, disability, extended periods of separation and for the purpose of guardianship. In this way, the tangible and immaterial harm that is to come from the break up of a family are reduced to an absolute minimum. At the same time, certain individuals are protected from resorting to unlawful circumstances due to influences exerted by circumstance. Men married to more than one woman have been encumbered with **"observ[ing] their rights with exact fairness"**. A Qur'anic verse states: **"If you fear that you will not be able to observe their rights with exact fairness when you marry the orphan girls** (in your custody)**, you can marry, from among other women** (who are permitted to you in marriage and) **who seem good to you, two, or three, or four. However, if you fear that** (in your marital obligations) **you will not be able to observe justice among them, then content yourselves with only one... Doing so, it is more likely that you will not act rebelliously."** (Nisa 4:3) **"You will never be able to deal between your wives with absolute equality** (in respect of love and emotional attachment)**, however much you may desire to do so. But do not turn away altogether** (from any one of them)**, so as to leave her in a dangling state** (uncertain if she has or does not have a husband)**. If you act righteously** (between them) **and act in piety** (fearful of doing any deliberate wrong to any of them)**, then surely Allah is All-Forgiving, All-Compassionate."** (Nisa 4:129)
2) The Prophet's Marriages: The marriages of the Messenger of Allah, upon him be peace and blessings, were never conducted on the basis of self-interest. When he was twenty-five years-of-age, he accepted the marriage proposal of Khadija,

fifteen years his senior. All the notables of Makka sought to marry Khadija. She, however, desired to marry the Messenger of Allah, whose character and person she was in great admiration of. The Prophet accepted her proposal of marriage due to her elevated virtue, not for financial or earthly reasons. In a society where polygamy was widespread, he exemplified the bliss of marriage with one woman until in his fifties. However, towards the end of his life, certain conditions and wisdoms necessitating his conducting several marriages emerged:

a) The Messenger of Allah, upon him be peace and blessings, conducted some of his marriages in order to form ties of kinship with various tribes and spread and consolidate the message of Islam through relationships of sincerity. For instance, his marriage with daughter of Khaybar Jewish chief **Safiyya**, may Allah be well pleased with her, was for the purpose of mending the existing relationships with the Jews by means of the formation of familial ties. Again, his marriage with daughter of a tribal chief, **Juwayriya**, may Allah be well pleased with her, resulted in the simultaneous release of thousands of prisoners of war and, consequently, the guidance of an entire tribe.

b) The Messenger of Allah, upon him be peace and blessings, contracted the majority of his marriages for the transferral of his practices and Sunna within the home to the people and for the communication and instruction of Islam among the women. The Prophet's wives fulfilled pivotal roles for an extended period of time, for the teaching and instruction of the laws and rulings of Islam.

c) Being the guardian of his community, Allah's Messenger, upon him be peace and blessings, contracted certain marriages for the purpose of honouring and protecting his self-sacrificing Companions who were among the first to enter Islam and consequently suffered great hardship. For instance, when he married Abu Sufyan's daughter **Umm Habiba**, his favouring this long-suffering believer was in question. This is because, despite her husband's defecting to Abyssinia and herself remaining in dire circumstances, Umm Habiba, may Allah be well pleased with her, defended her religion and, during this time, did not appeal to her father, Makkan leader Abu Sufyan, due to her self-possession and devotion towards her faith.

d) Certain erroneous beliefs, notions and suppositions in society needed to be deeply changed and corrected. The Prophet's marriage with **Zaynab bint Jahsh** was also conducted for this very reason. Based on these and similar wisdoms, Allah Almighty commanded His Messenger to contract several marriages and granted him leeway in this regard. (See: Ahzab 33:37, 50)

3) Women's Share in Inheritance and their Testimony: A just balance between shares and obligations has been maintained in inheritance law in Islam. A male whose expenditure is greater has been given a greater share in comparison with the woman. This is because the male is the individual responsible for all material expenses within the family, alongside shouldering the payment of the dowry when getting married. That is to say, the difference between men and women in Islam's law of inheritance is contingent upon obligation and responsibility. A balance between both of these has been established. The woman has not been held accountable for the material maintenance of the family due to such responsibilities as the protection of future generations, raising children and maintaining order in the family. This is the reason behind their share of inheritance being reduced by half. This share has been apportioned in consideration of such cases as a woman's being unable to wed, her divorce, or for certain personal needs. Women have also been granted such virtues as depth of emotion, delicacy, mercy, compassion, modesty, devotion and preservation of the generations. As they are of delicate constitution, remarkably powerful sensibility and with elevated feelings of compassion, they can sometimes fall physically and spiritually weak in the face of certain surprises they encounter in the various phases of life. It is for this reason that the woman's testimony is half that of a man. The fact is that Allah Almighty has created every creature and every part of that creature in line with a particular purpose and has bestowed them with a physical (biological) and spiritual (psychological) constitution enabling them to realise their purpose of creation. Holding the male morally and religiously responsible for the life-struggle and the maintenance of the home, Allah Almighty has made them stronger physically and more stoical spiritually in order for them to duly fulfil this duty. The woman, however, has been charged with protecting future generations, the upbringing of children, caring for and protecting them at their weakest and most helpless time. Consequently, their mission has necessitated that their spirit, not their body, is equipped with more profound feeling and sensibility. In order to embrace her child with a deep mercy and love in its first period of helplessness, the woman has been given a keen sensibility as a Divine favour. Being the wellspring of compassion with her emotional constitution, if an obligation outside a mother's power and purpose of creation is placed upon her shoulders, adverse affects are engendered. Consequently, the probability of a woman's taking pity on and feeling compassion towards an offender, and thus perverting the course of justice, is rather high. This is one of the wisdoms of the Divine ruling concerning her testimony being half that of a man.

From another standpoint, Islam regulates testimony in accordance with the psychology of the human being. While the testimony of men is not taken into account in certain cases, in yet others, the testimony of women is also accepted to be complete. For instance, in situations impossible for men to be aware of, only the testimony of women is deemed to be sufficient. (See: *Majalla*, '1685') While establishing a just balance between rights and responsibilities in these matters, Islam takes into account the entirety of the community alongside the immutable aspects of human nature.

A superficial and unjust equality has been generated between women and men in

2) His Striving for the Salvation of Humanity

All people, from the day the Messenger of Allah, upon him be peace and blessings, was sent as a Messenger up until the Last Day, are a part of his community. Some of these people accepted his invitation while others did not. Those who accepted his invitation are referred to as the recipient community (*ummat al-ijaba*) while those who did not are called 'those who did not respond' (*ummat al-ghayr al-ijaba*).

Allah's Messenger, upon him be peace and blessings, loves his community and exerted great efforts for their deliverance. He has described his state in a Prophetic Tradition in the following manner:

"The metaphor of me and people is like a man who lights a fire and when it lights up what is around it, the moths and these creatures begin to fall into it. He begins to drive them away from it, but they overpower him and rush into it. I take hold of the knots of your waist-wrappers to keep you back from the Fire while you are rushing into it." (Bukhari, Riqaq, 26)

The Prophet, upon him be peace and blessings, would constantly consider his community and entreat Allah for their eternal felicity and security. One day, he recited the Qur'anic verses:

"My Lord! They (the idols) **have indeed caused many among humankind to go astray. So, he who follows me is truly of me; while he who disobeys me, surely You are All-Forgiving, All-Compassionate."** (Ibrahim 14:36)

---

our day. Contradicting her innate characteristics, this competition debilitates her virtues of femininity and motherhood and harms the family. For this reason, the increasing number of abortions in our day constitutes the modernised version of burying baby girls alive in the Age of Ignorance and is thus the murder of the century. The only difference between the drained and exhausted woman of the current century and the Age of Ignorance is merely a difference of wardrobe, or dress and apparel. And this is the societal disaster brought about by a materialist education bereft of spirit.

"If You punish them, they are Your servants; and if You forgive them, You are the All-Glorious with irresistible might, the All-Wise." (Ma'ida 5:118) He then raised his hands and said, *"O Allah, my community, my community,"* and began to entreat Him, weeping. Upon this, Allah Almighty said,

"O Gabriel, go to Muhammad – and your Lord knows better – and ask him what makes him weep."

Gabriel, peace be upon him, came and the Messenger of Allah, upon him be peace and blessings, told him about his concern for his community and said that this was why he wept. Allah, glorified and exalted be He, said,

"O Gabriel, go to Muhammad and tell him: 'We shall please you concerning your community, and shall not cause you to be grieved.'" (Muslim, Iman, 346)

As reported by Abu Dharr, may Allah be well pleased with him, the Messenger of Allah, upon him be peace and blessings, repeatedly recited the 118th verse from the Qur'anic chapter Ma'ida in his prayer during the night, until daybreak. He also recited this verse when in the bowing position and in prostration... (Ahmad, V:149)

When 'A'isha, may Allah be well pleased with her, once saw the Prophet in good spirits, she said,

"O Messenger of Allah, please invoke Allah for me!" The Messenger of Allah, upon him be peace and blessings, said,

"O Allah, forgive Aisha all her past and future sins."

'A'isha was so pleased with this supplication that she was beside herself. The Messenger of Allah, upon him be peace and blessings, said,

"Has my supplication made you happy?" She replied,

"Certainly I am pleased with your supplication, shouldn't I be!"

Upon this the Messenger, upon him be peace and blessings, said,

"By Allah, this is the supplication I make for my community in every prayer." (Haythami, IX:243; Ibn Hibban, *Sahih*, XVI:47/7111)

Allah's Messenger, upon him be peace and blessings, used to encourage all Muslims to work and entreat Allah, like him, for the salvation of all humanity. He states in another narration:

"There is no supplication more pleasing before Allah than the servant's saying,

اَللّٰهُمَّ ارْحَمْ أُمَّةَ مُحَمَّدٍ رَحْمَةً عَامَّةً

"O Allah, have mercy on the entire community of Muhammad!" ('Ali al-Muttaqi, no. 3212, 3702)

Due to this sublime compassion, the Messenger of Allah, upon him be peace and blessings, would not invoke curses on those who did not believe in him and even those who showed open hostility towards him and would not wish for them to be killed. On the contrary, he would entreat Allah for them to find the true path and would strive to avert their evil without causing any harm to them. For he hoped that either they or their progeny would eventually worship Allah alone.

One day, some of the Companions who had become very frustrated by the persecution of the Makkan polytheists wanted the Prophet to invoke curses upon them. In response, the Messenger of Allah, upon him be peace and blessings, said,

"I was not sent as a curser, but as a mercy to all the worlds." (Muslim, Birr, 87)

Saying, *"My community, my community"* in hundreds of his traditions, the Prophet, upon him be peace and blessings, as though

THE ESSENTIALS OF BELIEF

received great delight in saying so. He became attached to his community with the heartfelt devotion. Allah's Messenger, upon him be peace and blessings, loved his community so much that he never wished to part from them. When he was informed of his impending demise, he entreated Allah saying,

"O Lord! Who will remain at the head of my community?" Thereupon, the following Qur'anic verse was revealed:

"We never granted everlasting life to any human being before you (O Messenger); **so if you die, will they live forever?"** (Anbiya 21:34) (Ibn Kathir, *Tafsir*, [Anbiya 21:34])

The Prophet's striving, upon him be peace and blessings, for the salvation of his community was not limited purely to his life in this world. He revealed that he would implore Allah Almighty after his demise, in his life in the intermediate realm, as well as after the Last Day, for the salvation of his community and would intercede on their behalf.

He has stated:

"My life is an immense good for you: you bring up new matters and new matters are brought up for you. My death, also, is an immense good for you: your actions will be shown to me; if I see goodness I shall praise Allah and if I see evil I shall ask forgiveness from Him for you." (Haythami, IX:24)

"Beware, I am a means of security for you in my life while after my death, I will beseech Allah in my grave saying, "O Lord, my community, my community," until the Trumpet is blown..." ('Ali al-Muttaqi, *Kanz al-'Ummal*, XIV:414)

When the world comes to an end, all the people that have come to earth from the first to the last will all be gathered on a flat terrain. The sun will be brought very close, human beings will be drenched in perspiration and will be subjected to great tribulation and hardship. People in fear of Divine wrath and punishment will be awestricken and in utter dread. Those wanting to escape this horrific state will appeal to previous Prophets, starting with Prophet Adam and, declaring that that the most qualified individual for intercession is Prophet Muhammad, upon him be peace and blessings, all these Prophets will direct human beings to him. Interceding on their behalf, the Messenger of Allah, upon him be peace and blessings, will deliver them from these horrendous fears. However, he will also exercise exclusive intercession for his own community.[120]

In short, just as Allah's Messenger who was sent as a mercy to the worlds, upon him be peace and blessings, exerted utmost effort for the salvation of all humanity throughout his entire lifetime, so too, in the intermediate realm and after the Last Day, he will pray and intercede for their eternal deliverance. That is, he perpetually endeavoured for human beings to be servants to their Creator and draw near to Him. His entire concern was for humanity to turn back from the wrong path and find their essence and for them to attain Divine mercy through obedience to Him.

3) His Miracles

Allah Almighty conferred upon His Messenger, upon him be peace and blessings, an exceptional rank and favoured him with all the miracles bestowed to the other Prophets.[121] However, the most important miracle of the Prophet is the **Qur'an**. This matter was elucidated in detail earlier. Following this comes his **blessed life** and **exalted morality**.

---

120. Bukhari, Anbiya 3, 9, Tafsir, 17:5; Muslim, Iman 302, 327, 328; Tirmidhi, Qiyama 10.
121. The following texts can be referred to for a discussion on the Prophet's miracles: Bayhaqi, *Dala'il al-Nubuwwa*, Beirut 1985; Abu Nu'aym, *Dala'il al-Nubuwwa*, Aleppo 1970-1972; Suyuti, *al-Khasa'is al-Kubra'*, Istanbul 2003.

The unsurpassed life of the Prophet and his lofty morality earned the admiration of everyone, friend and foe alike. Just as nobody held any serious objection to this, far from it, many non-Muslims have openly acknowledged the exalted nature of his character and morality. Among these, famous Western thinker and scholar **Thomas Carlyle** says of Prophet Muhammad, upon him be peace and blessings:

"No emperor with his tiaras was obeyed as this man in a cloak of his own clouting."

Possessing such an exemplary life and character is without doubt the greatest miracle. This matter also was elucidated in depth earlier.

Another one of the Messenger's miracles is the Companions he raised in as short a time span as twenty-three years.[122] This truth has been expressed by a great many scholars. For instance, one of the most famous personalities of Islamic jurisprudence, **Qarafi** (d. 684) states as such.

"Had the Prophet possessed no other miracle, his Companions would have been sufficient as proof of his Prophethood."[123]

Mustafa Sadiq al-Rafi'i, one of the masters of Arabic literature, also states that the Companions are a living representation of the Qur'anic miracle.[124]

However, we will make mention of the Prophet's other miracles here. Only a few among his countless miracles will be offered below:

'Uthman ibn Hunayf, may Allah be well pleased with him, explains:

---

122. For further detail in relation to this topic, refer to, **Osman Nuri Topbaş**, *The Society of the Age of Bliss*, Istanbul 2011; *Rahmet Esintileri*, 359-370.
123. Qarafi, *Al-Furuq*, Darussalam, 2001, IV:305.
124. Rafi'i, *I'jaz al-Qur'an*, Dar al-Kitab al-'Arabi, Beirut 1990, 158-159.

"I have seen a blind man come to the Messenger of Allah, may Allah bless him and give him peace, and complain to him of the loss of his eyesight, saying,"

'O Messenger of Allah, ask Allah to cure my blindness. I have been afflicted in my eyesight.'

Allah's Messenger, upon him be peace and blessings, said,

'If you wish, you can be patient with your calamity, and if you wish, I will ask Allah to cure your blindness.'

The blind man, however, said,

'O Messenger of Allah, there is no one near to guide me around and the loss of my eyesight is a great hardship for me, so please pray to Allah for me.' Upon this the Messenger of Allah, may Allah bless him and grant him peace, said,

'Go make ablution, perform two rak'as of prayer and then say:

اَللّٰهُمَّ إِنِّى أَسْأَلُكَ وَأَتَوَجَّهُ إِلَيْكَ بِنَبِيِّكَ مُحَمَّدٍ نَبِيِّ الرَّحْمَةِ. يَا مُحَمَّدُ إِنِّى تَوَجَّهْتُ بِكَ إِلَى رَبِّى فِى حَاجَتِى هٰذِهِ لِتُقْضٰى لِيَ. اَللّٰهُمَّ فَشَفِّعْهُ فِيَّ

'O Allah, I ask You and turn to You through Your Messenger Muhammad, the Prophet of Mercy; O Muhammad, I seek your intercession with my Lord for my need, that it may be fulfilled. O Allah, grant him intercession for me.'

Ibn Hunayf continued, 'By Allah, we didn't part company or speak long before the man returned to us as if nothing had ever been wrong with him.'"[125]

---

125. See, Tirmidhi, Da'awat, 118:3578; Ibn Maja, Iqama, 189; Nasa'i, Kubra, VI:169; Ahmad, IV:138; Hakim, I:707-708; Bayhaqi, *Dala'il*, V:464; Haythami, II:279.

The Makkan polytheists had demanded a miracle from the Prophet, upon him be peace and blessings. The Messenger of Allah, upon him be peace and blessings, entreated his Lord and the **moon** was split into two; this miracle was witnessed from all around. When the moon split into two, one half was seen on the side of Mount Abu Qays, while the other half was seen beyond it. The Makkan polytheists asked caravans arriving to Makka from distant lands whether or not they had seen this incident. They too affirmed that they had indeed seen the moon split in two.[126]

In examining the past activity of the moon, French astronomer **Joseph Jérôme Lefrançois de Lalande** has confirmed the truth of this miracle.[127]

✻

In the early years of the Prophet's communicating the message of Islam, a Bedouin approached him and asked what the proof of his Prophethood was. The Messenger of Allah, upon him be peace and blessings, said,

"I will summon this cluster of dates and it will bear witness to my Prophethood," and then he summoned the cluster.

The cluster of dates hanging from a date palm began to descend from the tree and then stood before him, saying, "Peace be upon you O Messenger of Allah!"

The Prophet then remanded it to its place and the cluster returned to its original position.

Before this scene, the Bedouin immediately embraced Islam. (Tirmidhi, Manaqib, 6)

---

126. Qamar 54:1-3; Bukhari, Manaqib 27, Manaqib al-Ansar 38, Tafsir 54:1; Muslim, Munafiqin, 43, 47, 48; Tirmidhi, Tafsir, 54:3286; Ahmad, I:377, 413.
127. Zekâî Konrapa, *Peygamberimiz*, Istanbul 1987, 110.

The son of **'Umayr ibn Wahb** was taken prisoner during the Battle of Badr. 'Umayr was one of the shrewd minds and heroes of the Qurayshi idolaters, who subjected the Prophet and his Companions to a great deal of torment and suffering. When 'Umayr sat with **Safwan ibn Umayya** one day, in the semi-circular, open-air enclosure situated opposite the northwestern wall of the Ka'ba (*hijr*), discussing those killed at Badr and the disaster they faced,

'Umayr said, "By Allah, life has lost all its meaning now [that they are dead]." 'Umayr responded saying,

"By Allah, right you are. If I did not have a debt that I could not discharge and a family who I fear might perish when I am gone, I would have ridden to Madina and killed Muhammad. And I have a justifiable cause against his followers, for my son is held captive in their hands. I heard that he walks through the market sometimes." 'Umayr's words pleased Safwan and, seizing this opportunity, the latter said,

"I will take on your debt and discharge it for you, and I will look after your family in exactly the same way as my own, as long as they live. They will lack nothing that is within my means." Upon this, 'Umayr called for his sword, had it sharpened and dipped in poison. Safwan had his mount and provisions for the journey prepared. When 'Umayr reached Madina, he stood at the entrance of the Prophet's Mosque, tied his camel and girded on his sword. **'Umar,** may Allah be well pleased with him, noticed 'Umayr and having read his intentions on his face said,

"This is the enemy of God, 'Umayr ibn Wahb. By Allah, he has certainly only come for some evil purpose. Was he not the one who spied for the Makkan polytheists, estimating our numbers on the day of Badr and reporting them to the enemy?" He then went in to the Messenger of Allah, upon him be peace and blessings, and said,

"O Allah's Messenger, here is the enemy of God, 'Umayr, who has come wearing his sword." The Prophet, peace and blessings of Allah be upon him, said,

"Bring him in to me, then."

'Umar, may Allah be well pleased with him, went up to him, caught hold of the shoulder belt from which his sword was hanging and seized him round the neck with it. Then he said to the members of the Ansar who were present,

"Go in to the Messenger of Allah and sit near him, and watch out for this villain, for he is not to be trusted." When Allah's Messenger, peace and blessings of Allah be upon him, saw them, he said,

"Release him, 'Umar. Approach, 'Umayr." He then asked 'Umayr what it was that brought him to Madina. He said,

"I have come for my son who you hold captive, so treat me well over him." The Messenger of Allah, upon him be peace and blessings, asked,

"In that case, for what purpose is that sword around your neck?" 'Umayr said,

"May Allah curse all swords! What good have they done us?" The Messenger of Allah, upon him be peace and blessings, repeated:

"Speak the truth, for what purpose have you come?" 'Umayr insisted,

"I have come for nothing but for my son whom you hold captive." When Allah's Messenger, peace and blessings of Allah be upon him, asked,

"What was the condition you stipulated with Safwan while sitting in the Hijr?" 'Umayr became afraid and said,

"What condition had I imposed on him?"

Relating word-for-word the conversation they had held, the Messenger of Allah, upon him be peace and blessings, said,

"Allah has intervened, however, between you and what you plan to do and has prevented you." 'Umayr then said,

"I bear witness that you are without doubt the Messenger of Allah. O Allah's Messenger, we used to deny the tidings of Heaven which you conveyed and the revelation which came down to you." This is a meeting at which only Safwan and I were present and of which only we both were aware. By Allah, I know that no one but Allah could have informed you of it. All praise is due to Allah Who has guided me to Islam and led me along this path." He then pronounced the Declaration of Faith. The Messenger of Allah, upon him be peace and blessings, then said to those present,

"Instruct your brother well in his belief, teach him to read and understand the Qur'an and release his captive," and they did so immediately. 'Umayr later said:

"O Messenger of Allah, I used to work to extinguish the light of Allah and used to persecute those who believed. If you allow me, I would like to go to Makka and invite the Makkan polytheists to Allah, His Messenger and to Islam. Perhaps Allah will grant them guidance." The Messenger of Allah, upon him be peace and blessings, gave him permission and he set off for Makka.

In the meantime, Safwan ibn Umayya, unaware of developments, used to say to the Makkan polytheists,

"You will soon rejoice with good news that you are to receive in a few days, of an event that will cause you to forget the pain of Badr," and ask arriving caravans about any news from 'Umayr. Eventually, a rider arrived who told him that 'Umayr had become a Muslim.

On arriving in Makka, 'Umayr ibn Wahb, may Allah be well pleased with him, began inviting people to Islam and strove for their guidance. Many people accepted Islam through him. One day, 'Umayr, may Allah be well pleased with him, ran into Safwan ibn Umayya near the Ka'ba and said to him,

"You are one of our leaders. Do you not see that we worship stones and sacrifice animals for them? Is this religion? I bear witness that there is no god but Allah and that Muhammad is His servant and His Messenger."

Safwan spoke not even a single word to him and was left in silence.[128]

He too embraced Islam after the conquest of Makka.[129]

Jabir ibn 'Abd Allah, may Allah be well pleased with him, relates:

"...We were walking with Allah's Messenger, upon him be peace and blessings. We went down into a wide valley and Allah's Messenger, upon him be peace and blessings, searched for a place to relieve himself. I followed him with a container full of water. Allah's Messenger, upon him be peace and blessings, looked about and he found no privacy but two trees at the end of the valley. Allah's Messenger, upon him be peace and blessings, went to one of them and took hold of one of its branches and said,

"Be you under my control, with the permission of Allah," and so it came under his control like the camel with its nose string in the hand of its rider. Then he came to the second tree and took hold of a branch and said,

---

128. See, Ibn Hisham, II:306-309; Waqidi, I:125-128; Ibn Sa'd, IV:199-201; Haythami, VIII:284-286.
129. Abu Dawud, Buyu', 88:3563.

"Be you under my control, with the permission of Allah," and it too came under his control. When he came to the middle of the two trees he joined together the two branches and said,

"Join with the permission of Allah," and they immediately joined. I was afraid lest Allah's Messenger, upon him be peace and blessings, become aware of my nearness and go still farther. I sat down and began to think to myself. With a sudden glance, I suddenly found Allah's Messenger, upon him be peace and blessings, before me and the two trees were separated and each one of them was standing in its original place. I saw Allah's Messenger, upon him be peace and blessings, pause for a short time, nodding his head towards right and left. Then he came to me and said,

"Jabir, did you see the place where I was standing?"

"Yes, O Messenger of Allah," I replied.

He then said, *"Then go to those two trees and cut a branch from each. When you reach the place where I stopped, plant one branch on the right and the other branch on the left."* I immediately set out to carry out what he had requested of me. Then I met him and said,

"I have done as you so wished, O Messenger of Allah, but would you (kindly) explain to me the reason for such." Thereupon, he said,

"I passed by two graves, the occupants of which had been undergoing torment. I desired that they might be relieved of this torment, for as long as these branches remain fresh, by means of my intercession." We came back to the place where the caravan had camped and Allah's Messenger, upon him be peace and blessings, said,

"Jabir, is there any water for the performing of ablution?" He asked me to see if there was any water in the water-skins of those camped there. There was no water save the drop in the mouth of the water-skin which belonged to one of the members of the Ansar. And if I

were to draw that drop, it would be absorbed by the dry part of the water-skin. He took hold of it and began to utter something which I could not make out while at the same time squeezing it with both his hands. He then gave it to me and said,

"O Jabir, announce for a basin to be brought." Thereupon, Allah's Messenger, upon him be peace and blessings, placed his hand in the basin with his fingers stretched out, and then he placed his fingers at the bottom of the basin and said,

"O Jabir, take this (waterskin) and pour water over my hand, saying, 'In the Name of Allah' (Bismillah), and I immediately poured water over his hand and said, 'Bismillah'. *I found water gushing forth from between the fingers of Allah's Messenger, upon him be peace and blessings.* The water in that basin gushed forth until it was filled to its brim and Allah's Messenger, upon him be peace and blessings, said,

"O Jabir, call out to those in need of water." The people came and drank of that water until they were all satiated.

"Is there anyone left who is in need of water?" I called out, but no one came forward. Upon this, Allah's Messenger, upon him be peace and blessings, raised his hand from that basin and it was still full to its brim. Some time later, the people complained to Allah's Messenger, upon him be peace and blessings, about hunger and he said,

"Allah will provide for you." We reached (the shores of) **Sif al-Bahr** and the sea surged until it tossed to the shore a large animal. We lit a fire, cooked it and ate from it until we had eaten to our heart's content; however, we scarcely finished half of it..." (Muslim, Zuhd, 74)

Allah, glorified and exalted be He, immediately accepted the entreaties of His Messenger. Even the Makkan polytheists had realised this. For instance, when the Messenger of Allah, upon him be peace

and blessings, prayed for a person, the effect of this could be observed on them for a lifetime. **Abu Hurayra**'s not forgetting anything that he heard, the blessing in **Anas ibn Malik**'s life, wealth and children, **Bashir ibn 'Aqraba**'s attaining blessing; the supplications he made for **Abu al-Yasar** to have a long life and for his community to benefit from him, are just a few of these. The following two incidents can be offered as examples of this:

Ju'ayd ibn 'Abd al-Rahman relates:

"I saw **Sa'ib ibn Yazid** when he was ninety-four years old, quite strong and of straight figure. He said,

'I know that I enjoy my hearing and seeing powers only because of the supplication of Allah's Messenger, upon him be peace and blessings. My aunt took me to him in my childhood and said,

"O Allah's Messenger! My nephew is sick; will you invoke Allah for him?"

So he passed his hands over my head and prayed for Allah's blessings for me...'" (See, Bukhari, Manaqib, 21-22)

'Abd Allah ibn Hisham saw the Prophet when he was six years old. He relates that his mother Zaynab bint Humayd took him to the Messenger of Allah, upon him be peace and blessings, and said,

"O Allah's Messenger! Take the pledge of allegiance from my son." But he said,

"He is still too young for the pledge," and passed his hand on his head and invoked for Allah's blessing for him.

In his later years, 'Abd Allah ibn Hisham, may Allah be well pleased with him, used to go to the market to buy foodstuff. Ibn 'Umar and Ibn Zubayr, may Allah be well pleased with them both, would meet him and say to him,

"Allow us partnership to these goods, as the Prophet invoked Allah to bless you." So, he would accept them as partners, and very often he would acquire a complete camel's load (in profit) and send it home. (Bukhari, Shirka, 13)

❊

Abu Hurayra, may Allah be well pleased with him, relates:

"We were accompanying the Messenger of Allah, upon him be peace and blessings, in a military expedition (towards Tabuk). The people's provisions were almost depleted. And (the situation became so critical that) they wanted to slaughter some of their camels. Upon this **'Umar**, may Allah be well pleased with him, said,

"O Messenger of Allah, If I were to pool together what has been left of the people's provisions, would you invoke (the blessings of) Allah upon them?"

Allah's Messenger, upon him be peace and blessings, did as such. The one who had wheat in his possession brought wheat. He who had dates with him brought dates. He who possessed seeds of dates brought with them seeds."

Those present asked Abu Hurayra in great astonishment,

"What did they do with the seeds of the dates?" That great Companion replied,

"As the people could not find anything to eat, they sucked them and then subsequently drank water." He continued,

"The Messenger of Allah, upon him be peace and blessings, invoked the blessings (of Allah) upon the provisions. And (there was such a miraculous increase in the provisions that) the people replenished their provisions fully. Before this Divine grace, Allah's Messenger said,

"I bear witness that there is no god but Allah, and I am His messenger. One who meets Allah without entertaining any doubt about these (two fundamentals) will enter Paradise." (Muslim, Iman, 44)[130]

6. Belief in the Hereafter

Allah Almighty has decreed five stages for human life. The first of these is the **realm of (pure) spirits** (*'alam al-arwah*), the second is the **mother's womb**, the third is **worldly life**, the fourth is the **intermediate realm and the world of the grave**, while the fifth is the **Hereafter** and its resultant eternal life in **Paradise** or **Hellfire**. Of these, worldly life has been granted to the human being as a test and eternal bliss or punishment has been made contingent upon the actions and behaviour of human beings in this realm. For each servant to know that their every act and manner has a consequence, positive or negative, and be thus aware of their responsibility, the Hereafter has figured among the six essentials of belief, such that, in parallel with its importance, belief in the Hereafter has been mentioned alongside belief in Allah in many Qur'anic verses. Especially

---

130. For details on the Prophet's life, morality and miracles, see,
 Osman Nuri Topbaş, *The Prophet Muhammad Mustafa the Elect I-II, The Exemplar Beyond Compare Muhammad Mustafa, Civilisation of Virtues I-II*, (http://islamicpublishing.net/)
 http://www.islamiyayinlar.net
 http://rahmetesintileri.darulerkam.altinoluk.com
 http://hazretimuhammedmekkedevri.darulerkam.altinoluk.com
 http://hazretimuhammedmedinedevri.darulerkam.altinoluk.com
 http://hazretimuhammed.darulerkam.altinoluk.com
 http://faziletlermedeniyeti1.darulerkam.altinoluk.com
 http://faziletlermedeniyeti2.darulerkam.altinoluk.com
 Ibn Ishaq, *The Life of Muhammad*, Karachi: Oxford University Press, 1967; **Mawlana Shibli Numani**, *Sirat al-Nabi*, Lahore: Kazi Publications, 1979; **Afzalur Rahman**, *Muhammad: Encyclopedia of Seerah*, London: The Muslims Schools Trust, 1982; **Abdul Ahad Dawud**, *Muhammed in the Bible*, Doha: Presidency of Shariyah Courts and Religious Affairs, 1980; **Maulana Abdul Haq Vidyarthi**, *Muhammad in World Scriptures*, New Delhi: Deep-Deep Publications, 1988.

THE ESSENTIALS OF BELIEF

in the last three parts (*juz'*) of the Qur'an, belief in the Hereafter is frequently stressed.

Allah Almighty declares:

"Whoever truly believes in Allah and the Last day and does good, righteous deeds, surely their reward is with their Lord, and they will have no fear, nor will they grieve." (Baqara 2:62)

In commendation of the believers, He declares:

"...Those who believe in Allah and the Last Day..." (Tauba 9:128)

The Hereafter is the new, eternal and true life to begin after death. It is declared in a Qur'anic verse:

"The present, worldly life is nothing but a pastime and play, but the abode of the Hereafter is truly alive. If they but knew." (Ankabut 29:64)

Those cognisant of this reality make the most of every breath in this fleeting realm and do not remain heedless of the Almighty for even an instant. Their lives are lives of worship that are teeming with deeds of righteousness. They are constantly between fear and hope concerning their end. Their hearts tremble with the terror and dread of the great reckoning and they shed tears with fear of Allah.

The following story is very striking with regard to the intensity of Divine reckoning:

One of the righteous had gone to the market to purchase a few necessary items. Having calculated the price of these items at home, he drew the conclusion that the money he had was enough to buy these. However, when he reached the marketplace, that money was not enough to purchase what he needed. Upon this, that righteous man began to weep and this state continued for some time. Those around him were astonished by his state. They tried to console him, telling him that there was no point to his crying because he did not have enough money. Composing himself some time later, this pious man addressed the perplexed crowd, choking back his tears:

"Don't assume that my tears are for this world. I realised that not everything works out exactly how you expect it to. So how are the calculations we make in this world to work out in the Hereafter?"

The Last Day and the Resurrection

When the time allocated for worldly life comes to an end, Archangel Israfil, peace be upon him, will sound the trumpet and this universe will burst violently and the world will come to an end.[131]

Such horrific scenes will emerge with the end of the world that the heavens will be split asunder and become as molten rock, the sun and moon will turn black, the stars will disperse and crumble, the mountains will be like discarded wool, the seas will boil and burst, Hellfire will be enkindled and Paradise will be brought near. Eyes will be blinded by the horror; people will flee but will not be able to find any place of refuge. Due to this terrifying scene, even cherished ten-month pregnant camels will be set free, or in other words, prized possessions will have no value and wild animals will be gathered together. No loyal friend will ask after their friend, suckling mothers will forsake their infants in dread due to the deafening sound and violent tremor, pregnant women will miscarry and people will lose their senses from the horror of that Day. The wrongdoer will yearn to give their children, spouse, sibling, kith and kin and whoever else is on earth as ransom so as to save themselves from the extremely severe punishment on that Day.[132]

---

131. Naml 27:87; Zumar 39:68; Haqqah 69:14-16.
132. See: Hajj 22:1-2; Ma'arij 70:8-14; Qiyama 6-12; Takwir 81:1-13; Infitaar 82:1-5. For further information regarding the overwhelming nature of the final destruction of the world, see: Ibrahim 14:48; Ta-Ha 20:105-107; Qamar 7-8; Haqqah 69:14-16; Muzzammil 73:14; Mursalat 77:8-11; Abasa 80:34-42; Inshiqaq 84:1-5; Qari'ah 101:1-5.

Allah Almighty declares:

"**They have no true judgment of Allah as His right, such as His being Allah requires, and** (such is His Power and Sovereignty that) **the whole earth will be in His Grasp on the Day of Resurrection, and the heavens will be rolled up in His Right Hand. All-Glorified is He, and absolutely exalted above what they associate with Him. The Trumpet will be blown, and so all who are in the heavens and all who are on the earth will fall dead, except those whom Allah wills to exempt. Then it will be blown for the second time, and see, they have all stood upright, looking on** (in anticipation)." (Zumar 39:67-68)

Again, Allah Almighty declares:

"**And the Trumpet will be blown, and see, out of the graves they rush forth to their Lord. They will cry: 'Woe to us! Who has raised us from our place of sleep?** (We have come to know that) **this is what the All-Merciful promised, and that the Messengers spoke the truth!'**" (Ya-Sin 36:51-52)

According to certain scholars, much as the unbelievers and rebellious will be subjected to punishment in their graves, this punishment is rather light when compared to that which they will suffer in the Hereafter. From this perspective, life in the grave has been likened to sleep. When they rise from their graves, they will be subjected to such severe punishment that they will begin to cry in lamentation, "Woe to us!" (Ömer Nasuhi Bilmen, *Tafsir*, VI:2943)

After this, the Day of Eternity (*Yawm al-Khulud*) begins.

The resurrection of human beings on that Day is an easy matter for the Almighty, Who absolutely creates from nothing. Allah, exalted and glorified be He, declares:

"**And** (despite this, that disbelieving) **human says: 'What? once I am dead, will I then be brought forth alive?'** **Does** (that) **human not bear in mind that We created him before when he was nothing?**" (Maryam 19:66-67)

"**Has human not considered that We have created him from** (so slight a beginning as) **a drop of** (seminal) **fluid? Yet, he turns into an open, fierce adversary** (selfishly disputing against the truth). **And he coins a comparison for Us, having forgotten his own origin and creation, saying, 'Who will give life to these bones when they have rotten away?'**

Say: 'He Who produced them in the first instance will give them life. He has full knowledge of every (form and mode and possibility of) **creation** (and of everything He has created, He knows every detail in every dimension of time and space).' **He Who has made for you fire from the green tree, and see, you kindle fire with it. Is not He Who has created the heavens and the earth able to create** (from rotten bones) **the like of them** (whose bones have rotted under the ground)? **Surely He is; He is the supreme Creator, the All-Knowing.**

When He wills a thing to be, He but says to it 'Be!' and (in the selfsame instant) **it is. So, All-Glorified is He in Whose Hand is the absolute dominion of all things, and to Him you are being brought back.**" (Yasin 36:77-83)

"**He brings forth the living out of the dead, and brings the dead out of the living, and revives the earth after its death. It is in this way** (that He revives the dead earth) **that you will be brought forth from the dead.**" (Rum 30:19)

Abu Razin, may Allah be pleased with him, relates:

I once said,

'O Messenger of Allah, how will Allah bring the dead back to life? What is the sign of this in His creation?' He said,

'(O Abu Razin,) do you not pass through the valley of your people (and see it) arid and barren, then you pass through it (and see it) stirred (to life) and green)?' I said, 'Yes.'

He said, *'Thus will Allah bring the dead back to life.'"* (Ahmad, IV, 11)

These Qur'anic verses, declared by the One Who brings to life, causes to die and revives back to life, and the Prophet's hadith illustrate that resurrection will absolutely be realised. What bears importance, then, is to take lesson from the Prophetic Tradition, *"You will die as you live and will be resurrected as you die,"*[133] and reachxs that Day with such a consciousness.

The World Will Come to an End Unexpectedly

Allah Almighty declares:

"And they say (intending mockery)**: 'So, when is this promise** (of resurrection and Judgment)**, if you are truthful?' They should await only a single blast that will seize them unawares even as they are disputing** (heedlessly among themselves about their worldly concerns)**. Then they will not be able even to make a bequest** (so suddenly will the blast seize them)**, nor return to their families."** (Yasin 36:48-50, 53. See, Saad 38:15; Qaf 50:42)

This stupendous Doomsday event, the magnitude and violence of which we make mention, is so simple and slight before the majesty and power of Allah that He will realise it in a single blast and without delay.

Another matter at least as important as this is that this dumbfounding event will take place within a very short space of time. Allah, exalted and glorified be He, declares:

---

133. (Munawi, *Fayd al-Qadr*, V:663)

"...the matter of the Hour (of Doom) is (in relation with the Divine Power) but the twinkling of an eye, or even quicker. Surely Allah has full power over everything."[134]

The Messenger of Allah, upon him be peace and blessings, has explained the fact that Doomsday will occur unexpectedly using various examples. He once said,

"The Final Hour will not come until the sun rises from the west. When people see it, whoever is one the earth will believe. That is the time when,

'...When some clears signs of your Lord appear, believing will be of no avail to anyone who did not believe before, or who has earned no good through his belief.' (An'am 6:158)

The Final Hour will come while two men are spreading a garment between them and will not finish their transaction or fold it up. The Final Hour will come while a man is carrying the milk of his milk-camel, but will not be able to taste it. The Final Hour will come while someone is mending his water basin and will not be able to water from it. The Final Hour will come when someone is raising his food to his mouth but will not be able to taste it." (Bukhari, Riqaq, 40; Ahmad, II:369. See, Muslim, Fitan, 140)

The most important matter here is not when Doomsday will take place, but whether or not human beings are ready for their own Hour of Doom, their death, and their life beyond it. The world is a deceptive mirage while the Hereafter is immortal life. Let us wake before the Doomsday that is our death comes, so that we are not subjected to an irreparable regret, for it is certain that every mortal will meet Archangel Azrail at a time and place unknown. There is no place in which one can escape from death. In that case, taking heed of the

---

134. Nahl 16:77.

mystery in, **"So, flee to** (refuge in) **God,"**[135] the human being must know Divine mercy as the sole refuge.

The elect servants of Allah are those who see to procuring their provisions for the Hereafter before their own Hour of Doom arrives; for such people, there is neither grief, nor fear on that terrifying day.

Reckoning

On the Day of Judgement, human beings will face an extremely difficult and severe reckoning. Allah, exalted and glorified be He, declares:

"And so, whoever does an atom's weight of good will see it; And whoever does an atom's weight of evil will see it." (Zalzalah 99:7-8)

"The Day when neither wealth will be of any use, nor offspring, But only he (will prosper) **who comes before Allah with a sound heart** (free of all kinds of unbelief, hypocrisy, and associating partners with Allah)." (Shu'ara 26:88-89)

In sum, the Hereafter is a realm necessary for both those who are evil as well as the good for there cannot be anything more natural than the rewarding of the good and the punishment of the evil. If there had not been places even in this fleeting realm where the good could reside and the evil could be imprisoned, life would have been unbearable.

As a case in point: In a play, the curtain never drops after the first act, with no closure having yet being achieved. Were this to happen, what would the audience – who are mentally and emotionally engaged and eager to learn the objective and central theme of the play and playwright – think? Even an intelligent child would deem it inappropriate to end the play in this way. In that case, how can it be

---

135. Dhariyat 51:50.

possible for Allah, Who creates everything to perfection and Who is aware of all things, to end this grand story of the universe in a manner unbecoming to even a child!¹³⁶

Human beings are even angered by a mosquito biting their skin and wish to penalise it, while on the other hand they deem themselves to be indebted for life to a person who offers them a single cup of coffee. As a result, there can be no heedlessness more preposterous than the idea that evil and good actions issuing from a person throughout their life will remain without consequence before Allah. For in this world the oppressor has their oppression, the wronged their lament, the unbeliever their unbelief and the believer their belief.

The Most High declares:

"Does human think that he is to be left to himself (to go about as he pleases)?" (Qiyama 75:36)

"Or did you think that We created you in vain, and that you should devote all your time to play and entertainment, and that you would not be brought back to Us?" (Mu'minun 23:115)

"He asks: 'When is the Day of Resurrection?' When the eyesight is confounded (through fear), **And the moon is darkened, And the sun and the moon are joined together, On that day human will say: 'Where is the escape?' By no means! No refuge** (to flee to)**! To your Lord the journey's end will be on that Day. Human will be made to understand on that Day all** (the good and evil) **that he forwarded (to his afterlife while in the world), and all (the good and evil) that he has left behind."** (Qiyama 75:6-13)

The exact time of the Last Day has not been revealed, however, some of its minor and major signs have been provided. These can be summarised briefly as follows:

---

136. Muhammad Sa'id Ramadan al-Buti, *Kubra al-Yaqiniyyat al-Kawniyya*, 180.

Minor Signs:

1) Knowledge will be taken away and ignorance will increase. The drinking of intoxicants and adultery will be prevalent and perpetrated publicly.

2) There will be much killing for petty reasons and without cause.

3) Justice and competence will be taken away and the prohibited and the permissible will not be observed.

4) Disobedience to parents and obedience to wrongdoing women will increase.

5) Cheating in weighing out goods will become widespread and everyone will come to complain of such deception.

6) Respect and compassion towards human beings will greatly decrease and advice will not be heeded.

7) Emigration to the cities will increase and buildings will get taller. Wicked and unqualified people will be respected and they will hold power and authority.

8) Gambling, fortunetelling and gaming equipment will be in high demand and people will lose track of time.

9) Waste will increase and worldly gain and possessions will be preferred to happiness in the Hereafter.[137]

Major Signs:

1) The emergence of a smoke that is to last forty days;

2) The appearance of the Dajjal (Anti-Christ);

---

137. For the minor signs of the end of the world, see: Bukhari, Hudud 20, Fitan 25; Muslim, Iman 1; Fitan 18, 55; Tirmidhi, Fitan 34, 37, 39.

3) The appearance of a creature known as the 'Beast of the Earth' (*Dabbat al ard*);

4) The sun's rising from the west;

5) The global spread of Gog and Magog;

6) Prophet Jesus' descent to earth;

7) The emergence of a powerful fire from the Hejaz; and

8) Three landslides – one in the east, one in the west and one in the Arabian Peninsula.[138]

Belief in the Hereafter strengthens a sense of responsibility and ensures that one does justice to their duty and is respectful toward truth and justice. In this way, it is the means to a strong sense of morality, a most perfect concept of order and an exalted awareness of justice.

It is most certain that a person with strong conviction that they will account for every word, state and act before Allah Almighty and that they see the good and evil of all that they do, will possess an elevated morality and lofty understanding of justice.

A believer who knows the Tradition of Allah's Messenger, who said,

"The feet of a servant will not move on the Day of Judgement until he has been questioned about four things: his life – how he spent it; his knowledge – how he acted upon it; his wealth - where he earned it and how he spent it; and his body – how he used it,"[139] is most certainly mindful of right, truth and reckoning.

---

138. For the major signs of the end of the world, see: Al-'Imran 3:55, Nisa 4:157-159; An'am 6:158; Kahf 18:93-99; Anbiya 21:96-97; Naml 27:82; Zukhruf 43:61; Dukhan 44:10-13. Bukhari, Buyu' 102, Anbiya 49, Fitan 24, 25, 27; Muslim, Iman 247, Fitan 23, 42, 100-103, 118; Tirmidhi, Tafsir, 27; Ibn Maja, Fitan, 31.

139. (Tirmidhi, Qiyama, 1/2417)

A person who knows that Allah Almighty constantly sees them and who believes in the Hereafter cannot err even in places where others cannot see them. They become an honest, reliable individual in whom all others trust.

It is inevitable that people from whose hearts a belief in the Hereafter, fear and love of Allah are erased, become the most harmful element of this realm, due to their worship of personal gain and self interest. In the eyes of such people, virtues such as love of nation, common interest and good as well as taking lesson from history are the subject of ridicule. Superiority and virtue, for them, consists of deceiving others. For this reason, weakening the religion of the people and their notion of the Hereafter is an extremely dangerous undertaking which would drastically lead societies to ruin. Many examples of this have been encountered in recent and distant history.

For those who believe in the Hereafter and organise their life accordingly, there is no fear of death. Being delivered from tribulations and attaining eternal peace, and the ideal of earning Allah's good pleasure and approval cause a zest for life in a person and give them the power of perseverance in the face of the suffering in the world. Fleeting worldly desires can never satisfy the human spirit. The spirit's repose is possible only through the elevated delights and spiritual tastes that belief engenders.

In short, a true success and peace in this life cannot be in question without the belief in a return to Allah.

7. Belief in Divine Destiny

The Divine will is present in all acts of coming into existence. Nothing can be realised without His will and power. Even a dust particle cannot budge and a gnat's wing cannot quiver. Consequently, due to the fact that Allah Almighty possesses infinite knowledge, He knows everything that has been and will be. The Almighty's recording, in the eternal past, a thing that is to happen is **Divine Decree** (*Qadar*), while its actualisation is **Divine Destiny** (*Qaza*).

It is not possible for *Qadar* to be duly understood within the reach of human conception. For this reason, it has been misused often. Consequently, gaining profundity of awareness in this matter is of no avail to a person. For the Divine declaration, **"With Him are the keys to the Unseen; none knows them but He..."** does not allow for a deepened understanding in the matter of Divine Decree.[140]

In the same way that colours cannot be described to a blind person, the mysteries of such matters cannot be attained with human perception. Only those with Divinely inspired knowledge (*'ilm al-ladunni*) can receive a minuscule portion herein. This incident, mentioned in the Qur'an, is the most salient example of this:

Allah Almighty sends **Prophet Moses**, peace be upon him, to **Al-Khidr**, peace be upon him, who possessed intuitive, God-given knowledge in order for him to acquire this knowledge also. This knowledge is a knowledge that reflects gleams from beyond causes and pretexts, that is, from the Supreme Preserved Tablet (or Record). Prophet Moses and Al-Khidr set out on a journey. During the journey, certain events which baffled and caused horror to Prophet Moses, peace be upon him, were experienced. Al-Khidr, peace be upon him, made a hole in the boat they embarked upon and, as such, damaged it. He killed a young boy that they later came across without apparent cause. Subsequently, they asked the people of a township they come upon for food, but they were refused. However, al-Khidr, peace be upon him, repaired a wall on the verge of collapse in that very town, without taking any payment.[141]

---

140. An'am 6:59.
141. See: Kahf 18:60-82; Bukhari, Tafsir, 18:2-4.

As Prophet Moses, peace be upon him, did not have a grasp of the mystery of Divine Destiny and the future repercussions of events, he was unable to make sense of all these happenings and at each time raised objection to Al-Khidr, peace be upon him. Eventually, at the end of the journey, al-Khidr, peace be upon him, explained the inner meaning of these events:

Outwardly, the boat's having a hole drilled into it is an injustice and cruelty to its owners; in reality, however, it prevents the boat's – the means of livelihood for those poor seaman – being forcibly seized. For there was a King pursuing the boat who seized by force every boat that he saw.

Outwardly, the child's being killed was a murder; in reality, however, it constituted the protection of the eternal lives of both his parents, both righteous servants, as well as his own. For if that child had lived, he was in future going to drag his parents to transgression and ingratitude and was thus going to destroy both his eternal life in the Hereafter, as well as that of his parents.

Outwardly, repairing the wall belonging to the townspeople who had refused them hospitality was illogical; in reality, however, it constitutes the protection of the trust belonging to two orphan children. For lying buried underneath that wall was a treasure belonging to those orphan children. If the wall were to collapse, the treasure would be revealed and would become the property of usurpers. Allah Almighty, however, willed that that treasure be found by those two orphans when they had come of age.

The mysteries behind these states only become clear through spiritual knowledge direct from God. Consequently, the mystery of Divine Decree cannot be comprehended only through reason as a complete grasp of Divine Decree is a circumstance which transcends human perception. It is by virtue of this fact that the Messenger of Allah, upon him be peace and blessings, has instructed us to suffice with belief in Divine Decree and has forbidden idle debates in this matter. When he encountered a group of people debating on the topic of Divine Decree, he said,

"Is this what you have been commanded to do? Is this why I have been sent to you? Those who came before you were destroyed because they disputed about it. Do not to fall into dispute concerning this matter." (Tirmidhi, Qadar, 1:2133)

As a result, comprehending accurately the wisdom behind Divine Decree as opposed to deepening in knowledge concerning it constitutes the most important and adequate criterion. The essence of the matter is this:

Allah Almighty, has manifested the acts that He has willed for humankind in two parts:

1) Compulsory Acts (Af'al al-Idtirariyya)

These are realised independently of our own volition and desire and are comprised completely of the manifestation of Divine Decree and Divine Destiny. It is not at all possible to contravene these. Being born, dying, becoming resurrected, sleeping, getting hungry, our physical constitution, our lifespan and the like are all included among this part of Divine Decree. These are also referred to as Absolute Divine Decree, such that humankind is not responsible for these acts to which they are necessarily subject to.

When the set time for the matters included under this aspect of Divine Decree arrives, the seeing eye of the human being no longer sees, their hearing ear no longer hears and the servant's precaution taken in this regard is nullified completely. **Mawlana Jalal al-Din al-Rumi** states:

"When Divine Destiny strikes, fish throw themselves from the seas; Birds flying in the air begin to rush to the lures set up for them on earth.

Only those fleeing to Divine Decree and Destiny can be saved from such Divine Decree and Destiny."

Allah, the Most High, declares:

"...The command of Allah is a decree determined (in due measures for every thing, event and individual)." (Ahzab 33:38)

However, Divine Decree and Destiny must not be envisaged purely as disasters and the like befalling a person. Divine Decree in a sense expresses the balance in the universe and the Divine measure of that balance. Allah, the Most High, declares:

"Surely We have created each and every thing by (precise) **measure."** (Qamar 54:45)

Thus, criticism of the judgement of Divine Decree is an ignorance and, so to speak, idiocy, for its judgement is forever in its rightful place. For instance, no one has any concerns in relation to the **sun**, which perpetually rotates in the world that we live in without deviating for even a moment or a single millimetre and which illuminates our world. Everyone knows the sun to rise and set each day, without fail, within a set order. Similarly, in the event that the wisdom behind every event – good or bad – is known, the single thing that remains to be said, without exception, is, "This is what's best".

Even the staunchest unbelievers are in awe before the Divine symmetry, order and functioning decreed in their own constitutions. Far from criticism, each mystery from the master plan of Divine Will, solved to the extent of the Almighty's permission, drives every person of sound judgement – unbelievers included – to wander, as it were, through the eternal valley of amazement and bewilderment. Those who complain in regard to this matter are only those deprived of reason and perception who are unaware of the mystery of Divine Will. They are victims of ignorance insensible to good and evil, right and wrong and truth and falsehood.

On the other hand, it is known that Divine Decree and Destiny is an unknown. This, in itself, is a Divine favour bestowed upon the human being who is in reality a mortal. If a person were to know everything, good and bad, that is to befall them, life would become unbearable for them. They would pull away from eating, drinking and working. However, it is by virtue of the Almighty's concealing Divine Decree and Destiny that humankind can carry the hope of life even when within a whisker of death, and do not sever themselves from life-sustaining activity. This, too, is a stupendous and perfect Divine system that makes it possible for one to 'live' in this worldly life.

In short, the repose of the heart has been hidden within resignation to Divine Decree. No other deed or doing can avail a person. How beautifully **Rumi** puts it when he says:

"So long as you are not content with what Allah has given you, wherever you flee for relief and safety, you will be confronted by calamity, disaster will strike and again find you.

Know that no corner of this fleeting world is trap-free. There is no deliverance except finding Allah in one's heart, seeking sanctuary with Him and living in His spiritual presence. Look, are not those living in the most secure places of this fleeting realm and seeing themselves to be invincible in the end falling into the trap of death?

Look to seeking refuge in Allah, not beings secure of transient traps. If He wills, He can render poison a remedy for you and if He wills He can make water a poison.

2) Volitional Acts (Af'al al-Ikhtiyariyya)

Allah Almighty has bestowed upon His servants a partial and relative willpower. The servant is responsible for the actions that come into existence through the use of this willpower. If what they do is good, they will be rewarded while if it is evil, they will suffer the punishment thereof. Allah Almighty creates the action that the

THE ESSENTIALS OF BELIEF

servant desires to carry out using his or her own will. In such actions, alongside Allah Almighty's attribute of creating there is the acquisition [of Divinely created actions by individual human beings]' (*kasb*). This pertains to the servant. However, Allah Almighty does not create everything that the servant wishes.

From another standpoint, as there is no time for Him, there is no difference for Allah Almighty between knowledge of something that is to occur and knowledge of something that has occurred. Due to the fact that we contemplate and think in a world constrained by time, we are inclined to think that His knowing what is to happen as it were compels us to act. This is a weakness and failing born of our inability to conceive of anything outside of time, due to the time-space dimensions in which we find ourselves. Whereas, when the veil of time is lifted, everything is observed simultaneously. Hence, when the Messenger of Allah, upon him be peace and blessings, imparted his observations during the Ascension (*Mi'raj*), having on the one hand become acquainted with the Eternal from which humankind has come (*azal*), he stated:

"*Then Gabriel ascended with me to a place where I heard the creaking of the pens.*"[142] On the other hand beholding the realm of the eternal to which humankind will journey after death (*abad*), he has made mention of the kinds of people who will enter Paradise and Hellfire. (Bukhari, Riqaq 51, Muslim, Zuhd 93)

This truth that the Prophet, upon him be peace and blessings, was favoured with on the night of the Ascension, having been lifted from the restrictions of time, is valid for the Almighty perpetually. For He is above and beyond time and space.

Thus, when we begin to unveil our weakness and failing in relation to time, we see that Allah Almighty has given His servants a

---

142. Bukhari, Salat, 1.

willpower and capacity commensurate with their responsibility and a responsibility commensurate with their willpower and capacity. Had this not been the case, Allah, the All-Merciful and All-Compassionate would not have burdened His servants with any responsibility and would not have held them to account in relation to His commandments and prohibitions. Hence, it is declared in a Qur'anic verse:

"(O believers, if you are worried that Allah will take every soul to account even for what the soul keeps within it of intentions and plans, know that) **Allah burdens no soul except within its capacity: in its favor is whatever** (good) **it earns, and against it whatever** (evil) **it merits…**"

Immediately after, the Almighty teaches the following supplication:

"**…Our Lord, take us not to task if we forget or make mistakes. Our Lord, lay not on us a burden such as You laid on those gone before us. Our Lord, impose not on us what we do not have the power to bear. And overlook our faults, and forgive us, and have mercy upon us. You are our Guardian and Owner** (to Whom we entrust our affairs and on Whom we rely) **so help us and grant us victory against the disbelieving people!**" (Baqara 2:286)

Allah Almighty's decreeing responsibility and account for His servants illustrates that He has favoured them with the will, power (to make decisions) and capacity necessitating this. **Rumi** calls out to those who cannot see this truth, from the realm of reflection:

"If you move jaggedly, the pen will write jaggedly; if you proceed in a straight fashion, this will breed happiness.

When a thief was caught by the police, he said to the officer arresting him, "What I have done is the decree and will of God." In response, the police officer said, "What I have done is also the decree and will of

God." First do wrong and then refer it to Divine Decree – this is not the business of the wise!"

The sum of the matter is this: Satan shows the human being evil, while the spirit shows them goodness. If there were no capacity to choose, then why should they bother!

O Jabri (defender of absolute predestination)! In saying, "The servant is not a free agent," you supposedly seek to disassociate weakness from the Lord, but you do not see that by denying the mystery in His holding His servant to account – Allah forbid! – you ascribe to the Divine an attribute which pertains to an ignorant and senseless humankind. Could that Creator of all the Worlds demand from His servants the manifestation of a quality that He has not bestowed and thus oppress them? Come to your senses and grasp the wisdom behind Allah Almighty's addressing commands and prohibitions to His servants. Even this is a sign of the willpower He has granted.

And turn and look to your own world. If none other than Allah possesses will, then why do you anger at the thief who steals your property? Why do you deem certain people as foes and bear endless hostility to them? How is it that you brand those without agency with the stamp of crime and sin? In this case, willpower indeed exists! Otherwise, what need would there be for prisons?"

There is another point worthy of mention at this juncture:

It is not right to place excessive importance on the will and agency bestowed upon the servant and raise reason above everything else. For as wisdom, rather than knowledge increases, it becomes easy to discern just how trifling human will and agency is before the cosmic Divine Will. Eventually, minor human will – being the likes of a small crumb in comparsion – decreases in servants attaining **annihilation in Allah** (*fana fi'llah*) to the point of extinction. In particular, for those advancing upon the path of annihilation in Allah with His being the *eyes with which His servant sees, the hands with which His servant holds*,[143] partial (human) will is, so to speak, like the dwindling candle flame beneath the sunlight.

Good and Evil are from Allah

In reference to evil also being created by Allah, it is important to note that no evil is realised with His approval. However, Allah Almighty occasions the occurrence of evil – despite His displeasure at such – as a requirement of trial in the world. Will and desire is from the servant while the act of creating and generating is from Allah. Moreover, His placing a 'visa', so to speak, for the appearance of evil by **'granting permission'** for it to transpire, constitutes yet another manifestation of His boundless mercy towards His servants. This is because this 'visa' does not allow for the realisation every evil that we wish to carry out and protects us, whether we are aware of it or not, from many a material and spiritual abyss. Otherwise, who knows how many more misdeeds and offences committed via the intrigues of the carnal self and Satan, humankind would add to their lot, as they aspire evil just as much as they aspire good, willingly or unwillingly. Allah Almighty reveals this truth in the following way:

"**Yet human** (through his actions as well as his words) **prays and calls for evil just as he prays and calls for good. Human is prone to be hasty**" (Isra' 17:11)

"**If Allah were to hasten for human beings the ill** (which they have earned) **in the same manner as they hasten** (the coming to them of what they consider to be) **the good, their term would indeed have been decreed over for them...**" (Yunus 10:11)

The extent to which humankind engages in self-reflection is the extent to which they will have a grasp of the truth of these Qur'anic

---

143. See, Bukhari, Riqaq, 38.

verses. For instance, when a liar utters such statements as "Cross my heart and hope to die," in order to convince others of the 'truth' of what they are saying, they for the most part do not die and the period for examination granted to them continues as per usual. Again, many people voice rather severe, conditional statements, damning themselves if they do or fail to do such-and-such, momentarily and unfeignedly; however, the time comes when they contradict the vows they made and despite this, they are not damned and do not die. There are many such examples in a person's life. Thus in such cases, Allah Almighty does not allow for the realisation of this evil due to His mercy.

Sometimes, however, such unbecoming wants of a person are fulfilled. In such cases, that person faces the repercussions of their foolishness and what their tongue utters. Consequently, we must be wary of making such incorrect statements and choose very carefully every word that comes out of our mouths.

While Allah Almighty is pleased with good works and deeds, He does not approve of evil. He allows for and creates it only as a requirement of examination in this world.

He declares:

"Assuredly, Allah wrongs (no one) **not even so much as an atom's weight..."** (Nisa 4:40)

"Whatever affliction befalls you, it is because of what your hands have earned; and yet, He overlooks many (of the wrongs you do)." (Shura 42:30)

Consequently, perceiving this mercy and compassion of Allah Almighty and before every manifestation of thus, the Gnostics say:

"Pleasing to me is whatever comes from You,

Whether rosebud or thorn,

Whether robe or shroud,

Pleasing to me is whatever comes from You.

Moreover, Allah Almighty demands this state of resignation from His servants:

"Say: 'Nothing befalls us except what Allah has decreed for us; He is our Guardian and Owner'; and in Allah let the believers put all their trust." (Tauba 9:51)

"If Allah touches you with affliction, there is none who can remove it but He; and if He wills any good for you, then there is none who can hold back His bounty. He causes it to reach whomever He wills of His servants. He is the All-Forgiving, the All-Compassionate." (Yunus 10:107)

However, at no time does this situation prevent one from taking the required precautions. As Divine Decree is unknown, the human being must do everything in their power to attain the best of everything.

A deeper examination of these key principles reveals a good deal of matters requiring explanation, but these would amount to nothing more than material for theological debate. The essence of the matter is this:

The servant possesses willpower. This willpower or agency has been bestowed upon them by Allah Almighty. While the Divine Will is present in every act and occurrence, His pleasure and approval lies only in the good. A teacher's objective is for their student to be equipped with knowledge and pass their subject. If the student fails to study, then there is nothing that the teacher can do. Again, a doctor's duty is to heal their patient. If the patient fails to administer the given

THE ESSENTIALS OF BELIEF

prescription, they are the only party responsible for any adverse effect to ensue. No shortcoming can be ascribed to the doctor.

In this respect, we cannot use Divine Decree as an excuse to justify ourselves in matters involving our own will and which thus make us accountable.

A person's saying, after failing to perform worship or going astray, "It can't be helped, this was my fate," can only be due to their heedlessness. The Almighty favours the person wishing to observe the Prescribed Prayer or perform other acts of worship with the necessary causes.

Our excusing ourselves in relation to the sins that we commit amounts to calumny against Divine Decree, and this can only be the manifestation of foolishness and shamelessness.

Part 3

Worship

The preservation of belief is possible not with dry information and theory, but by means of deepening in one's inner world through reflecting upon the embroidery of Divine power and majesty exhibited upon the Qur'an, the universe and the human being, by observing acts of worship in a state of rapture and devoted reverence and with an elevated morality. There is no delight and degree loftier than servanthood to God. Acts of worship are akin to the vitamins of the life of our heart. On the other hand, if a heedless life beneath the yoke of base and carnal desires, with a purblind, sullen, coarse and ungraceful constitution of heart is being lived, than this implies the debilitation of belief.

WORSHIP

The essence of Islam is belief, while its objective is deeds of righteousness and good character. Islam is not something which should be concealed only within the conscience, for any truth which is relegated to the field of thought and feeling and which is not actively experienced, no matter how lofty it may be, does not have much value. If a person cannot verbally articulate a truth in which they believe and put it into practice, their belief in and love of it gradually diminishes. For this reason, Islam has not only inculcated theoretical and theological principles, but also practical rulings. That is to say, Islam is in the complete sense of the term a 'religion of life'. Belief, which is to begin in the deepest point in the heart and envelop a person entirely, is to flow from the tongue like the water of life and then become diffused to the whole body and its surroundings.

Belief is preserved not through dry facts and theory, but as a result of the enhancement of reflection before existent truths, a spiritual deepening and the observation of worship with this increasing spirituality. If the outward citadel of worship is weakened, the inner citadel of belief is also threatened. If we were to liken belief to a lamp, worship resembles the glass lantern protecting it from blowing out in the face of winds coming from various directions and which serves to enhance its light.

Knowledge can only develop through implementation and experience and, taking root, becomes expertise. While the protection of dry information that has not been put into practice is most difficult, its benefit is little if any. Similarly, belief's becoming established in a person is possible only through worship.

In blessed and elect servants of Allah, the joy and pleasure of belief has surpassed all fleeting joys and pleasures. It has virtually annihilated the burning, unbearable and deleterious force of worldly pain, suffering and hardship:

When the sorcerers who challenged Prophet Moses, peace be upon him, professed their belief, the tyrannical Pharaoh had their hands and feet cut off alternately and had them crucified all together. In the face of this great persecution of the Pharaoh, these new Muslims raised their hands towards the heavens in fear of demonstrating human weakness and weakening in faith, and entreated Allah Almighty:

"Our Lord! Pour out upon us persevering patience, and take our souls to You as Muslims (wholly submitted to You)!"[144] And finally, they returned to their Lord in the spiritual exuberance of declaration of Divine Unity.

The first followers of **Prophet Jesus**, peace be upon him, each sincere Muslims, displayed persevering patience and steadfastness in their belief in Allah's Oneness, even at the risk of being mutilated between the teeth of lions at the circus. They attained martyrdom in a state of spiritual rapture, overcome by the sublime delights they had tasted.

After having tasted the pleasure of belief, the Prophet's Companion **Sumayya**, may Allah be well pleased with her, showed great

---

144. A'raf 7:126.

perseverance in the face of the Makkan polytheists branding her body in torture, when she formerly had feared of the prick of a single needle. She made not the slightest concession from her belief. After having been subjected to barbaric torture, her body was savagely brutalised by having each foot tied to a separate camel. Her husband **Yasir**, may Allah be well pleased with him, displayed extraordinary patience, despite himself being elderly and weak. Eventually, he too was martyred. In this way, the Yasir family, may Allah be well pleased with all of them, became the first martyrs of Islam.¹⁴⁵ They paid the price of their belief by practising it with great love and devotion and with their own lives.

The illustrious state of the Companion **Bilal**, may Allah be well pleased with him, is by virtue of the same exhilaration of meeting with Allah (*liqa' Allah*). Bilal too, may Allah be well pleased with him, despite being covered in blood under the brutal torture of the Makkan polytheists, proclaimed, "One, One... Allah is One, Allah is One!" Rather than feeling the pain and agony, he experienced the rapture of meeting with Allah with a heart which had tasted the exalted pleasure of belief. For he, as with all the others, had perceived to the utmost the greatness of the blessing of Islam. In this way, they knew just how they were to open the doors of Divine Exaltedness in both worlds with their love and rapture. With their ephemeral lives ending within the spirit of the Divine command, **"O you who believe! Keep from disobedience to Allah in reverent piety, with all the reverence that is due to Him, and see that you do not die save as Muslims** (submitted to Him exclusively),"¹⁴⁶ they attained the life true and eternal.

---

145. See, Ibn Hajar, *al-Isaba*, III:648; Zamakhshari, *Kashshaf*, ed. Muhammad Musa 'Amir, Cairo 1988, III:164.
146. Al-'Imran 3:102.

The believing generations that came after them, too, were exalted at each time they crowned themselves with Islam.

A belief that is not consolidated with acts of worship however, due to its diminishing with time, loses the positive effect that it exerts over the behaviour of a person. As the effect of belief weakens, the person begins to commit various sins and vices by being dragged into negative feelings and evil character.

Touching upon the wisdom of worship, Allah Almighty declares:

"Now O humankind! Worship your Lord Who has created you as well as those before you (and brought you up in your human nature and identity), **so that you may attain reverent piety toward Him and His protection** (against any kind of straying and its consequent punishment in this world and the Hereafter)." (Baqara 2:21)

A servant protected from wrongdoing and who continues their worship is thus becoming nearer to Allah with every passing moment. The Messenger of Allah, upon him be peace and blessings, has expressed this as follows:

"Allah, glorified and exalted be He, said

'Whoever shows hostility to My saintly servant, I will surely wage war on him. My servant cannot draw near to Me with anything more loved by Me than fulfilling the things I have made incumbent on him. Then, My servant draws nearer and nearer to Me through supererogatory acts of worship until I love him. When I love him, I become his ears with which he hears, his eyes with which he sees, his hands with which he grasps and his feet on which he walks. Were he to ask [something] of Me, I would surely grant it to him, and were he to seek refuge (from something), I would surely take him under My protection..." (Bukhari, Riqaq, 38.) Also see, Ahmad, VI:256; Ibn Hibban, *Sahih*, II, 58:347)

WORSHIP

There is the following inclusion in some narrations:

"...his heart with which he reasons and his tongue with which he speaks." (Tabarani, *Kabir*, VIII, 221:7880; Haythami, II:248)

By enabling spiritual advancement, acts of worship save a person from Hellfire and carry them to Paradise. The sole capital that will benefit the human being in the Hereafter is the worship performed with belief and their deeds of righteousness. We will be buried with nothing other than our deeds of righteousness in the bosom of the earth.

How beautifully **Rumi** expresses this:

"If you do not wish to be alone where you are headed, then take a child (i.e. a helper) of goodness and worship (along with you)." (*Divan al-Kabir*, II:692)

Acts of worship have many positive effects on a person's psychological make up. Each of the different acts of worship retain a distinct quality and each of them amount to spiritual sustenance and nutrients given to spirits. A believer who carries out their worship is psychologically strong and lives their life in peace of mind and heart. They do not despair or undergo stress before the obstacles, difficulties and hardship they face throughout their lives. A person who neglects their worship, however, cannot find peace in two abodes. It is stated in a Prophetic Tradition:

"When a person lapses in their duties of servanthood, or fails to perform sufficient worship, instead decreasing it, Allah afflicts him with grief and sorrow." ('Ali al-Muttaqi, *Kanz al-'Ummal*, no: 6788)

Moreover, through their worship, a person is freed from becoming swept up in materiality, ascends spiritually and attains the honour of true humanity through grace, refinement and sensibility. To the extent that they draw near to Allah with their worship, worldly transactions and good character, they attain the honour of being the treasured of the universe.

From another standpoint, acts of worship also have physical benefits for Islam does not neglect any of the domains of human activity and establishes a magnificent balance between these. Islam is a perfect system which envelops life in all its facets.

For instance, Allah's Messenger, upon him be peace and blessings, has stated that believers who are mindful of their worship are granted abundance in their provisions.[147]

Again, Allah's Messenger, upon him be peace and blessings, has stated:

"Your Lord, exalted and glorified be He, has said: 'If My servants were to obey Me, I should give them rain by night, make the sun rise on them by day, and not cause them to hear the sound of thunder.'"
(Ahmad, II:359; Hakim, IV, 285/7657)

As is evident, Islam places great importance on worship. It is for this reason that deeds of righteousness are mentioned, in the main, alongside belief in the Qur'an and in the Prophetic Traditions. This situation, at the same time, illustrates the vital role of worship in the protection of belief and its centrality in religion.

It also be remembered that worship mainly benefits people themselves. Allah Almighty is in no need whatsoever of the worship and devotion of any other. Worship can perhaps be an expression of gratitude for the innumerable worldly and otherworldly bounties that Allah Almighty has bestowed upon us. What great ingratitude is a person in, who fails to express thankfulness towards the Almighty despite all these bounties, favours and blessings, if not at the very least by performing their worship.

---

147. See, Muslim, Munafiqin, 57.

WORSHIP

However, everything in the universe is in a state of worship toward Allah Almighty, before His majesty. The Qur'an declares that whatever is in the heavens and the earth glorifies Allah with praise.[148] The stars, mountains, trees, animals[149], the birds flying in patterned ranks in the skies[150] and indeed all other beings prostrate themselves to Allah Almighty, in the way which He demands and in a manner beyond our comprehension. This is known as the **"worship of the universe"**.

In short, a life without worship is meaningless for Allah Almighty has created humankind for servanthood and worship.[151] And He has designed human nature accordingly. For this reason, the human being is in need of seeking refuge in their Lord and Creator, asking help from Him and worshipping Him. It is for this reason that the life of the human being is filled with manifestations of the search for truth in way of reaching their Creator.

On the basis of the statement, "Humankind has been created for worship," it must not be supposed that Muslims are constantly serious and in hardship. The Messenger of Allah, upon him be peace and blessings, always had a smiling countenance and informed the Muslims that they would be rewarded for smiling at one another.

The Companions would joke among themselves, utter words of cheer and the Prophet, upon him be peace and blessings, would smile at them.

Again, Allah's Messenger, upon him be peace and blessings, would recommend the display of happiness and cheer on days of festivity and at weddings. That is to say, Muslims too have their times for relaxation, rest and recreation. However, all of these are realised

---

148. See, Isra' 17:44.
149. See, Hajj 22:18.
150. See, Nur 24:41.
151. See, Dhariyat 51:56.

in their lives in due measure and harmony, without any room for heedlessness and carnality.

Islam has ordained worship in different forms and has sprinkled these throughout various times. This enables the person to maintain constant togetherness with Allah Almighty. Experiencing constant nearness to the Almighty grants great tranquillity and security to the believer.

As a final point, let us note that the sole Being Who is worthy of worship is Allah Almighty for worship is the highest of the ranks of reverence, obedience and homage. This is only done towards Allah and only He is entitled to this, as it is only He Who bestows the body, life and all the bounties pertaining to these. For this reason, prostrating to any other than Allah has been absolutely forbidden.

1. Ablution (*Wudu'*) and Cleanliness

Islam places importance on both physical as well as spiritual cleanliness. It demands of human beings to be clean, organised, mannerly and sensitive in every way. It lists the use of scents pleasing to human beings among the most important elements of the elevated practices of the Prophet. For this reason, it deems cleanliness as worship and places it at the head of all acts of worship. It stipulates that a person who has newly entered Islam take the full body ritual ablution (*ghusl*).[152] Islam informs human beings that such worship as the Prescribed Prayer, circumambulation of the Ka'ba and recitation of the Qur'an are not acceptable without the ritual ablution.

The Messenger of Allah, upon him be peace and blessings, advised the washing of hands[153] before and after meals and the taking

---

152. See, Abu Dawud, Tahara, 129:355.
153. See, Tirmidhi, At'ima, 39:1846.

of ablution before retiring to bed.[154] He even encouraged believers to be in the ritual state of ablution as much as possible.[155]

One morning, the Messenger of Allah, upon him be peace and blessings, called his *Mu'addhin* (the reciter of the Call to Prayer) **Bilal al-Habashi**, may Allah be well pleased with him, and said:

"O Bilal, With what (deed) have you preceded me to Paradise? I have never entered Paradise (in my dreams) except that I have heard the sound of your footsteps in front of me. Last night (in my dreams) I entered Paradise and I heard the sound of your footsteps in front of me..."

Bilal, may Allah be well pleased with him, said:

"O Messenger of Allah, I have never recited the Call to Prayer except that I prayed two units of prayer (afterwards) and I have never broken my ablution except that I renewed it (immediately) and I believed that I should offer two units of prayer to Allah (i.e. after every ablution)."

The Messenger of Allah, upon him be peace and blessings, then said:

"It is because of those two (units of prayer)." (Tirmidhi, Manaqib, 17:3689; Ahmad, V:354)

At the end of the Qur'anic verse in which Allah Almighty commands and describes the ritual ablution, He declares:

"...Allah does not will to impose any hardship upon you, but wills to purify you (of any kind of material and spiritual filth), **and to complete His favor upon you, so that you may give thanks**

---

154. Bukhari, Wudu', 75; Muslim, Dhikr, 56.
155. Ibn Maja, Tahara, 4; *Muwatta'*, Tahara, 36; Ahmad, V, 276, 282; Darimi, Tahara, 2.

(from the heart, and in speech and action by fulfilling His commandments)." (Ma'ida 5:6)

Again, it has been stipulated that both the garments as well as the place in which one is to perform the prayer is to be clean.

An examination of the ablution, full body ablution and other acts of cleanliness enjoined by Islam reveals that these hold a great many benefits and wisdoms from the perspective of health and hygiene. In the simplest terms, human beings both keep their surroundings and themselves clean in a great spirit of worship and also maintain their health and wellbeing. For the Prophet, upon him be peace and blessings, has said:

"Cleanliness is half of belief." (Muslim, Tahara, 1)

Just as Muslims show meticulousness attention to cleanliness during their lives, after their deaths, they seek to embark on the journey to the Divine in a state that is pure and clean. Consequently, the body of a Muslim who has died is washed carefully, they are made to take the full body ablution, their body is enshrouded with a pure white cloth and is scented, and it is then entrusted again to the pure soil. Supplications are made for the person to rise from their grave at the Resurrection in the purest possible state.

2. The Prescribed Prayer

The greatest and most important of the springs of worship leading the servant to the ocean of union with their Lord is undoubtedly the Prescribed Prayer. The Prescribed Prayer holds the position of being the pinnacle and essence of all forms of worship, with respect to scope, content and rank.

All beings in the universe – the sun, stars, meadows, grass, trees and animals – are all in a state of glorification and remembrance of

Allah. The birds flying in fancy formations, the mountains and rocks are all in servitude to Allah in a glorification unknown to us. The worship of trees and plants are in the standing position of prayer (*qiyam*), that of animals is the bowing position (*ruku'*) and the position of those deemed inanimate is that of being face down, that is, in the position of prostration (*sajda*). The situation of the inhabitants of the heavens is also thus. A certain group among the angels are in the upright position, a group in the bowing position, another group in prostration and yet another in praise and glorification. As for the prayer that Allah Almighty has favoured the believers with as an Ascension, however, it merges all these forms of worship within itself. Consequently, those who duly observe the prayer attain the incalculable rewards and spiritual manifestations of having performed an act of worship which encompasses that of all other beings in the earth and the heavens.

There is no worship that resembles the Prescribed Prayer. One who observes the prayer cannot be preoccupied with anything other than the prayer itself. The prayer severs their connection with everything else and enables the person to experience an indescribable union with Allah Almighty. This is not the case with the other forms of worship. For instance, one who fasts can simultaneously work and a person performing the pilgrimage can engage in buying and selling when necessary. However, both the physical being and the spirit of a person performing the prayer are in the Divine presence. As affirmed in a Qur'anic verse:

"**...Prostrate and draw near** (to Allah)." ('Alaq 96:19)

In the physical sense, the Prescribed Prayer enables the human body's inner and outward movement. Through causing a person to pursue their life in an organised fashion, it enables them to acquire a time discipline and punctuality.

Spiritually, the Prescribed Prayer is filled with such favours and blessings as being in the Divine presence, reflection, consolation during times of fear, consolidation of spirituality during times of joy, preservation of belief and intimacy with Allah Almighty.

From the standpoint of its social benefits, the Prescribed Prayer is a means to unity and solidarity, acquaintance, intimacy, familiarity and the strengthening of the ties of belief and brotherhood. In particular, not differentiating human beings on the basis of race, colour, language, rank and status, the prayer that is performed in congregation – namely the Friday Prayer and the specific prayers on days of religious festivity – facilitate people's coming together on the same level, as well as their integration, cooperation and the development of a social conscience.

In terms of its spiritual manifestations and through taking the person to the Divine presence, the Prescribed Prayer is a form of worship that adorns the human being with such meritorious qualities as sincerity, piety and faithfulness. In prayer, a person transforms the world of their heart into a spiritual climate of spring.

Due to the fact that it is repeated at least five times every day, the Prescribed Prayer constantly reminds one of Allah Almighty and connects the heart and conscience to Him. It firmly establishes the infinite power of Allah, His absolute will, His mercy and compassion, favour and grace, and His wrath and punishment in the human being's heart. In this way, it keeps the person away from sin, wrongdoing and injustice. As stated in a Qur'anic verse:

"Recite and convey to them what is revealed to you of the Book, and establish the Prayer in conformity with its conditions. Surely, the Prayer restrains from all that is indecent and shameful, and all that is evil. Surely Allah's remembrance is the greatest (of all types of worship and not restricted to the Prayer). **Allah knows all that you do."** (Ankabut 29:45)

WORSHIP

Coming to the Prophet one day, a person said:

"So-and-so performs the Prayer in the night but steals when it is morning." Allah's Messenger, upon him be peace and blessings, said:

"If they are observing the Prayer truly, then this Prayer and the verses of the Qur'an that they recite during their Prayer will pull them away from that act of wickedness." (Ahmad, II:447)

The crime rate among Muslims is rather small and the countries in which the least murders are committed are the Muslim majority nations. Western researchers continue to conduct important studies on the reasons behind the low murder rates in Muslim societies.[156]

The most important reasons behind this are the principles of belief, worship and the ethics and morality established by Islam. A person who receives an Islamic education and training fears Allah and believes that they will have to account in the Hereafter for even every atom's weight of good and evil they carry out. Consequently, it becomes a padlock for evil and a key for goodness.

The Prayer observed at set times frees a person, at regular intervals, from the intensity of a heavy workload and the monotony of life, thus giving them respite. It enables the servant to express their obedience, submission and feelings of gratitude to their Lord. A person who prostrates finds the opportunity of turning to their inner world, confronting himself or herself directly therein.

A critical illness in our world today, where people are becoming more and more estranged from one another, self-interest comes to the fore and individualism reigns supreme, is the sense of **loneliness**. The best remedy for this disease, which drags the human being into the clutch of various mental disorders, is the Prayer. Whether the Prayer

---

156. For instance, see Ana Cordova, "An Examination of Causes of Low Murder Rates in Islamic Societies," American Society of Criminology (ASC), 2006.

is performed individually or in congregation with a view to increasing its merit, it dispels a person's sense of loneliness, at least five times every day. This is because the Prescribed Prayer, carrying a person to the Divine presence, reminds them that they are not alone, even if they observe the prayer on their own. When performed in congregation, however, it both takes a person to the presence of Allah and also brings them together with their fellow believers.

Sociologist **Professor Ümit Meriç** has stated:

"A society that performs the Prescribed Prayer has no need for psychology and a society that pays the prescribed annual alms (zakat) has no need for sociology."

In relation to the Prayer, the Almighty declares, **"Prostrate and draw near."**[157] He informs us that His prosperous servants perform the Prayer in devoted reverence.[158] By virtue of one single Prayer performed in such humble submission, a person's reliance and surrender to Allah Almighty increases. As a result of this surrender, the person is protected from psychological disorders and mental illness. For, through submission to Allah Almighty, the greatest power, they have left themselves at the mercy of the infinite Presence.

A believer who observes the Prayer feels themselves to be under the Divine protection and lives in a great sense of peace and security. The Messenger of Allah, upon him be peace and blessings, stated in relation to those who neglected the Prayer:

"...Whoever neglects the Prescribed Prayer, they will be deprived of the protection of Allah." (Ibn Maja, Fitan, 23)

Consequently, a society that observes the Prescribed Prayer is physically and psychologically sound. A doctor had come to the city

---

157. 'Alaq 96:19
158. See, Mu'minun 23:1-2.

of Madina during the Age of Happiness but was unable to find work. Eventually, the Messenger, upon him be peace and blessings, advised him to return home to his family.[159] Again, when we examine the narrations, we do not encounter any case of psychological illness during the Age of Happiness.

Allah Almighty has sent His Messenger, upon him be peace and blessings, as an exemplar. Just as he served as a model in every other way, he was an example in the matter of psychology and psychotherapy. Similarly, he is an example in regard to the reform of society. The greatest demonstration of this is the society of the Age of Happiness.

Furthermore, the Prescribed Prayer is, after belief, the most meritorious[160] of deeds carried out for the invocation and remembrance of Allah and also the most perfect. It is the most important pillar of Islam after the Declaration of Faith and the major sins of a person who observes the Prescribed Prayer will be forgiven.

The Messenger of Allah, upon him be peace and blessings, once said to his Companions,

"What do you think would happen if there was a river by someone's door in which he washed five times every day? Do you think that any dirt would remain on him?" The Companions said,

"Not a scrap of dirt would remain on him." He said,

"That is a metaphor of the five prayers by which Allah wipes out wrong actions." (Muslim, Masajid, 283. See, Bukhari, Mawaqit, 6)

The Messenger of Allah, upon him be peace and blessings, informs us that this river gushing forth plentifully is just at our doorstep. In other words, it is very close to us and our taking water from it

---

159. See, Halabi, *Insan al-'Uyun*, III:299.
160. See, Muslim, Iman, 137-140.

and entering it to bathe is most easy. With slight effort, we are able to attain the immense grace and favour promised by Allah.

As the Prayer is the **key to Paradise**[161], Allah's Messenger, upon him be peace and blessings, advised those wanting to enter Paradise and be his neighbour to prostrate much.[162]

The prostration is, at the same time, a means of **deliverance from Hellfire**. This truth is expressed in a Prophetic Tradition as follows:

"...When Allah wishes to show mercy to those He chooses among the people of the Fire, He will command the angels to take out all those who worshipped Allah. They will bring them out, recognising them by the mark of prostration (sajda). Allah has forbidden the Fire to consume the mark of sajda. Thus they will come out of the Fire. The Fire consumes every part of the son of Adam except for the mark of sajda."
(Bukhari, Adhan, 129)

Implied in the *sajda* is largely the Prescribed Prayer. In some Qur'anic verses and Prophetic Traditions, the Prayer has been mentioned with the prostration, its most important element.

One of the other benefits of the Prayer, more important than all the others is its being the means for the believers entering Paradise being favoured with vision (*jamal*) of the Almighty. The Prophet's Companion **Jarir**, may Allah be well pleased with him, relates:

We were with the Prophet, may Allah bless him and grant him peace, one night and he looked at the full moon and said,

'You will see your Lord as you see this moon and you will not be harmed by seeing Him. If you can manage not to be overwhelmed to

---
161. See, Ahmad, III:340.
162. See, Muslim, Salat, 225, 226; Ahmad, III:428, 500.

the point of missing the prayer before the sun rises and before it sets, don't be.'

Then he recited,

'**...and glorify your Lord with praise before sunrise and before sunset, and glorify Him during some hours of the night – as well as glorifying** (Him) **at the ends of the day – so that you may obtain Allah's good pleasure and be contented** (with what Allah has decreed for you).'" (Ta-Ha 20:130)[163] (Bukhari, Mawaqit 16, 26; Tafsir, 50:1; Tawhid, 24; Muslim, Masajid, 211)

Hence, the Prescribed Prayer is the most important act of worship enabling the human being to realise their purpose of creation. The human being's skeletal make up being created in a form facilitating the bowing and prostrating position, is in a sense to ease the observance of the Prayer and, as such, to allow them to reach their true purpose. For this reason, the human being must organise their entire life in accordance with the times for Prayer and must make the Prescribed Prayer the axis around which their life revolves.

3. Fasting and the Month of Ramadan

Fasting is a form of worship which entails obedience to the Divine command and refraining from eating, drinking and sexual relations from pre-dawn until sunset, in order to earn the good pleasure of Allah.

The month of **Ramadan**, observed with such forms of worship as the fast first and foremost as well as the Prayer, prescribed annual alms, spending in Allah's way, remembrance of Allah, recitation of the

---

163. This Qur'anic verse reveals the times for the Prescribed Prayer. For further information, see, Hud 11:114; Isra' 17:78; Rum 30:17-18; M. Kamil Yaşaroğlu, "Namaz", TDV Encyclopedia of Islam, XXXII:351.

Qur'an, cooperation and hospitality, is a blessed month of reward and spiritual gifts. It is the master of all the other months[164] wherein Allah Almighty honours His servants with great favour and kindness. The doors of forgiveness are wide open and He bestows immense rewards for even the slightest of deeds. Allah's Messenger, upon him be peace and blessings, has stated:

"When Ramadan comes, the gates of the Garden (Paradise) are opened, the gates of Hellfire are closed and the satans are chained."
(Bukhari, Bad'u al-Khalq, 11; Muslim, Siyam, 1, 2, 4, 5)

The Wisdom of Fasting

The mystery of forsaking fleeting pleasures and attaining everlasting pleasures is realised in this month through the Divinely ordained worship of **fasting**. A believer who fasts constantly struggles against the obstacle of the carnal self within the consciousness of worship and, holding it under control, reduces its effect to an absolute minimum.

Fasting perfects our morality through the training of such states necessary in the struggle of life as "determination, patience, perseverance, willpower, contentment, resignation, steadfastness and detaching oneself from carnality". Fasting serves as a protective shield for a person's honour and dignity against the never ending desires of the carnal soul in the way of eating, drinking and lust.

Again, by means of deprivation and hunger, fasting reminds a person of the innumerable bounties bestowed to them by Allah. Causing us to consider the plight of the poverty-stricken, it sensitises our hearts with feelings of mercy and compassion, and revives our feelings of gratitude. Through this quality, fasting is a form of worship

---

164. See, Bayhaqi, *Shu'ab al-Iman*, III:314-315; Haythami, III:140.

most effectual in eliminating such elements engendering disorder in society as hatred, envy and covetousness.

Fasting has been enjoined not only for this community, but for earlier ones as well. Allah, exalted and glorified be He, declares:

"O you who believe! Prescribed for you is the Fast, as it was prescribed for those before you..." (Baqara 2:6183-184)

The worship prescribed by Islam function as remedies for myriad spiritual diseases. Carnal desires, being deceived by the attractions of the world, inclining to pleasure and amusement are among the causes of spiritual and psychological illnesses. Regulating one's diet is necessary if one is to be protected from contracting such spiritual diseases. Fasting is the best method of this treatment, for fasting is enjoined by Allah Almighty, the Creator of human beings. Assuredly, He knows best His servants' needs.

Indeed fasting serves as a sort of curative for a great many physical and spiritual ailments. It is for this reason that it is observed on **"days that are numbered"** for if medicine is used for prolonged periods of time, the body becomes accustomed to it and its benefits are no longer evident. Thus, the Messenger of Allah, upon him be peace and blessings, warned one of his Companions who said that he would spend the rest of his life fasting:

"Someone who fasts all the time does not fast at all," and repeated this statement three times. (Bukhari, Sawm, 55-57)

From the medical point of view, it is observed that fasting nonstop becomes habitual, which does not engender the same effect as fasting at particular intervals. To fast for less than a month does not produce great effect, yet a fast for more than forty days becomes a habit.

Fasting enables the person to acquire a discipline of eating and drinking and the habit of controlling one's appetite. It prevents obesity, greed and consequently many diseases. If a person who observes the fast is overweight, they are able to lose their extra kilos and grant respite to their digestive system, which works non-stop throughout the year.

A look at the universe also reveals many examples of fasting:

Biological studies have shown that during times of snowfall, wild beasts cannot find anything with which to fill their stomachs. As a result of this, these animals spend the entire winter in hibernation or fasting, as it were.

The same is true for trees. In winter, they shed their leaves and enter into a long sleep and cannot even absorb water to their roots until the arrival of spring and the ensuing melting of the snow. At the coming of spring, following these several months of fasting, they thus become rejuvenated are productive, as can be gleaned from the abundance of their leaves and flowers.

Even metals and minerals are in need of the fast. Engines and machines are given rest after having worked for extended periods of time. This rest facilitates the reacquisition of their former strength and power.

In a new method of medical treatment implemented recently, the chronically ill are treated, depending on the situation of the patient, via extended or short-term fasts.[165]

Moreover, the fast's being observed during a set month is significant with respect to fostering the unity and solidarity between Muslims. In addition, the tasks undertaken with others are easier for individuals to perform and the sacred month of Ramadan is realised

---

165. Muhammad Hamidullah, *Introduction to Islam*, 87.

in unison, in a spirit of festivity. As a result, the fast, which is comprised of a set period of days, adds an especial refinement, profundity and grace to our lives that are again numbered.

In addition, the fact that the month of Ramadan rotates throughout the seasons of the year represents another one of its wisdom. Ramadan falls upon the hot, cold, cool and warm as well as the long, short days experienced throughout the various seasons of the year respectively. In this way, the fast gives blessings to all the days of the year at regular intervals. This situation at the same time serves, for those who observe the fast, as a means to manifestations filled with various difficulties and ease and allows the believers to experience a great many spiritual delights. Again, this state is the best illustration of the believers' obedience to Allah Almighty under any circumstances.

Allah Almighty declares in relation to the month of Ramadan and the fast:

"The month of Ramadan, in which the Qur'an was sent down as guidance for people, and as clear signs of Guidance and the Criterion (between truth and falsehood). **Therefore whoever of you is present this month must fast it, and whoever is so ill that he cannot fast or is on a journey** (must fast the same) **number of other days. Allah wills ease for you, and He does not will hardship for you, so that you can complete the number of the days required, and exalt Allah for He has guided you, and so it may be that you will give thanks** (due to Him)." (Baqara 2:185)

According to this Qur'anic verse, Allah Almighty wills that the fast be observed in gratitude for the Qur'an's being sent down. However, as with all other matters, He has made fasting easy for His servants and has never left them in a difficult situation. In the last section of the verse, He declares, so to speak, that which must be engendered from the fast. Accordingly, the human being perceives the majesty and favours of Allah and learns the best way of expressing gratitude to Him.

Thus, the actual meaning and essence of the fast, in addition to refraining from certain bodily desires, is to purge the consciousness of worldly attachment and all other than Allah, and to thus reach the highest limit possible in spiritual concentration in the way of togetherness with Him.

The Virtue of the Fast

Mawlana Jalal al-Din al-Rumi, may Allah sanctify his secret, says:

"The true sustenance of the human being is the light of Allah. It does not befit them to give them excessive bodily sustenance. The true sustenance of the human being is Divine love and reason.

The human being is uneasy as they have forgotten their true spiritual sustenance and have become attached to bodily sustenance. They are voracious. They have grown pale, their legs quiver and their heart pulsates in panic. Where is the sustenance of the earth, the sustenance of infinity!

Allah, glorified and exalted be He, declares concerning those killed in His way, **"With their Lord they have their sustenance."** For this spiritual provision there is neither mouth nor body."

There are ten advantages of eating little and, in particular, in hunger and fasting.

1) In hunger is ease of heart and strength of memory, while in satiation is folly and forgetfulness.

2) In hunger, the heart softens and one derives joy and blessing from supplication and worship. In satiation, however, the heart becomes hardened and no pleasure is derived from worship.

3) In hunger there is tenderness of heart, delicacy and humility, while in satiation there is extravagance, pride, conceit and self-praise.

4) In hunger, the poor and hungry are remembered, while they are forgotten and dismissed from the mind in satiation.

5) In hunger, carnal and bodily desires are crushed. In satiation, however, the carnal soul strengthens.

6) In hunger, the body is alert and awake. In satiation, sleep and heedlessness take precedence.

7) In hunger, it is easy to continue worship and servanthood. In satiation, however, there is laziness and laxity.

8) The body is healthy in hunger, while in satiation the body is worn down and becomes beset by illness.

9) The body is light and refreshed in hunger, while heavy and lethargic in satiation.

10) An enthusiasm for giving in charity, generosity and spending in Allah's way accompanies hunger. And this allows the servant cool shade in the horrendous heat of Judgement Day. Stinginess or wastefulness surface in satiation and this ruins the servant spiritually.

In other words, while satiation rouses carnal desires, hunger – as long as one does not go to extremes – strengthens the capacity for reflection and feeling.

In sum, fasting enables the human being to be healthy in all respects. The Messenger of Allah, upon him be peace and blessings, states:

"Observe the fast so as to attain (physical and spiritual) health."
(Haythami, III:179)

The most perfect illustration of the physical and spiritual health and qualities acquired through hunger is this: Allah Almighty prepared His Messengers for the spiritual effusion of Prophethood through the fast. When they reached the peak of spiritual perfection, they withdrew from the people for a certain amount of time and angelic qualities became manifested in them. In this way, their hearts and minds overflowed with the spiritual outpouring of Divine revelation. For instance, the precious Prophet of Mount Sinai **Prophet Moses**, peace be upon him, fasted for forty days and forty nights until the revelation of the Torah.

The great Prophet of Mount Sa'ir, **Prophet 'Isa (Jesus)**, upon him be peace, also fasted for forty days and nights until he heard the first words from the Gospel.

Prior to the first revelation of the Qur'an, **Prophet Muhammad**, upon him be peace and blessings, spent extended periods of time alone at Mount Hira, in Makka's surrounds, and spent his days observing various kinds of worship. In the end, he received glad tidings from the voice of Archangel Gabriel and the light of Divine effusion began to rise in his heart.

Again, prior to his Ascension to the heavens and his personal encounter with Allah Almighty, which is of a nature unbeknownst to us, he reached the zenith of spiritual perfection through patiently enduring the severe hunger and hardship that the Makkan polytheists inflicted on them during a three-year boycott.

These facts illustrate that the actual aim and advantage of the fast is spiritual. Consequently, as fasting is a form of worship, it must be observed with purely this objective. If only the external benefits are made an objective, then fasting is no longer worship. That is to say, our fasts must not have such objectives preventing filling our stomachs completely and losing weight; earning the good pleasure of Allah cannot be conceived of in such fasts. Benefits such as these will emerge automatically with the fast that is observed for the sake of Allah.

A Muslim who fasts with this intention must shield the life of their heart from carnal desire, inclination and thoughts. Not being content with merely avoiding bodily tendencies such as eating and drinking, they must protect their inner world from every kind of baseness such as backbiting, lying, hatred and jealousy.

Allah Almighty has encouraged His servants to observe the fast due to a great many more benefits and virtues that cannot possibly be all enumerated here. In order for human beings to have an inclination to fasting, He has multiplied its virtue several fold. Every good deed is given from ten up to seven hundred times the reward; however, fasting is not included in this. Its reward will be granted by Allah Almighty in a measureless fashion and, pleasing His fasting servants both in this world and in the Hereafter, He will receive them personally in His Paradise. The Messenger, upon him be peace and blessings, has stated:

"Allah, glorified and exalted be He, said, 'Every action of the son of Adam is for himself except for fasting. It is Mine and I repay it.'

Fasting is a shield. When someone is fasting, he should not have sexual relations nor quarrel. If someone fights him or insults him, he should say, 'I am fasting'.

By the One in whose hand the self of Muhammad is, the changed breath in the mouth of the faster is more fragrant to Allah Almighty than the scent of musk. The faster experiences two joys: when he breaks his fast he rejoices and when he meets his Lord he rejoices in his fasting."
(Bukhari, Sawm, 9; Muslim, Siyam, 163)

In short, fasting is one of the best nourishments of the spirit. It enables the servant to live in a state of austerity, both physically and with respect to their worldly possessions. By accustoming them to use even the permissible to a bare minimum, it develops the spirit. A believer who uses even the permissible in a state of austerity shuns even more those things that are doubtful and never approaches the prohibited.

4. The Alms-Tax (*Zakat*)

The **prescribed annual alms (*zakat*)** is comprised of those possessing more than a given amount of possessions and property giving 2.5 percent of their wealth – annually, according to the Hijri calendar – in the way of Allah. The Prescribed Purifying Alms (*zakat*) is given to the poor, the destitute, officials in charge of collecting the alms-tax, those whose hearts are to be warmed to Islam, to free slaves, those overburdened with debt, those working in Allah's cause and wayfarers in need of help. (Tauba 9:60)

Animals and agricultural produce are also subject to the alms-tax. All these are calculated separately. The prescribed annual alms on agricultural produce is referred to as *'ushr*.

Islam has left the spending in God's way in addition to the prescribed alms for those with lofty aims up to the individual, to be given in accordance with their own respective situations.

Responsibilities of the Wealthy and the Poor

The fact that individuals and communities assume differing positions such as powerful and weak, healthy and unhealthy, wealthy and poor, hold many deep and subtle wisdoms of the Divine will. Before all else, Allah Almighty has bestowed all the bounties that we possess in life as each a means of trial. To the degree of the bounties we possess, even the deprivations we undergo are each a means of examination. Allah, exalted and glorified be He, declares:

"And so, human – when his Lord tries him by bestowing favors on him – says: 'My Lord has honored me. But whenever He tries him by straitening his means of livelihood, then he says, 'My Lord has humiliated me.'" (Fajr 89:15-16)

Accordingly, riches are not, for instance, an honour and poverty abasement; these amount to Divine apportionment and distribution. Allah Almighty declares:

"...it is We Who distribute their means of livelihood among them in the life of this world, and raise some of them above others in degree, so that they may avail themselves of one another's help? But your Lord's mercy (in particular Prophethood) is better than what they amass (in this life)." (Zukhruf 43:32)

While the Almighty has distributed among His servants differently, He has ordered their responsibilities accordingly and, as such, has on no account wronged them. Moreover, we also understand from this Qur'anic verse that the differences among human beings play a vital role in the establishment of social harmony and order.

The wealthy will be called to account before Allah in regard to where they earned and spent their wealth – or concerning their lawful or unlawful earnings – as well as their alms-tax, charity and good works. They are charged with giving a determinate portion of their property to the poor and are subject to a great trial with respect to their wealth. However, in the event of their success in this examination, they will earn Divine approval and attain the blessings of Paradise.

As for the poor, they will be called to account in such affairs as patience, complaint, rebellion, hatred, jealousy and honour. If the outcome of all these accords with the good pleasure and approval of Allah, their worldly suffering will be transformed into an eternal happiness in the Hereafter.

Just as the poor are in need of the material support of the wealthy in this world, the wealthy are in need of the supplication of the poor both in this world and the next.

The magnanimous wealthy, the people of thankfulness, and the poor and dignified are together in the honour of humanity and Divine approval. However, the arrogant miserly affluent, as well as the impatient poor who have made a habit of begging, have been openly condemned in Islam. Hence, the Prophet, upon him be peace and blessings, used to entreat Allah saying,

"O Lord, I seek refuge with You from the evil of the affliction of wealth and from the affliction of poverty." (Muslim, Dhikr, 49)

This being the case, in whomsoever contentment, reliance, surrender and obedience prevail, they are the true wealthy...

Working and earning property and possessions through lawful means are of course a virtue. That which is right is to spend these in the way of Allah without embedding these in the heart, or in other words without deifying them. Otherwise, wealth will amount to nothing other than porterage in the world and the cause of woeful punishment in the Hereafter.

The following report is exemplary in terms of illustrating the significance of spending, giving in charity as well as of service and endeavour in Allah's way.

Bashir ibn Khasasya, may Allah be well pleased with him, relates:

"I came to the Messenger of Allah, upon him be peace and blessings, to pledge my allegiance to him. He enjoined upon me to bear witness that there is no god but Allah and that Muhammad is His servant and His Messenger, to observe the Prescribed Prayer, to pay the prescribed annual alms, to perform the pilgrimage, to observe the fast during Ramadan and to struggle for the sake of Allah.

I said,

'O Messenger of Allah, two of those I cannot do. The first is charity. I only have ten camels. They constitute my entire wealth. The second is struggling in the way of Allah (*jihad*); I heard that whoever runs away from the battlefield has incurred the wrath of Allah.[166] I am afraid that if I reach the battlefield I might fear death and my spirit would fail me."

Allah's Messenger, upon him be peace and blessings, grabbed his hand, waved it and said,

'No charity and no jihad! How then can you enter" Paradise?'

I then said,

'O Messenger of Allah, I pledge my allegiance to you!' The Messenger of Allah took my pledge on every term he mentioned." (Ahmad, V:224; Hakim, II, 89:2421; Bayhaqi, *Shu'ab*, V:8; Haythami, I:42)

Wisdoms of Zakat and Spending in Allah's Way

The prescribed annual alms and spending in the way of Allah prevents the well to do from being deceived by their riches and transgressing, and prevents the needy from breeding feelings of hatred and envy towards the wealthy. In this way, social life is protected and individuals in society are bound together with ties of solidarity and affection. The gap between the rich and the poor is reduced to the

---

[166]. It is declared in a Qur'anic verse:
"For whoever turns his back on them on the day of such an engagement – except that it be tactical maneuvering to fight again or joining another troop of believers (or taking up a position against another enemy host) – **has indeed incurred Allah's condemnation, and his final refuge is the Fire; how evil a destination to arrive at!"** (Anfal 8:16)

bare minimum. Consequently, with the great decrease in the number of poor, a great many problems, which arise due to poverty and desperation, will be prevented.

The following example, which illustrates the way in which the prescribed annual alms brings diverse people together, is noteworthy:

'Umar, may Allah be pleased with him, passed by the door of a house in front of which he saw a beggar who was an old blind man. He tapped his arm from behind and asked,

"To which People of the Book do you belong?" The old man said that he was a Jew. Upon this 'Umar, may Allah be well pleased with him, said,

"What is it that has reduced you to such a state?" The blind Jewish man replied,

"Being in need of money to pay the poll tax (*jizya*), my poverty and my old age has reduced me to this state (of begging)."

'Umar, may Allah be well pleased with him, held the man by the hand and took him to his own house. He gave the man some things that he could find in his house as well as some money. 'Umar, may Allah be well pleased with him, then summoned an official from the public treasury (*bayt al-mal*) and instructed him as follows:

"Attend to this man and the likes of him. By Allah, if we have benefited from the productive time of his youth and have thus forsaken him in his old age, we would not have acted justly..."

After this incident, Caliph 'Umar, may Allah be well pleased with him, exempted such individuals from paying the poll tax.[167]

Non-Muslims are our partners in humanity. As the last breath is an unknown for everyone, it is essential to treat all people in the best

---

167. Abu Yusuf, Kitab al-Kharaj, Dar al-Salah, n.d., 259-260.

way and to approach unbelievers with the hopeful attitude that they might one day believe. For this reason, a share can be apportioned to them from charity, if not from the alms-tax. These kindnesses and favours can be a means to their guidance. We see the most vivid example of this again in the life of Allah's Messenger, upon him be peace and blessings:

In the seventh year after the Emigration, the Messenger of Allah, upon him be peace and blessings, sent various items in aid to the people of Makka who had faced severe drought and famine following the conquest of Khaybar. Abu Sufyan received all of these and distributed them to the Qurayshi poor. Despite himself being a polytheist at the time, he was struck with admiration and expressed the joy he felt saying,

"May Allah reward the son of my brother with goodness as he observed the rights of kinship!"[168]

Softening the hearts of the Makkans, such benevolence facilitated their collectively embracing Islam at Makka's conquest.

Many people were guided in this way throughout the history of the Ottoman Empire also.

The property received as alms-tax is gradually transferred to society's suffering and downtrodden. In this way, balance, justice and social harmony ensue. Being purified, the fortune of the wealthy becomes completely lawful for its owner.

The conflict between rich and poor has existed since time immemorial. For the most part, the poor have looked to the wealthy with hatred and envy and the wealthy have snubbed the poor and have held them in contempt. The exception to this has only been possible in periods where the prescribed annual alms have been duly

---

168. Ya'qubi, Tarikh al-Ya'qubi, Beirut 1992, II:56.

observed. In such times, the alms-tax and charity used to be offered in great secrecy and grace for as declared in a Qur'anic verse, "**... surely Allah is He who welcomes His servants' turning to Him in repentance, and accepts what is offered as charity** (prescribed or voluntary) **for His sake...**" (Tauba 9:104) If the prescribed annual alms were to be duly observed today, there would be next to no needy and suffering in society. And so, during the caliphate of **'Umar ibn 'Abd al-'Aziz**, people used to bring their alms but could find no one to whom to give it.[169] 'Umar ibn 'Abd al-'Aziz once sent an official charged with distributing goods given in alms to Africa. The official returned without having distributed the goods, as he was unable to find anyone who would accept alms. Upon this, he emancipated a great many slaves with this money.[170] This situation is a reward of spending one's wealth and life for the sake of the Almighty.

Thus, while Islam dresses the physical and spiritual wounds of humanity in such a way and restores them to health, other systems have been unsuccessful in this, going to extremes in either aspect. Some have completely forbidden asking others for anything, while begging has become rife in others. Islam, however, has approached this wound with exceptional wisdom through the prescribed annual alms and spending in God's way, and has offered the most feasible solution.

Indeed, *zakat* is one of the loftiest values which Islam adds to humanity. One of the ways of removing the yoke of **slavery** that was once a bitter reality for humanity is the prescribed annual alms, as one of the eight places in which the property given in alms can be used is to emancipate slaves.

Another wisdom behind the alms-tax and spending in Allah's way is the prevention of abnormal growth of individual capital. The

---

169. See, Bayhaqi, *Dala'il al-Nubuwwa*, VI:493.
170. See, Muhammad Sa'id Ramadan al-Buti, *Fiqh al-Sira*, 434.

prescribed annual alms and spending in the way of Allah is the best remedy and cure preventing capital becoming a cancerous growth.

Again, it is by virtue of zakat that people striving in the way of Allah can be supported and good works be pioneered. By means of supporting the education of students, the use of knowledge in the way of servanthood to Allah is facilitated.

Thus, peace becomes established in a society which gives in alms. We see that society experienced a universal peace in both various Muslim societies and in the Ottoman communities. The Ottoman Empire stood tall for 620 years with this peace.

When the social fabric is destroyed by not giving the alms-tax, such ills as theft, indulgence and pretension are compounded. As one digresses from spirituality, carnal desires are stirred and, as a result, the peace of the entire society is disturbed. In such a case, sociology's laws remain merely in words.

Dominion Belongs to Allah

We live in the dominion of our Lord. We are sustained with His bounties. Do not those who display negligence in their financial worship consider whose wealth they are withholding from whom?

In reality, dominion belongs to Allah absolutely. The property and possessions of human beings, however, resembles time share. Worldly wealth is a trust given by Allah to His servant. On no account can individuals' use of this at will be condoned. It must be used in line with the commandments of the True Owner of that property.

In this case, one who spends in the way of Allah in actual fact spends of the wealth that Allah has bestowed again for one of His servants.[171] Consequently, Allah Almighty has apportioned the alms-

---

171. See, Baqara 2:3; Ra'd 13:22; Nur 24:33; Hadid 57:7.

tax as a right that those who are able to are required to give to those in need. It is declared in a Qur'anic verse:

"And those in whose wealth there is a right acknowledged (by them) **for such as have no means other than begging, and such as are denied help** (because, having self-respect, they cannot beg and are thought to be well-off)." **"And in their wealth the poor** (who had to beg) **and the destitute** (who did not beg out of shame) **had due share** (a right they gladly honored)." (Ma'arij 70:24-25; Dhariyat 51:19)

Hence, a servant wishing to acquire Divine morality and favour are obliged to allow the needy and suffering to benefit from the worldly wealth from which they themselves benefit. For the true aim is to become a believer from whom all others benefit and to thus attain Divine approval and good pleasure.

The Blessing in Zakat and Spending in God's Way

The prescribed annual alms, which gladdens society's downtrodden, in actual fact avails the giver more than the receiver. Literally meaning **cleanliness**, **purity** and **blessing**, the word '*zakat*' possesses such exceedingly important benefits as the human being's being purified of particular spiritual diseases and evils and the cleansing and increase of one's wealth.[172] Such that this cleansing, which includes the heart's purification, the spirit's growing in purity and the refinement of the carnal soul, is one of the wisdoms behind Prophets and Messengers being sent to humankind.

Through abating avarice and covetousness of one who is predisposed to attachment to wealth, the prescribed annual alms enables them to turn to Allah Almighty Who is worthy of true love and devotion. It facilitates a person's experiencing the meaning of Divine Unity by purging everything that casts a cloud over love of Allah and,

---

172. See, Tauba 9:103; Saba 34:39; Abu Dawud, Zakat, 21:1619.

being freed from miserliness, to show thankfulness to Allah for the provisions He has bestowed upon them. And thankfulness increases the bounty. Allah Almighty declares:

"...**If you are thankful** (for My favors), **I will most certainly give you more...**" (Ibrahim 14:7)

"**The parable of those who spend their wealth in Allah's cause is like that of a grain that sprouts seven ears, and in every ear, there are a hundred grains. Allah multiplies for whom He wills. Allah is All-embracing** (with His mercy), **All-Knowing.**" (Baqara 2:261)

Explaining the expansive and far reaching spiritual blessings of charity and spending one's wealth in Allah's way, the Messenger of Allah, upon him be peace and blessings, has stated:

"Allah, glorified and exalted be He, admits three people into His Paradise by means of a single morsel of bread, a handful of dates or the like from which the needy can benefit:

1) The owner of the house who instructs that it (i.e. charity) be given;

2) The woman of the house who prepares that which is to be given; and

3) The domestic servant who personally conveys the charity to the needy."

After enumerating these, Allah's Messenger, upon him be peace and blessings, completed his words as follows:

"All praise is due to Allah Who omits none of us!" (Haythami, III:112)

From another standpoint, charity averts a great many worldly and otherworldly afflictions. Allah's Messenger, upon him be peace and blessings, refers to a group of these:

"Charity extinguishes (the fire of) sin as water extinguishes fire." (Tirmidhi, Iman, 8:2616). Also see, Ibn Maja, Fitan, 12)

"Charity extinguishes the wrath of Allah and saves a person from an evil death." (Tirmidhi, Zakat, 28:664)

"The charity of a Muslim lengthens their life (i.e. makes it fruitful), prevents a bad death and, through it, Allah Almighty removes arrogance, poverty and self-praise." (Haythami, III:110)

"Hasten in giving charity as calamity cannot exceed it." (Haythami, III:110)

"On the Day of Reckoning, everyone will be under the shade of their charity until judgement is delivered."

Abu al-Khayr, may Allah be well pleased with him, one of the narrators relating this Prophetic Tradition, strove to the utmost to give in charity every day, even if that which he gave was a single onion or the like. (Ahmad, IV:147-8; Haythami, III:110)

According to a Prophetic account, a group of people visited **Prophet 'Isa** (Jesus), peace be upon him. After they left, Prophet 'Isa, peace be upon him, said to those with him,

"One of them will die today, if Allah wills."

At nightfall, those people again came to Prophet 'Isa with the bundle of branches they carried on their backs. Prophet 'Isa, peace be upon him, commanded them to, "Place the branches on the ground." Then, to the person about whom he said would die on that day, he said:

"Unbundle your branches." When that man unbundled his branches, a black snake emerged from among them. Prophet 'Isa, upon him be peace, asked,

"Which deed of righteousness did you perform today?" The man responded,

"I did not perform any righteous deed today." Prophet 'Isa, peace be upon him, said,

"Think long and hard. What had you done?" Upon this, the man said,

"I did not perform any deed, but I had a piece of bread in my hand and at that point, a person in need came to me and asked if I had anything to give them. I then gave a portion of this bread to them."

Upon hearing this, **Prophet 'Isa**, peace be upon him, said:

"This is the reason why disaster was averted from you." (Haythami, III:109-110; Ahmad, *Zuhd*, I:96)

How beautifully **Mawlana Jalal al-Din al-Rumi** expresses the blessing of spending in Allah's cause:

"Wealth never decreases by giving in charity. Far from it, giving in charity protects one's wealth from loss and waste. Your charity serves to guard your pocket. Your prayer serves as your shepherd and protects you from the wolves and evil.

The storehouse of one who plants crops is emptied, but when the time comes, they receive many times its return in yield. In return for a single storehouse, they receive many more. However, if the wheat is not used fittingly and is instead kept in the storehouse, it will become feed for pests, maggots and mice which will, in turn, completely destroy it."

The Proper Manner of Zakat and Spending in God's Way

Observing the proper conduct when giving in the prescribed and voluntary alms is very important. In particular, the giver must feel a sense of indebtedness to the receiver as they have relieved them of a religious obligation and have been the means for them to attain a great many blessings.

When giving obligatory or voluntary alms, one must at the very least give of the average in quality of one's property and possessions. We must not give to others as charity what we ourselves would not take save with disdain.[173]

Again, one must not place the receiver under any obligation or taunt them for Allah Almighty has forbidden such repugnant behaviour absolutely.[174]

It is not right to ask for something back after having given it to the needy. This conduct has been deemed to be extremely repulsive.[175]

Another important matter that needs to be regarded in almsgiving, charity and good works is observing secrecy. This is because charity that is given openly diminishes the sense of modesty of the receiver and when it in time becomes habit, it removes the desire and effort to work. In addition, it prevents the giver's falling prey to such bad character traits as arrogance, pride and self-conceit.

Charity must be given in sincerity and earnestness, purely for the sake of Allah. Spending that is done for show and for worldly interests come to naught and cannot avail the human being.[176]

Danger of Neglecting the Prescribed Annual Alms

Great dangers, both material and spiritual, await societies that fail to pay the prescribed annual alms. Drawing attention to this threat, Allah Almighty declares:

---

173. See, Baqara 2:267; Abu Dawud, Zakat, 5:1582.
174. See, Baqara 2:262-264; Insan 76:8-11.
175. See, Muslim, Hibat, 5.
176. See, Baqara 2:264.

"(So) spend in Allah's cause (out of whatever you have) and do not ruin yourselves by your own hands (by refraining from spending. Whatever you do,) do it in the best way, in the awareness that Allah sees it. Surely Allah loves those who are devoted to doing good, aware that Allah is seeing them." (Baqara 2:195)

The Hand that Gives is Superior to the Hand that Takes

Islam does not prohibit a person in need from asking something from others. It does not, however, encourage such from an ethical perspective, only allowing asking from others in dire circumstances and times of great need, for begging degrades a person. For this reason, when the Companions pledged allegiance to the Messenger of Allah, upon him be peace, he stipulated, *"that [they] would not beg people of anything"*.[177]

That is to say, one must endeavour not to take alms but to give it. For Allah's Messenger, upon him be peace and blessings, has stated:

"The upper hand is better than the lower hand. Begin with your dependents. The best charity is that given by the wealthy. Anyone who refrains [from asking], Allah will spare him the need to and anyone who seeks to be independent, Allah will give him independence." (Bukhari, Zakat 18; Muslim, Zakat 94-97, 106, 124)

Furthermore, Allah Almighty draws attention to the sensibility of heart of the righteous believers who spend in His way, in alms and charity. Indicating that their inner worlds which are like a court of mercy, must become a spiritual x-ray machine, so to speak, with respect to identifying the true needy, He declares:

"That (which you spend) **is for the poor who, having dedicated themselves to Allah's cause, are in distressed circumstances. They are unable to move about the earth** (to render service in Allah's

---

177. See, Muslim, Zakat, 108; Abu Dawud, Zakat, 27:1643; Ahmad, I:11.

cause and earn their livelihood). **Those who are unaware** (of their circumstances) **suppose them wealthy because of their abstinence and dignified bearing, but you will know them by their countenance – they do not beg of people importunately. And whatever good you spend, surely Allah has full knowledge of it."** (Baqara 2:273)

The Harms of Interest

With its rulings such as the Prescribed Purifying Alms and spending in Allah's cause, Islam has gratuitously extended out a hand to people in difficult circumstances and has completely healed many a bleeding wound. In addition, it has prohibited the scourge of interest, which on the surface appears to be assistance and ease for human beings, but which in reality amounts to nothing more than exploiting the circumstances of those in difficulty.

For the usurer seeks to take advantage of the difficult circumstances of others. One who gives alms, however, is the fellow sufferer of those in need and in difficulty. Their sole aim is to earn the good pleasure of the Almighty. Consequently, they constantly strive to be of assistance to His suffering servants.

The wealth of a person who is ambitious and avaricious, however great it may be, constantly appears in their eyes to be slight. However, those who are used to almsgiving and charity are generous and big-hearted. They make do with a small amount of worldly possessions. The vision of a usurer, however, has been clouded with ambition to such an extent that they seek to increase their own wealth at the expense of destroying others. However, their end is always bankruptcy and ruin, for Allah, exalted and glorified be He, has declared:

"Allah deprives interest (which is thought to increase wealth) **of any blessing, and blights it, but makes alms-giving** (which is thought to decrease wealth) **productive..."** (Baqara 2:276)

Allah's Messenger, upon him be peace and blessings, has warned his community thus:

"Whoever increases their wealth through interest, their end is assuredly their being dragged to ruin." (Ibn Maja, Tijarat, 58; Hakim, IV, 353:7892; Bayhaqi, *Shu'ab al-Iman*, IV, 392:5512; Tabarani, *Kabir*, X, 223:10539)

Due to the fact that interest involves taking from one and giving to another, or in other words draws the blood of one to strengthen the teeth of another, it damages the foundation of society. It increases inflation. It makes the rich richer and the poor poorer. It drags the people into a quagmire, financially, socially, religiously and morally.

In contrast, due to the fact that the charity and donations given to assist the poor and aggrieved in society ensure the perpetuation of social harmony and order, they are a means for blessings in the world and the Hereafter.

In sum, with feelings of solidarity diminished, social peace and tranquillity destroyed and hatred and hostility on the rise in our day, there is a great need for a serious campaign of spending in the way of Allah. We must not forget that we could have been in the situation of those who are impoverished and needy. Hence, our spending on them is at the same time our debt of thankfulness to our Lord.

5. Pilgrimage (*Hajj*)

The pilgrimage (*hajj*) is an act of worship observed by every Muslim who is financially and physically able, once in a lifetime and through visiting the Ka'ba in Makka on certain days of the year. Allah, exalted and glorified be He, declares:

"...Pilgrimage to the House is a duty owed to Allah by all who can afford a way to it..." (Al-'Imran 3:97)

The pilgrimage had also existed in the time of previous Prophets. In time, however, the polytheists reduced it, from its sacred status of worship, to a show of strength by the wealthy to the poor and virtually an indecent ceremony. Islam restored the sacredness of the pilgrimage once again.

The pilgrimage has many wisdoms, both worldly and transcendental.

The pilgrimage transpires in a blessed and glorious climate wherein Allah's infinite mercy is manifested. For this reason, one of the names of the city of Makka is **"Umm al-Ruhm"** (Mother of Beneficence), or the place upon which Divine mercy pours.[178]

The sacred spaces in which the Pilgrimage is undertaken are the spiritual climates of an exalted realm. These climates are filled with Divine signs. The mercy and favour of Allah are forever remembered therein. These blessed lands have been nourished with the spirituality of believing hearts since the time of **Prophet Adam**, and have been watered with their tears of love. Those who perform the Pilgrimage gnostically seek these blessings and follow the footprints of the many Prophets who came before, experiencing the spiritual blessings of their memories. This is because these sanctified places, as singular wellsprings of Divine grace, are filled with the honoured memories of the chain of Prophets.

In this respect, one purpose of the Pilgrimage is reverence to those blessed spaces and to adorn hearts with the recollection of the sacred stations therein.

The Pilgrimage is to receive a spiritual share in the reliance and surrender in Allah of **Prophet Abraham** and **Prophet Ishmael**, upon them both be peace.

---

178. See, Bukhari, Tafsir, 18:4.

It is to stone the enemy within, known as the carnal self, as well as the satanic tendencies externally.

It is to shed differences in class, don the shroud and to be able to seek refuge in our Lord.

It is to shudder with that horrendous scene of the Day of Judgement and, by bringing together Muslim communities distant and foreign to one another, to establish a brotherhood of faith.

Again, the Pilgrimage is to strive to cast off carnal craving by shedding the garment of the body and penetrating the depths of the spirit.

The city of Makka is the place where the reality of such conceptions as race, colour and dress are lifted and all believers' being one nation under the Islamic brotherhood is manifested. There, chief, official, destitute, wealthy, poor, ignorant, scholar, sultan and subject, all are together, wearing the same garments, in the same space and standing together. That blessed city is the bosom of security, peace and love and the hearth of Prophets filling hearts with blessing and mercy. The unity displayed in those blessed spaces during the major and minor pilgrimages despite all the pangs felt in the Muslim world, those summits of brotherhood and love, are magnificent scenes indeed. Muslims favoured with forgiveness and mercy merge therein with a profound love of belief, rapture and rhapsody.

The pilgrimage is the observance of a servitude filled with love.

The essence of the Pilgrimage is to dedicate oneself solely to Allah, pulling away from everything else in one's actions and behaviour. It is in a sense preparation for death and the journey to the Hereafter and a rehearsal for the states to be experienced after death.

The Pilgrimage constitutes the servant's being stripped of all worldly ranks, with just two towels wrapped around them and their heads and feet exposed, a representation of their gathering at the place of Judgement so to speak and, as such, their state of heartfelt entreaty and complete submission to their Lord. The Pilgrimage vividly demonstrates that the shedding of sins can only be realised after the blessing of a form of worship observed after entreaty, reliance in God and submission to Him.

The Pilgrimage directs the person to a spiritual life, as this delicate form of worship is replete with many manifestations of compassion, mercy and love. Hunting, hurting Allah's creatures and even plucking a single blade of grass is forbidden during the Pilgrimage. There, a love and courtesy by virtue of the Creator prevails. Hence, the Messenger of Allah, upon him be peace and blessings, once said to **'Umar**, may Allah be well pleased with him,

"O 'Umar, you are a strong man, do not crowd around the Stone and disturb the weak. If you find space, then touch it, otherwise just face it and gesture, reciting the Declaration of Faith and saying 'Allahu Akbar." (Ahmad, I:28; Haythami, III:241)

As the Pilgrimage is performed at a specific time and place, it enables Muslims to acquire the concept of time and space and the consciousness that everything in the world transpires within a certain order. It reminds human beings that when they miss certain important windows of opportunity in life, they will lose a great deal. Thus, it instructs the human being that they must perpetually be alert and must carry out every task at its particular time.

The Farewell Pilgrimage and Farewell Sermon of Allah's Messenger, upon him be peace and blessings, serves as an exemplar for all the Pilgrimages that his community will perform until the Last Day. At the same time, during his Farwell Pilgrimage, love exuded from the Prophet, upon him be peace and blessings. The guidelines of the reciprocal rights between human beings have been reinforced with the mortar of love and compassion.

6. Other Forms of Worship

In Islam, there are other forms of worship alongside those mentioned thus far. These include supererogatory worship, invocation, remembrance, supplication and recitation of the Qur'an. Set times have not been allocated for such forms of worship, with people being encouraged to perform these to their own ability. People will acquire a degree according to the sincerity and earnestness with which they perform these acts of worship.

Allah Almighty created humankind and the jinn for worship (servanthood) to Him. For this reason, life in all its facets must be adorned with minor and major forms of worship.

Allah Almighty forever wills ease for His servants. Thus, he has made servanthood easy, opening a great many doors of good works accessible to people of all degrees. Every person of sound judgement can earn His good pleasure and approval through readily fulfilling His commands.

The Messenger of Allah, upon him be peace and blessings, states:

"Your meeting your brother with a smile is a charity. Your enjoining the right and forbidding the wrong is a charity. Your guiding a man who has lost his way is a charity for you. Your guiding a person with defective vision is a charity for you. Your removing a stone or thorn or bone from the road is a charity for you. Your emptying your bucket of water into your brother's (empty) bucket is a charity for you." (Tirmidhi, Birr, 36:1956)

"Let not any one of you regard any good deed insignificant, even if it is that you meet your brother with a cheerful countenance. If you buy meat or prepare broth, add (extra) water to that and give that (as a present) to your neighbour." (Tirmidhi, At'ima, 30:1833)

A sincere believer gains significant ground with a small step that they take in Allah's path and, in so doing, attains great rewards. As is declared in a Qur'anic verse:

"**Whoever comes to Allah with a good deed will have ten times as much, and whoever comes with an evil deed will be recompensed with only the like of it; and they will not be wronged.**" (An'am 6:160)

In a Hadith Qudsi, Allah Almighty declares:

"*If (My servant) comes near Me by a handspan, I come near him a cubit. If he comes near Me by a cubit, I come near a fathom. When he comes to walking, I come to him running.*" (Bukhari, Tawhid, 50; Muslim, Dhikr, 2, 3, 20-22, Tauba 1)

Even one's daily activities can become worship commensurate with their intention and sincerity. For instance, if a believer who observes their obligatory worship works with the intention of earning a lawful living to maintain their family and raise them with an Islamic grounding, then they both earn money and obtain the rewards of worship. If a person who eats aims to maintain a life of worship through the preservation of their health, they too receive rewards in line with their intention.

Hence, whoever places more importance on the Islamic forms of worship – the supererogatory as well as the religiously mandatory – they acquire greater degree and merit and they see the reward for their endeavour both in this world and in the Hereafter. For this reason, the Companions were in a race toward worship and good works. **Abu Hurayra**, may Allah be well pleased with him, relates:

The poor amongst the Emigrants came to the Messenger of Allah, may Allah bless him and grant him peace, and said,

'The rich people have obtained the highest degrees of Paradise and everlasting bliss.' He said,

'How is that?'

They said, 'They pray as we pray and fast as we fast and they give charity but we do not give charity, and they set slaves free but we do not set slaves free.' Upon this the Messenger of Allah, upon him be peace and blessings, said,

'Shall I tell you something which will enable you, if you take it on, to catch up with those who have gone ahead of you. No one coming after you will be able to catch up with you and you will be the best of those you live among, except someone who does the same thing?' They said,

'Yes, O Messenger of Allah!' He, upon him be peace and blessings, said,

'Say after every prayer, "Glory be to Allah," "All Praise is due to Allah" and "Allah is the Greatest" thirty-three times each.'

The poor amongst the Emigrants returned to the Messenger of Allah, may Allah bless him and grant him peace, saying,

'Our wealthy brethren have heard what we have done and they have done the same.' So the Messenger of Allah, upon him be peace and blessings, said,

'This is Allah's Grace which He gives to whom He wishes.'" (Bukhari, Adhan 155; Da'awat 18; Muslim, Masajid 142; Abu Dawud, Witr 24)

❈

Thus, there are a great many wisdoms and benefits of each form of worship enjoined in Islam. We have not been able to exhaust all of these here. Just as the wisdom and benefit of some of these will be discovered with time, a great portion of these will be truly perceived in the Hereafter.

However, it must not be forgotten that it is not correct to consider such physical and worldly benefits of worship when performing them. For the Prophet, upon him be peace and blessings, has said:

"Actions are judged according to intentions, and every man shall have what he intended..." (Muslim, Imara, 155)

A Muslim must perform their worship only for the sake of earning the approval and good pleasure of Allah Almighty. They must consider these other benefits as being Allah's grace and favour to His servants and must additionally praise and thank Allah for these.[179]

Again, it ought not be forgotten that intentions are superior to actions. The situation of Khorasan's great ruler **'Amr ibn al-Layth** is a clear example of this. After his death, a righteous individual saw Layth in his dream. The following conversation then took place between them:

"How did Allah treat you?"

"Allah forgave me."

"Through which of your deeds were you forgiven?"

"I once climbed to the peak of a mountain. When I looked at my troops from above, their great numbers pleased me and, overcome by emotion, I said:

'If only I had lived during the time of Allah's Messenger, upon him be peace and blessings, and supported him.' It was due to this intention and fervour that Allah, exalted be He, forgave me." (Qadi 'Iyad, *al-Shifa'*, II:28-29)

---

179. In relation to the virtue of worship, see, Osman Nuri Topbaş, *Islam: Spirit and Form,* 2006. (http://islamicpublishing.net/; http://www.hudayipress.com/books_en/islamimanibadet_ing.pdf)

Part 4

Worldly Transactions and Morality

*I*slam is not a life comprised only of belief and acts of worship. In addition to belief and worship, it is the system of exceedingly delicate balances minutely regulating every field of life, such as social relations, morality and especially rights and justice. For Islam is the religion of truth that Allah Almighty, Who created human beings and Who therefore knows them better than they know themselves, revealed in order to teach them how to live in this world.

Every discerning believer must deepen in pondering upon the following questions: What is this world? Why did we come here? In which direction are our fleeting days flowing? How must I live and die?

WORLDLY TRANSACTIONS (MU'AMALAT) and MORALITY (AKHLAQ)

Islam is not solely a way of life comprised of belief and worship. In addition to belief and worship, it is a system of exceptionally delicate criteria minutely arranging every sphere of life such as civil obligations, morality and in particular observing rights and rule of law. For Islam is the religion of truth sent by Allah Almighty – Who created humankind and Who, therefore, knows them better than they know their own selves – to instruct them how they are to live in this world.

Consequently, one of the most important parts of Islam is *mu'amalat*, or the practices in worldly affairs, which regulate the relationships among people.

Mu'amalat, expresses the part of Islamic jurisprudence which falls outside the domain of worship, or the completion of the law. We can also express this as "the principles of Islamic jurisprudence which regulate the relationships of a person with other people and with society".

Islam has delineated the roles, responsibilities and rights of human beings as well the penal sanctions to be implemented in the event of violations of these, in every sphere from the private and daily life to the domestic life of individuals making up society, from kinship and relationships with one's neighbours to commercial and economic activities, from instruction, training and educational services to the rules of social intercourse ensuring social peace and order.

That is to say, just as a Muslim must live their individual life in line with Islam, they are required to regulate their social life and relationships with others according to the Divine commandments. Hence, they must enable Islam to prevail in every facet of their lives. One who is unsuccessful in this cannot attain the disposition of a righteous believer. Allah's Messenger, upon him be peace and blessings, has stated:

"One who mistreats those under his authority and care will not enter Paradise." (Tirmidhi, Birr, 29:1946; Ibn Maja, Adab, 10; Ahmad, I:7)

'Umar, may Allah be well pleased with him, says:

"Do not be misled by a person's prayers and fasting.

[Consider instead], are they true in speech,

Are they trustworthy when something is entrusted to them (for safekeeping),

Do they observe the limits of the religiously permissible and prohibited in their worldly engagements?" (Bayhaqi, *Kitab al-Sunan al-Kubra*, VI:288; *Shu'ab al-Iman*, IV:230, 326)

A man praised another when in the presence of 'Umar. 'Umar, may Allah be well pleased with him, asked,

"Have you ever travelled with the person whom you praise?" The man answered,

"No."

"Have you conducted business with him?"

"No."

"Have you been their neighbour?"

WORLDLY TRANSACTIONS and MORALITY

"No."

Upon these, 'Umar, may Allah be well pleased with him, said,

"By Allah – there is no god but He – you do not know him!"[180]

Our books of jurisprudence elucidate the rulings pertaining to civil obligations at full length. By virtue of these rulings, worldly life is regulated and all people, Muslim and non-Muslim alike, are protected from injustice and oppression.

In order for the rulings pertaining to worldly transactions to be implemented, Allah Almighty has established penal sanctions in both the world and the Hereafter and has declared these. Considering not merely the worldly dimension of their dealings but also the otherworldly dimension, a true believer strives to live in piety, in line with Allah's approval.

Morality

Islam also has a dimension of morality that adds profundity and consistency to personal and social life.

The aim of Islam is to transform humankind into a virtuous civilisation. The realisation of this is possible only through the acquisition of an elevated level of morality and, in so doing, to acquire virtue. Hence, after belief and action, Islam has placed most importance on ethics and morality.

Encompassing sincerity in belief and worship, morality also comes to mean the reflection of this attitude on relationships with other human beings and treating them with compassion, magnanimity, respect, justice, sincerity and grace. This is because it is not possible to totally isolate a person's relationship with Allah Almighty from their relationships with other human beings.

---

180. Ghazali, *Ihya' 'Ulum ad-Din*, III:312.

Good character perfects belief, embellishes life and enables one who possesses it to draw near to Divine approval. As being a person of high morality amounts to being adorned with the beautiful Divine attributes, it is at the same time an indicator of nearness to Allah Almighty.

Allah's Messenger, upon him be peace and blessings, has stated:

"Allah, glorified and exalted be He, has allotted you your characters just as He has allotted you your provisions. Allah Almighty gives worldly things to those whom He loves and those whom He does not love, but He gives religion only to those whom He loves, so he who is given religion by Allah is loved by Him..." (Ahmad, I:387)

In this Prophetic Tradition we see how intimately connected are 'religion and morality' and how they are even used interchangeably.

Again, Allah's Messenger, may Allah bless him and grant him peace, states:

"Gabriel, peace be upon him, said that Allah said, 'Verily, Allah has chosen this religion for Himself. Thus nothing is appropriate for your religion except generosity and good character. Ornament, therefore, your religion with them'." (Haythami, VIII:20; 'Ali al-Muttaqi, Kanz, VI:392)

The true jewel, which makes a person human, is good character. **How beautifully Shaykh Sa'di** puts it:

"All that possesses eye, ear and mouth is not Adam. Many satans there are who appear in the form of the children of Adam. The true Adam is the person with good character. Beauty in countenance and other adornments resemble the fleeting embroideries in the world."

Mawlana Jalal al-Din al-Rumi describes the evil predicament of those deprived of good character and morality in the following way:

WORLDLY TRANSACTIONS and MORALITY

"If hundreds of savage lions came together, they could not commit the evil perpetrated by those corrupt and ignorant who seize eminent positions." (Mathnawi, IV, couplet 1441)

"Whatever befalls one by way of grief, sorrow and hardship, these come by way of presumptuousness, shamelessness and insolence. One who is shameless, presumptuous on the path of the Beloved is also an obstacle on the path of others. Such a person is not brave but cowardly.

By means of (spiritual) propriety, the Heavens became full of light, and by means of (such) propriety the angels became innocent and pure." (Mathnawi, I, couplets 89-91)

For this reason, Muslims have placed great importance on propriety and good character. Traveller to the Ottoman lands, **Ogier Ghiselin de Busbecq**, relates how the Turks followed their Prophet's path of peace in their day-to-day lives and how they resented profanity and quarrel.[181]

Islam has brought the best of character in every field of life. A few of these will be touched upon by way of example:

1. Humility

The start of good character is a person's knowing their place, their being humbled and even seeing themselves to be lower than they are so as to stifle their carnal self. This situation at the same time ensures that a person becomes more assiduous and hardworking in life.

Above and beyond everything else, a sense of humility leads a person to spiritual reverence and humble submission before Allah Almighty. A person who feels the power and majesty of the Almighty

---

181. Esther Kafé, "Rönesans Dönemi Avrupa Gezi Yazılarında Türk Miti ve Bunun Çöküşü," *Tarih İncelemeleri Dergisi*, II, Izmir 1984, 232.

even slightly, understands their own weakness and impotence. They contemplate the fact that they have come to the world with zero capital, that is, without having paid any price. They realise that all the possibilities and capacities they possess belong to Allah, glorified and exalted be He. In every state, they turn to and seek refuge in Him saying, "O my Lord!" They come to understand that Allah Almighty, the Creator of all things, knows, hears and sees all thoughts, words and actions. They live in the consciousness of constantly being under Divine watch, so much so that they reach the point where they spend their every moment as though they were seeing Him. They are freed of all wrongs and attain a distinguished life with each moment adorned with deeds of righteousness.

A humble person places value on Allah's servants, loves them, approaches each of them with affection and displays the virtue of being able to forgive their shortcomings. However, it is exceedingly difficult for these states to be observed in a self-conceited person.

Allah Almighty declares:

"Spread your wings (to provide care and shelter) **over the believers who follow you** (in practicing Allah's commandments in their lives)."** (Shu'ara 26:215)

"The (true) **servants of the All-Merciful are they who move on the earth gently and humbly, and when the ignorant, foolish ones address them** (with insolence or vulgarity as befits their ignorance and foolishness), **they response with** (words of) **peace,** (without engaging in hostility with them)." (Furqan 25:63.)

Allah's Messenger, may Allah bless him and grant him peace, has also stated:

"Allah revealed to me that we should be humble amongst ourselves and none should show pride upon the others. And it does not behove one to do so..." (Muslim, Janna 64)

WORLDLY TRANSACTIONS and MORALITY

"He who is humble for the sake of Allah by one degree, Allah will elevate him one degree, until he reaches the highest degrees and he who is arrogant toward Allah, Allah will lower him one degree until he reaches the lowest of low degrees." (Ibn Maja, Zuhd, 16)

Allah's Messenger, may Allah bless him and grant him peace, held servanthood to Allah above everything else. One of the narrations detailing this preference is the following:

Gabriel, peace be upon him, sat with the Prophet, peace and blessings of Allah be upon him, and looked at the sky, and he saw an angel descending. Gabriel, peace be upon him, said: 'This angel has never before descended, since he was created.' When he came down, he (i.e. the angel) said:

'O Muhammad, your Lord has sent me to you and He asks, Shall He make you a Prophet-king or a Prophet-slave?'

Allah's Messenger, upon him be peace and blessings, turned to Gabriel, peace be upon him, who said:

'Be humble before your Lord, O Muhammad.'

The Messenger of Allah, may Allah bless him and give him peace, said:

"I wish to be a Prophet-slave," and thus displayed an extraordinary example of humility. (Ahmad, II:231; Haythami, IX, 18, 20)

After this incident until his demise, Allah's Messenger never took his meals while leaning against something. (Haythami, IX:20)

To those who paid him excessive honour, the Prophet, upon him be peace and blessings, used to say,

"Do not elevate me above the rank which Allah, the Exalted, has determined for me, for He has made me a servant before making me a Messenger." (Haythami, IX:21)

Even if slaves used to invite him to share bread made of barley, he would accept their invitation[182] and would even greet children.[183]

According to **Anas**' accounts the Prophet would visit the Helpers (Ansar) from time to time and upon arriving at their homes would greet the children separately, place his hand upon their heads and make supplication for them. (Nasa'i, *Kitab al-Sunan al-Kubra*, VI:90)

Anas, may Allah be well pleased with him relates the following concerning the Prophet's humility and moral perfection:

"I served the Prophet of Allah, upon him be peace and blessings, for ten years. **During that time, he never once said to me as much as 'uff' [i.e. in disappointment] if I did something wrong.** He never asked me, if I had failed to do something, 'Why did you not do it?' and he never said to me, if I had done something wrong, 'Why did you do it?'"

During one of his expeditions with his Companions, the Prophet, may Allah bless him and grant him peace, asked them to slaughter a sheep when it was time to have food prepared. One of the Companions said,

"O Messenger of Allah, I will slaughter it." Another one of the Companions said,

"O Messenger of Allah, allow me to skin it." A third said,

"O Messenger of Allah, I will cook it." So, Allah's Messenger, upon him be peace and blessings, said,

"*I will collect wood for the fire.*" The Companions said,

---

182. See, Haythami, *Majma' al-Zawa'id*, IX:20.
183. See, Bukhari, Isti'zan, 15.

WORLDLY TRANSACTIONS and MORALITY

"O Allah's Messenger! We can do that too! There is no need for you to exhaust yourself." But despite their insistence, the Prophet, upon him be peace and blessings, said,

"I know that you can do it for me, but I do not like to be privileged. Allah dislikes seeing a slave of His privileged among others." So he went and collected fire-wood.

Again, during one of his travels, the Messenger of Allah, may Allah bless him and grant him peace, set up camp in order to perform the prayer. He proceeded to the place where they would observe the pray and then returned. The Companions asked,

"O Messenger of Allah, where are you going?"

"I am going to tie my camel," he replied. The Companions said,

"We can tie your camel, O Allah's Messenger! Do not trouble yourself thus." Upon this the Messenger of Allah, upon him be peace and blessings, replied,

"Let one (who is able) not seek help from people, even if it be to chew the end of their tooth stick (miswak) [i.e. until the twig forms bristles]."[184]

The Companions, who were raised in the educational climate of the Messenger of Allah, upon him be peace and blessings, were of the same character and morality. During his Pilgrimage, 'Umar, may Allah be well pleased with him, would serve those with him and would take their camels out to graze while they were asleep. This was the result of his (moral) perfection and the beauty of his character.

Tabi'un scholar **Mujahid ibn Jabr** says:

---

184. Muhib al-Din al-Tabari, *Khulasa Siyar Sayyid al-Bashar*, 19; Qastallani, *Kitab al-Mawahib al-Laduniyya*, Cairo 1281, I:385.

"When I was in the company of **Ibn 'Umar** I wished to serve him, but he used to serve me." (Abu Nu'aym, *Hilya*, III:285-286)

Allah's Messenger, may Allah bless him and grant him peace, once went out with some of his Companions to send **Mu'adh ibn Jabal**, may Allah be well pleased with him, off to Yemen as Governor. Mu'adh, may Allah be well pleased with him, was upon the mount while the Messenger of Allah, upon him be peace and blessings, walked alongside his riding beast. Mu'adh expressed his unease saying,

"O Messenger of Allah! I am riding, while you are walking. Can't I get down and walk with you and your Companions?" Consoling him, Allah's Messenger, upon him be peace and blessings, revealed to him the actual concern weighing on his mind:

"O Mu'adh, I desire that these steps of mine be steps taken in the way of Allah." (Diyarbakri, *Tarikh al-Khamis*, Beirut n.d., II:142)

Such an exemplar was the Messenger, upon him be peace and blessings, in humility. His concern was not in regard to his own person but was – even to the detriment of his own health – that humankind be guided and attain happiness in this world and the Hereafter.

The Messenger of Allah, upon him be peace and blessings, used to see to his own tasks himself and would help his family in household chores. An examination of the relevant narrations reveals the following:

The Prophet used to wash his own clothes, milk his sheep, mend his own garments, repair his shoes, sweep his house, tie and feed his camel, eat together with his servants, knead dough and carry home the goods that he purchased from the market. On one occasion, when **Abu Hurayra**, may Allah be well pleased with him, attempted to carry the garment that he had bought, he said,

WORLDLY TRANSACTIONS and MORALITY

"It is more proper that a person carry their own things themselves; however, if they are unable to do so, their Muslim brother (or sister) can assist them," and did not allow him to do so. (Haythami, V:122)

The Prophet's entering the city during the **conquest of Makka**, the Prophet's greatest conquest, with his army more that ten thousand strong is a monumental model of humility. The Companions who were present describe this state thus:

"During Makka's conquest, the Messenger of Allah, may Allah bless him and grant him peace, was at the head of the army. On his triumphant entry into Makka, such was his deep submission and humility before Allah that his beard touched the packsaddle of his camel. He was prostrating before Allah in thankfulness and saying constantly,

"O Allah, there is no life, but the life of the Hereafter." (Waqidi, II:824; Bukhari, Riqaq, 1)

The following example of **'A'isha**, may Allah be well pleased with her, is another illustration of such humility:

It is related from 'Abd Allah ibn Abi Mulayka that Ibn 'Abbas asked permission to visit 'A'isha before her death, while she was on her deathbed. She said,

"I fear that he will praise me," *(and thus did not want to grant him permission).* When it was said to her,

"He is the cousin of the Messenger of Allah, may Allah bless him and grant him peace, and one of the leading Muslims," she said, "Give him permission."

He asked,

"How are you feeling?" She replied,

"Good, if I am God-revering and pious."

He said,

"Allah willing, you are upon (the path of) goodness, being the wife of the Messenger of Allah, may Allah bless him and grant him peace, and he did not marry any virgin other than you and proof of your innocence was revealed from heaven."

'Abd Allah ibn Zubayr entered after him and she said,

"Ibn 'Abbas came and praised me. 'Would that I had died before this, and had become a thing forgotten, completely forgotten!' (Maryam 19:23)" (Bukhari, Tafsir, 24:8)

As is evident, 'A'isha's every word and action exudes her noble character, humility, fear of Allah and piety.

Let us end this discussion with a final example:

The Prophet's beloved grandson **Hasan**, may Allah be well pleased with him, once circumambulated the Ka'ba and then performed two units of prayer beside the Station of Abraham (*Maqam al-Ibrahim*). He then placed his face against the Station and began to weep, repeating the words,

"O Lord, this weak servant has come to Your door. O Allah, this helpless slave begs at Your door, this beggar, this needy soul…"

He then left on his way stumbling across some people who were trying to placate their hunger with dry pieces of bread. He greeted them and they in turn invited him over to join their humble meal. Hasan, may Allah be well pleased with him, sat with them and said,

"Had I not known that this bread was charity, I would have joined you."

He instead invited them to join him at his own house and they set off together. The Prophet's grandson fed and clothed them, placing some money in the pockets of their garments." (Abshihi, *al-Mustatraf*, Beirut 1986, I:31)

2. Altruism and Generosity

Selfishness or egocentrism has no place in Islam. Islam has forbidden selfishness. In this world that we share, we are obliged to consider others at least as much as we consider ourselves. We must wish for them what we wish for ourselves. In particular, we must take a close interest in the weak, needy and forlorn for we are all the servants of the One God. Our Lord demands us to be of assistance to one another:

"**And spend** (in Allah's cause and for the needy) **out of whatever We provide for you before death comes to any of you and he says: 'My Lord! If only You would grant me respite for a short while, so that I may give alms, and be one of the righteous!' But never will Allah grant respite to a soul when its appointed term has come. Allah is fully aware of all that you do.**" (Munafiqun 63:10-11)

"**O you who believe!** (So that you may enjoy solidarity and discipline, as a cohesive, peaceful community) **spend** (in Allah's cause and for the needy) **out of what We have provided for you** (of wealth, power, and knowledge, etc.) **before there comes a Day when there will be no trading nor friendship** (which will bring any benefit), **nor intercession** (of the sort you resort to unjustly in the world). **The unbelievers – it is they who are wrongdoers (those unable to discern the truth, who darken both their inner and outer world, and who wrong, first and most of all, themselves).**" (Baqara 2:254)

"**...Whatever you spend (in Allah's cause and in alms), He will replace it.**" (Saba 34:39)

The Messenger of Allah, may Allah bless him and grant him peace, has encouraged altruism with the following words:

"The Muslim is the brother of the Muslim. He should not oppress him, nor should he hand him over to an oppressor. Allah will take care of the needs of anyone who takes care of the needs of his brother. Allah will dispel the anxiety on the Day of Judgement of anyone who dispels the anxiety of another Muslim. On the Day of Judgement Allah will veil (the faults) anyone who veils (the faults of) another Muslim." (Bukhari, Mazalim, 3; Muslim, Birr, 58)

It does not befit the Muslim to think only of themselves and disregard others for the Messenger of Allah, upon him be peace and blessings, has stated:

"One who sleeps while his neighbour is hungry is not a (perfected) believer." (Hakim, II:15; Haythami, VIII:167; Bukhari, *al-Adab al-Mufrad*, 112)

Muslims have centred their lives around this Prophetic warning. **Ibn 'Umar**, may Allah be well pleased with him, explains:

"There were seven homes, all of which were needy. Someone sent a sheep's head to one of these homes. The owner of the house sent it to his neighbour, believing them to be more in need of it than they were. With the same thought, the second neighbour sent it to the third. After the sheep's head had gone from house to house, it came back to the first home to which it was sent." (Hakim, II:526)

Spending their wealth for the servants of Allah is higher in the eyes of Muslims than spending it on themselves. One of the most poignant examples of this is the following episode:

The Prophet's household once slaughtered a sheep. Allah's Messenger, upon him be peace and blessings, asked,

"What remains of it?" 'A'isha, may Allah be well pleased with her, said,

"Only the shoulder blade remains." Upon this the Messenger of Allah, upon him be peace and blessings, replied,

WORLDLY TRANSACTIONS and MORALITY

"In reality, only the shoulder blade is gone and all the rest remains." (Tirmidhi, Qiyama, 33:2470)

Allah's Messenger, may Allah bless him and grant him peace, advised 'A'isha as follows:

"Do not turn away the needy O, 'A'isha, even if all you can give is half a date. If you love the poor and draw them near to you, Allah will draw you near Him on the Day of Judgement." (Tirmidhi, Zuhd, 37:2352)

After hearing these words, she displayed exemplary altruism and selflessness throughout her life. Her nephew 'Urwa ibn Zubayr said of her:

"...She would not keep anything which came to her from the provision of Allah but that she would give it in charity..." (Bukhari, Manaqib, 2)

Allah's Messenger, may Allah bless him and grant him peace, used to advise his entire community in selflessness. One such example is related by **Abu Sa'id al-Khudri**, may Allah be well pleased with him:

"Once when we were on a journey with the Prophet, a man came on a camel of his and began to look to his right and left. The Messenger of Allah, may Allah bless him and grant him peace, said,

'Anyone who has a spare mount should prepare it for someone who does not have a mount to ride, and anyone who has extra provision should prepare it for someone who does not have any provision,' and he mentioned the different categories of property until we thought that none of us had any right to anything in excess of our needs." (Muslim, Luqata, 18)

Allah, exalted and glorified be He, declares:

"...They also ask you what they should spend (in Allah's cause and for the needy). **Say: "What is left over** (after you have spent on your dependents' needs).**" Thus does Allah make clear to you His Revelations, that you may reflect."** (Baqara 2:219)

That is to say, Allah Almighty tests us, His servants, with regard to whether we spend out of the bounties that He has bestowed upon us.

Spending in Allah's cause is one of the most important means bringing a believer near to their Lord. Hence, the Almighty declares:

"You will never be able to attain godliness and virtue until you spend of what you love (in Allah's cause, or to provide sustenance for the needy)..." (Al-'Imran 3:92)

An All-Encompassing Altruism

Altruism necessitates engagement with not only the material needs of human beings, but all their problems and hardships.

Allah's Messenger, upon him be peace and blessings, was at the forefront when embarking upon military expeditions and during battle and everyone else used to take refuge in him.[185] On the return, he would follow the convoy from behind, assist those enfeebled and with difficulty walking, allow them to ride pillion on his camel and would entreat Allah for them.[186]

A noteworthy example in this regard is the following incident:

Allah's Messenger, may the peace and blessings of Allah be upon him, went to the market to buy a shirt for himself for four dirhams. He put it on, praised Allah and returned. On his return from the market, he encountered one of the Helpers who said,

"O Allah's Messenger, clothe me and Allah will clothe you with garments of Paradise."

---

185. See, Muslim, Jihad, 79; Ahmad, I:86, 126.
186. See, Abu Dawud, Jihad, 94:2639.

WORLDLY TRANSACTIONS and MORALITY

Then the Prophet, upon him be peace and blessings, took off his shirt and put it on that Companion. Then he himself went to the market to buy another shirt for himself for another four dirhams. He had two dirhams remaining.

On his way back, he came across a slave-girl who was crying.

"Why are you crying?" he asked. She replied,

"O Messenger of Allah! My master gave me two dirhams with which to buy flour from the market. I don't know where I lost that money. Now I don't have the courage to go back home."

He gave her the remaining two dirhams in his possession. He later saw that the girl was still crying and asked her,

"Why didn't you go home?" She said,

"O Messenger of Allah! It is too late for me to return and I am afraid that they might beat me."

Allah's Messenger, upon him be peace and blessings, walked with her until they reached her house. He stopped at the door and called out its residents with greetings of peace. They recognised his voice but did not respond. He offered greetings a second time and again there was no response. Upon his third greeting they came out in great joy. The Messenger of Allah, upon him be peace and blessings, asked,

"Did you not hear my first greeting?"

"O Messenger of Allah!" they exclaimed, "Indeed we heard you! We loved to hear your voice again and again. And your greeting is a means of blessing for us. This was the reason for our delay. May our father and mother be your ransom, O Allah's Messenger! What is it that brings you here?"

The Messenger of Allah, upon him be peace and blessings, said,

"This young girl feared that you might punish her."

Upon hearing these words, the master of the house said,

"O Allah's Messenger! Seeing that you have honoured our home, we have set her free!" The Messenger of Allah, upon him be peace and blessings, then gave them the glad tidings of Paradise and said,

"All praise is due to Allah. I have not seen any ten dirhams more blessed than these. With them, Allah clothed His Messenger and one of the Helpers and freed a slave-girl. All praise is due to Allah! It is He Who has favoured us thus through His power." (Haythami, IX:13-14)

The Companions possessed the same nobility of character. **'Abd Allah ibn 'Abbas**, may Allah be well pleased with him, was once in retreat (*i'tikaf*) in the Prophet's Mosque, when a man approached, greeted him and sat down beside him. Ibn 'Abbas said,

"You appear sad and downcast," and the following conversation took place between them:

"Indeed, O cousin of Allah's Messenger. I am indebted to So-and-so but, by the one who lies buried here (i.e. Allah's Messenger), I do not have the means to repay it."

"Shall I speak to them on your behalf?"

"If you please."

Ibn 'Abbas, may Allah be well pleased with him, put on his shoes and was about to leave when his companion called out to him saying,

"Have you forgotten that you are in retreat? Why have you left the mosque?" Ibn 'Abbas, may Allah be well pleased with him, said with tears swelling in his eyes,

"No, I have not forgotten, but I heard the words of the Noble One who has only recently departed from among us, upon him be peace and blessings, who said:

WORLDLY TRANSACTIONS and MORALITY

"Whoever works to fulfil the needs of his brother, this is better for him than performing i'tikaf for ten years. And whoever performs i'tikaf for (just) one day, seeking Allah's good pleasure, Allah will create three trenches between him and the fire of Hell. Each trench is wider than the distance between the Two Wings (the expanse of the East and West)."
(Bayhaqi, *Shu'ab al-Iman*, III:424-425. Also see, Hathami, VIII:192)

Bayazid al-Bistami, may Allah sanctify his secret, relates another notable example of the altruism introduced with Islam.

"There were thousands of friends of Allah in our day, but the mission of the *Qutb* (Supreme Saint) of the Age was given to a blacksmith by the name of Abu Hafs. I went to his shop to ascertain the wisdom behind this. I found him to be extremely troubled and asked him the reason why. In intense grief, he said,

"I wonder if there is anyone who has a greater affliction than mine, a person who is more troubled than I am? I wonder what will be the state of all these servants of Allah on the Day of Judgement?"

He then began to weep and caused me to weep along with him. In curiosity, I asked,

"Why are you so grieved at the people's being subjected to punishment?"

Abu Hafs replied,

"My nature was kneaded with the yeast of compassion and mercy. If all the punishment of the denizens of Hellfire were placed on me and they were forgiven, I would be excessively pleased and rid of all my worry..."

With this, I understood that Abu Hafs was not one of those who said, "Me, me, me!" but was of the temperament of Prophets who said, "My community, my community!" I stayed with him for some time during which I taught him some chapters of the Qur'an. I reached a spiritual degree, however, that I could not in forty years of learning and insight. My inner world was filled with spiritual blessing. I came to understand yet again that the status of Supreme Sainthood is another mystery entirely. Virtue is acquired not only through knowledge and a great amount of worship, but through these being transformed into wisdom and with Divine grace and regard. It must also not be forgotten that in his being the focus of this Divine regard and grace is the blessing of compassion and mercy having becoming his nature."

Generosity in Ottoman Society

Fifteenth century traveller to Anatolia **Bertrandon de la Broquière** states:

"The Turks were well-meaning people who respected one another. More often than not, I witnessed them inviting a poor person who was passing by to join them for their meal. This is something that we just never do."[187]

English traveller **Sir Charles Fellows** also relates that he was received with hospitality from people in every sphere of Ottoman society, from the Pasha to the Turkish peasant living in his tent pitched in the mountains, and that treated him thus without expecting anything in return. According to him, the sole concern of the Turks, their "universal law" was to "feed the stranger" without any differentiation of religion, nation, rich or poor.[188]

Nineteeth century English traveller **Frederick Gustavus Burnaby** praises the hospitality and generosity of the Turkish peoples even affirming that they "carry this virtue to excess". He states:

---

187. B. Broquiére, *Deniz Aşırı Seyahat*, Istanbul 2000, 174.
188. Sir Charles Fellows, *Travels and researches in Asia Minor*, London 1852, 222.

"Sometimes after having admired a horse, I have been surprised to find that the steed has been sent to my stable, with a note from the owner, entreating my acceptance of the animal."[189]

Thus, the human being must be filled with compassion, mercy, love and feelings of altruism towards all the creation of Allah, and especially human beings. These qualities will be the means to their reaching a lofty rank before Allah Almighty.

3. Faithfulness and Trustworthiness

Faithfulness denotes constancy in intention, word and deed, and to act in sincerity and earnestness.

Trustworthiness refers to being reliable and demonstrating a dependable character.

Islam has considered lying as one of the cardinal sins and has absolutely prohibited it. Failure to keep one's word, inconsistency in action and seeing the deception of others as acceptable are extremely harmful qualities that are signs of hypocrisy. The greatest source of the affliction and tribulation which befalls human beings are such evil qualities, or in short, lying. This being the case, accustoming others to truthfulness and trustworthiness and raising new generations upon this elevated character, is a duty incumbent upon each and every one of us. For the foremost of all the beautiful qualities of the Prophets, sent as an example to all humanity, and the righteous are truthfulness and trustworthiness.

Allah Almighty shows the path of deliverance and prosperity as follows:

---

189. See, Fred Burnaby, *On Horseback Through Asia Minor*, Cambridge University Press, 2001, 215.

"O you who believe! Act in reverence for Allah and piously, without doing anything to incur His punishment, and always speak words true, proper and straight to the point, that He will make your deeds good and upright and forgive you your sins. Whoever obeys Allah and His Messenger has surely attained to a mighty triumph." (Ahzab 33:70-71)

"O you who believe! Keep from disobedience to Allah in reverence for Him and piety, and keep the company of the truthful (those who are also faithful to their covenant with Allah)." (Tauba 9:119)

"...and fulfill the covenant: the covenant is surely subject to questioning (on the Day of Judgment you will be held accountable for your covenant)." (Isra' 17:34)

Allah's Messenger, upon him be peace and blessings, has stated:

"Promise me the following six things and I will promise you Paradise:

1. Speak the truth when you talk;

2. Keep a promise when you make it;

3. When you are trusted with something fulfill your trust;

4. Avoid sexual immorality;

5. Lower your gaze (in modesty); and

6. Restrain your hands from committing injustice." (Ahmad, V:323)

Truthfulness and trustworthiness are the essence of Islam. And so, **Sufyan ibn 'Abd Allah**, may Allah be well pleased with him, said to Allah's Messenger, upon him be peace and blessings:

"Messenger of Allah, tell me something about Islam which I could not ask from anyone but you." He said,

WORLDLY TRANSACTIONS and MORALITY

"Say, 'I have believed in Allah' and then and then be upright." The man said,

"Messenger of Allah, what is the thing you fear most for me?"

He took hold of his tongue and then said, "This." (Ahmad, III:413. Also see, Muslim, Iman, 62; Zuhd, 61; Ibn Maja, Fitan, 12)

Abu Musa, may Allah be well pleased with him, had asked:

"Messenger of Allah, whose Islam is best?" He said,

"The one from whose tongue and hands the Muslims are safe." (Bukhari, Iman, 4, 5, Riqaq 26; Muslim, Iman 64, 65)

Again, Allah's Messenger, may Allah bless him and grant him peace, said:

"He who is not trustworthy has no Belief." (Ahmad, III:135)

The Messenger of Allah, may the peace and blessings of Allah be upon him, happened to pass by a heap of eatables (corn). He thrust his hand in that (heap) and his fingers were moistened. He said to the owner of that heap of eatables (corn):

"What is this?" He replied,

"Messenger of Allah! These have been drenched by rainfall." To which the Prophet, upon him be peace and blessings, remarked,

"Why did you not place this (the drenched part of the heap) over the corn so that people might see it? **He who deceives is not of us.**" (Muslim, Iman, 164)

Islam has taken truthfulness as a basis even in matters that people deem to be trifling. **'Abd Allah ibn 'Amir**, may Allah be well pleased with him, narrates:

My mother called me once, whilst the Prophet, upon him be peace and blessings, was at our home and she said,

"Come here, I will give you something." Thereupon the Prophet, upon him be peace and blessings, asked,

"What did you want to give to him?" She replied,

"Dates." The Prophet then said,

"Had you not given him anything, it would have been recorded (for you) as a lie." (Abu Dawud, Adab, 80:4991; Ahmad, III:447)

Lying has even been prohibited when speaking in jest. Some of the Prophet's words of counsel and warning in this regard are as follows:

"A servant's belief in Allah is not complete until he abandons lying, both in jest and earnestness, and arguing even if he be in the right." (Ahmad, II:352, 364; Haythami, I:92)

"Woe to him who lies to make people laugh. Woe to him, woe to him!" (Abu Dawud, Adab, 80:4990; Tirmidhi, Zuhd, 10:2315)

Even unbelievers have benefited from the truthfulness and trustworthiness of the Muslims. The Prophet's Companion **Hudafa**, may Allah be well pleased with him, narrates:

"I set out with my father Husayl (from Makka to Madina), but we were caught by the Qurayshi polytheists. They said,

'(Do) you intend to go to Muhammad?' We said,

'We do not intend to go to him, but we wish to go (back) to Madina.' So they took from us a promise in the name of Allah that we would turn back to Madina and would not fight on the side of Muhammad, upon him be peace and blessings. So, we came to the Messenger of Allah, upon him be peace and blessings, and related the incident to him. He said,

'Both, of you proceed (to Madina); we will fulfil the covenant made with them and seek Allah's help against them.' This is the reason why I could not participate in the Battle of Badr." (Muslim, Jihad, 98)

One of the countless examples that can be provided in this regard is the following:

After the Battle of Uhud, leader of the enemy Abu Sufyan shouted loudly, saying,

"I adjure you by Allah, 'Umar, have we killed Muhammad?" **'Umar**, may Allah be well pleased with him, said,

"By Allah, you have not, he is listening to what you are saying right now." Abu Sufyan replied,

"I regard you as more truthful and reliable than Ibn Qami'a."
(Ibn Hisham, III:45; Waqidi, I:296-297; Ahmad, I:288; Haythami, VI:111)

Those who live as truthful and reliable people in the world will receive their true due on the Day wherein everyone will be in most need and where no one will be of any avail to anyone else. They will attain salvation by means of these noble characteristics which will run to their aid in their most trying times. Allah Almighty describes that Day saying,

"...This is the Day when their truthfulness (faithfulness and steadfastness) **will benefit all who were true to their word** (to Allah)."[190] Again, as stated in a Qur'anic verse:

"...and all men and women honest and truthful in their speech (and true to their words in their actions)**... for them Allah has prepared forgiveness** (to bring unforeseen blessings) **and a tremendous reward."** (Ahzab 33:35)

---

190. Ma'ida 5:119.

"In consequence, Allah will reward the truthful ones for having been true to their covenant..." (Ahzab 33:24)

Allah's Messenger, upon him be peace and blessings, states that truthfulness will lead a person to eternal happiness:

"Truthfulness leads to piety and piety leads to the Garden. A man should be truthful until he is written down as truthful with Allah. Lying leads to deviance and deviance leads to the Fire. A man will lie until he is written down as a liar with Allah." (Bukhari, Adab, 69; Muslim, Birr, 103-105)

Islam prohibits the doing unto others those things that one does not wish upon themselves. In that case, a person who does not want to be deceived or be treated unjustly must embrace truthfulness and trustworthiness for deliverance is in honesty and truthfulness. Consequently, the Messenger of Allah, upon him be peace and blessings, has stated:

"Speak the truth even if it entails your own ruin, for assuredly therein is deliverance and prosperity." ('Ali al-Muttaqi, III:612/6855)

4. Grace and Refinement

Islam demands a sincere grace removed from show to be dominant in the life of a Muslim. It is necessary to observe the rules of courtesy and cultivation in one's dress, manner of one's sitting and standing, walking and talking, gaze, in giving and asking for something, in short in every kind of social intercourse, even in thought and feeling. So much so that a Muslim must not hurt anyone in anyway whatsoever and must not be hurt by anyone. How beautifully a poet expresses not hurting others and the virtue of being able to forgive those that hurt you:

WORLDLY TRANSACTIONS and MORALITY

The true purpose of human beings in this garden of the world is thus:

Neither is anyone offended by you, nor you by anyone.

In other words, a Muslim must know how to forgive the coarseness that is committed against their person. They must be engaged in the constant endeavour to become deserving of Divine forgiveness by constantly forgiving others. As declared in a Qur'anic verse:

"Let not those among you who are favored with resources swear that they will no longer give to the kindred, the needy, and those who have emigrated in Allah's cause, (even though those wealthy ones suffer harm at the hands of the latter). **Rather let them pardon and forbear. Do you not wish that Allah should forgive you? Allah is All-Forgiving, All-Compassionate."** (Nur 24:22)

An excellent example in every way, the Messenger of Allah, may Allah bless him and grant him peace, is also a perfect model for us in grace and refinement. 'A'isha, may Allah be well pleased with her, states:

"There is no one more exalted in character that Allah's Messenger. Such that whenever one of his Companions or household called him, he readily responded. It is by virtue of his exalted character that Allah Almighty revealed the verse, **"You are surely of a sublime character, and do act by a sublime pattern of conduct."** (Qalam 68:4) (Wahidi, *Asbab*, 463)

The Messenger of Allah, upon him be peace and blessings, was a compassionate, polite, gentle, soft-hearted individual. In response to a vulgar man's repeatedly shouting out to him, "Muhammad, Muhammad!" he replied each time, in a gentle and compassionate manner,

"What is it that I can do for you?" and fulfilled his need. (See, Muslim, Nadhr, 8; Abu Dawud, Ayman, 21:3316; Haythami, IX:20)

Allah's Messenger, upon him be peace and blessings, used to educate a person who displayed coarseness in behaviour without embarrassing or insulting them. Even if he knew the individual in the community who did something unbecoming, he would direct focus to his own person, beginning his sentence with,

"*What is it that I see you [doing such-and-such]?*"[191]

Sometimes he would employ the third person, saying,

"*What is the matter with the people that they say such and such?*" (Abu Dawud, Adab, 5:4788)

Another one of the innumerable examples of the Prophet's grace and courtesy is the following:

While the Messenger of Allah, upon him be peace and blessings, was walking a man who had a donkey came to him and said,

"Messenger of Allah, ride," and the man moved to the back of the animal. Allah's Messenger, upon him be peace and blessings, said,

"*No, you have more right to ride in front on your animal than me unless you grant that right to me.*" He said,

"I grant it to you." So he mounted. (Abu Dawud, Jihad, 58:2572)

Another one of the requirements of Islamic decorum is to exercise utmost care not to cause trouble or anguish to others. **Mu'adh ibn Anas** relates:

"I fought along with the Prophet, may Allah bless him and grant him peace, in such and such battles. The people occupied much space and encroached on the road (by randomly placing their belongings). The Prophet, may Allah bless him and grant him peace, sent an announcer to announce among the people:

---

191. See, Bukhari, Manaqib, 25; Muslim, Salat, 119; Abu Dawud, Khatam 4, Adab 14.

WORLDLY TRANSACTIONS and MORALITY

"*Those who occupy much space or encroach on the road (or cause injury or hardship to a believer) will not be credited with jihad.*" (Abu Dawud, Jihad, 88:2629; Ahmad, III:441)[192]

In another Tradition in which he invites human beings to gentility, Allah's Messenger, upon him be peace and blessings, says:

"*Whoever steps over the necks of the people on Friday (in order to reach the front row of the mosque), he has taken a bridge to the Fire.*" (Ahmad, III:437)

The Prophet's kindness to women can be illustrated with the following example:

During a journey, the driver of the camels, by the name of **Anjasha** goaded them on with his singing.[193] In view of the possibility that the delicate constitutions of the females seated on the camels might be affected, the Messenger of Allah, upon him be peace and blessings, said:

"*O Anjasha, take care lest the crystals break!*" (Bukhari, Adab, 95; Ahmad, III:117)

The Companions were such gentle people that **Anas ibn Malik**, may Allah be well pleased with him, reported, "that people knocked

---

192. It should also be noted at this point that in Islam, Jihad is conducted in order to remove oppression and thus restore peace for human beings, as well as to be a means to the guidance of the people. Otherwise, the sword cannot be used to shed blood, for a show of strength or to earn wealth. The true conquest is the conquest of hearts. Conquests based upon the sword and brute force are the shame of humanity. The real conquest is the conquest of hearts, the conquests of service and love and those which carry hearts to Allah. These conquests can only be realised by those who have attained the mystery of humanity and the truths of the human heart.
193. Camels are charmed by singing and chanting and camel drivers employ such a device in order to spur on their herds. These songs of the cameleers are referred to as *hida'* or *huda'*.

on the door of the Prophet, may Allah bless him and grant him peace, using the tips of their fingernails." (Bukhari, *al-Adab al-Mufrad*, 1080)

This incident also serves as vivid demonstration of the delicacy and grace of the Companions:

Caliph 'Umar, may Allah be well pleased with him, sat with some people in a house wherein Jarir ibn 'Abd Allah, may Allah be well pleased with him, was also present. 'Umar detected an odour and said to those present:

"Let the one from whom this smell comes take the ablution at once." Jarir then said,

"O leader of the believers, would it not be better for everyone present here to take the ablution?"

Filled with admiration for his civility, 'Umar said to him,

"May Allah have mercy on you! How noble you were in the Age of Ignorance, and how noble you are in Islam!" ('Ali al-Muttaqi, *Kanz*, 8608)

Great courtesy is required when helping the needy and one must be in a state of gratitude towards them for it is through their means that one is able to attain Divine approval and pleasure. When my late father **Musa Efendi**, may Allah sanctify his secret, and my uncles used to spend in the way of Allah, they used to display great care and grace. On the envelopes in which the prescribed annual alms and charity was placed they would write, "Thank you for your acceptance."

When they were to present something to the poor, they would first package these in the finest possible way and would present these with an admirable delicacy, without causing any offence and in a manner pleasing to those who were to receive them. The receiver would be joyous and the giver at peace. One would accept the offering acknowledging its coming from Allah, and the other would be jubilant at having consigned this Divine trust to its rightful place.

Similarly, in Ottoman society, the distribution of food to martyrs' families in sealed containers and in the dark is an immensurable example of sensitivity and delicacy. This serves as an exceptional lesson in grace and propriety for generations to come.

Furthermore, the **"Stones of Charity"** invented to enable the impoverished to receive the money required to fulfil their needs without any discomfort is the result of an unrivalled refinement.

Having a small hole burrowed on top, these stones would be placed in suitable places throughout the neighbourhood. Those well-to-do could spend in the way of Allah *'without their left hand knowing what their right hand has given,'* by placing their charity in the holes at the top of these stones, under the cover of darkness.

The virtuous and honourable poor of the neighbourhood would later take only as much money as they needed and nothing more. When their situation improved, they would place many times more than what they had taken from there, in return.

None other than those in need would take of these monies despite their being left out in the open. Hence, a seventeenth century French traveller reports that he monitored a stone with money on it for exactly one week and that he did not observe anyone come to take from it in charity.

Manner of Speech

Courtesy and grace holds especial importance in one's speech. Commanding His servants to possess refinement in their manner of walking and talking, Allah Almighty declares:

"Be modest in your bearing, and subdue your voice. For certain the most repugnant of voices is braying of donkeys." (Luqman 31:19)

Again, He declares:

"...and speak kindly and well to the people..." (Baqara 2:83)

"And say to My servants that they should always speak (even when disputing with others) that which is the best..." (Isra' 17:53)

Islam forbids superfluous and vulgar speech and disapproves of excessive speech. Allah's Messenger, upon him be peace and blessings, has said,

"Let one who believes in Allah and the Last Day either speak of good or keep silent." (Muslim, Iman, 77)

Allah and His Messenger advise human beings to speak in a language that is concise and eloquent, and with words that are very carefully selected.[194]

Again, Allah's Messenger, may Allah bless him and grant him peace, has stated:

"Some eloquent speech possesses the power of magic." (Bukhari, Nikah, 47)

That is to say, some words produce a bewitching effect on the heart. This is only possible through command of language and effective word choice. The pinnacle of such power is observed in the Qur'an with the Qur'anic verses each at the peak of eloquence and rhetoric, constituting a profound miracle. It is essential, therefore, to benefit from the Qur'an's wisdom-laden address.

---

194. Baqara 2:104; Nisa 4:46; Bukhari, Adab 100, Da'awat 6.

The Qur'an places great importance on what needs to be said where, or the etiquette and manner of speech, such that it commands the following:

- Speaking even to the oppressor 'with gentle words';
- Speaking to those in need 'gently and well-meaning';
- Addressing one's parents 'in gracious words';
- Speaking 'words true, proper and straight to the point' to all people;
- Speaking in 'an honourable way' to the orphan and the needy; and
- Using 'profound words touching their very souls' when guiding others.

Thus, Islam has introduced the most effectual principles enabling human beings to be polite, graceful, understanding and genteel. Muslims who observe these principles will lead felicitous lives in both abodes and will attain neverending prosperity. As for those who reject these principles and seek to live according to the principles placed by mortal beings, their felicity is short-lived and they are consequently dragged to an eternal wretchedness.

5. Service

Belief in Allah requires one to be compassionate for one who believes in Allah Almighty loves Him and obeys His commands. Moreover, in time, they gradually come to love everything that is concerned with Him. In the Qur'an, Allah Almighty reminds of His attributes **All-Merciful and All-Compassionate** the most and incessantly commands compassion towards His creation. In this case, both a believer's obedience to the Divine command as well as their assuming the character traits of God. A heart deprived of compassion, however, is an unfortunate heart estranged from Allah.

Allah's Messenger, may Allah bless him and grant him peace, once affectionately kissed his grandson **Hasan**, may Allah be well pleased with him, on his cheek. Aqra' ibn Haris, who was seated next to him, said,

"I have ten children and have never kissed any of them."

The Messenger of Allah, upon him be peace and blessings, looked at him and said,

"The one who does not show mercy will not be shown mercy." (Bukhari, Adab, 18)

Again, Bedouin came to the Prophet and said,

"Do you kiss children? We do not kiss them." The Prophet, may Allah bless him and grant him peace, said,

"There is nothing I can do if Allah has removed mercy from your hearts." (Bukhari, Adab, 18)

After the Battle of Hunayn, some captives were brought to the Prophet, may Allah bless him and grant him peace, among whom was a woman who had lost her own child. Whenever she found an infant among the captives, she held affectionately it to her chest and suckled it. Before this great tableau of compassion, the Prophet, may Allah bless him and grant him peace, said,

"Can you imagine this woman casting her child into the Fire?"

The Companions replied, "No, no long as she has the power not to cast it."

Then he said,

WORLDLY TRANSACTIONS and MORALITY

"Allah is more merciful to His slaves than this woman is to her child." (Bukhari, Adab, 18)

The Messenger of Allah, upon him be peace and blessings, later unconditionally released these captives numbering six thousand.

Thus, serving the servants of Allah most loved by Him and whom He always approaches with compassion is one of the most fundamental principles of Islam. **Service to the created with a view to worshipping Allah is tantamount to worship of Allah itself.**

Service is meeting the need of a powerless or impoverished person. It implies rushing to the aid of everyone and concerning oneself with their plight and hardship for the Messenger, upon him be peace and blessings, has stated:

"The best amongst you is the one who is most beneficial to human beings." (Bayhaqi, *Shu'ab al-Iman*, VI:117; Ibn Hajar, *Matalib*, I:264)

Abu Musa, may Allah be well pleased with him, narrates:

"Allah's Messsenger, upon him be peace and blessings, would wear a garment of coarse wool, milk his own sheep and entertain and honour his guests." (Hakim, I, 129:205)

Service is a social duty of servanthood that the Almighty demands from His servants. Just as Allah has absolutely prohibited arrogance, pride and self-conceit, He does not want His servants to lead selfish lives. He wills His servants to be altruistic and pledges enormous rewards for the believers who engage in service to others. Hence, Allah's Messenger, upon him be peace and blessings, states:

"...Allah helps the servant so long as he helps his brother... and he who is slow to good deeds will not be hastened by his lineage." (Muslim, Dhikr, 38; Ibn Maja, Muqaddima, 17)

"Whoever attains a white hair while in the path of Allah, it will be a light for him on the Day of Judgment." (Tirmidhi, Fada'il al-Jihad, 9:1635; Nasa'i, Jihad, 26)

"An evening spent in the way of Allah or an morning is better than this world and everything it contains..." (Bukhari, Jihad, 6)

It is a given that **one who serves, as opposed to one who is served, will be more prosperous in both the world and in the Hereafter.** Hence, the people of wisdom have said:

"The people who are truly happy are those who know how to be of service to others."

In that case, we are in need of service to others in order to attain perfection and felicity in both worlds. ***Consequently, we must be deeply indebted to those people we serve for they are a means to our acquiring nearness to Allah Almighty.***

6. *Jihad* and the Struggle against Terror

a. Islam is a Divine and True Religion

It is Allah, glorified be He, Who created human beings, animals and all other beings alongside the entire universe and Who sustains and regulates it in wondrous order and fashion. He has sent the religion of Islam to regulate the relationships of human beings – to whom He has bestowed reason and will – with one another and their treatment of other creatures. That is to say, Islam is a Divine and true religion. Anyone who examines Islam with a fair mind would acknowledge this.

Allah, exalted and glorified be He, is beyond all deficiencies, limitations and imperfections. Thus, He never wills disorder and corruption, or terrorism and evil. And so, when making mention of the hypocrites and the wicked, He declares:

WORLDLY TRANSACTIONS and MORALITY

"**When he leaves (you) or attains authority, he rushes about the land to foment disorder and corruption therein, and to ruin the sources of life and human generations. Surely Allah does not love disorder and corruption.**" (Baqara 2:205)

Again, prohibiting His servants to seek, condone or wait for an opportunity for such disorder and corruption, Allah Almighty declares:

"**...Do not seek corruption and mischief in the land, for Allah does not love those who cause corruption and make mischief.**" (Qasa 28:77)

Allah, glorified be He, is most compassionate to His servants and always wills goodness, mercy and prosperity for them. He deems violations of the rights of others as being of the greatest of crimes. So long as the servant does not forgive such a crime, Allah will not forgive it either. The Almighty approaches even His sinning servant with forgiveness and compassion. He makes known the fact that speaking ill of them behind their back is a major sin and fiercely warns against this.

Accordingly, it is not at all possible for Islam – sent by Allah Almighty for the peace and happiness of humanity – to desire and condone the killing of innocent people.

Islam sees the protection of the life property, honour, intellect and progeny of every human being as indispensable.

For this reason, an examination of history reveals that the person who struggled most with terrorism was the Messenger of Allah, upon him be peace and blessings. His twenty-three years of Prophethood were invariably a struggle against terror. The Prophet, may Allah bless him and grant him peace, constantly struggled against terror levelled against the human being, terror against animals and terror against the environment. He always held observing the rights of each and every individual, whether unbeliever or believer, as fundamental. Consequently, through his efforts, the entire world attained repose; the deserts that had formerly become a blood bath found peace and the history of humanity witnessed a civilisation of virtue the likes of which it had never seen before.

This being the case, certain groups set out to use Islam in juxtaposition with the word terror, one of the greatest calamities of our time. Whereas terrorism and anarchy have been established upon heartlessness and in no way do they require such exalted sensibilities as morality and principle. Terrorism has no tears, no compassion and conscience. Islam, however, is predicated upon mercy and compassion. In the Qur'an, Allah Almighty instils His Names **All-Merciful** and **All-Compassionate** the most, or in other words His universal mercy encompassing all creatures. Islam is a religion of humanity and civilisation which issues law and justice. Those who learn Islam properly perceive immediately the unfounded nature of even using its name in the same sentence as the word terror.

b. Every Life is Sacred

It is Allah Who has given life and it is only He Who can take it. It follows that unjustly taking a life is a most great crime committed against Allah for in the eyes of Islam, every life holds a value equal to all humanity. Allah, glorified be He, declares in the Qur'an:

"...He who kills a soul unless it be (in legal punishment) **for murder or for causing disorder and corruption on the earth will be as if he had killed all humankind; and he who saves a life will be as if he had saved the lives of all humankind..."** (Ma'ida 5:32)

A powerful deterrent that Islam has placed with a view to discouraging members of society from committing murder is retaliation wherein the violation of the law is proportionate to the infliction of punishment which such violence entails. In the event of there being several accomplices to the crime, each and every one of them are dealt the same punishment.[195] Killing someone else to one side, a person's taking their own life has even been prohibited and suicide has been counted among the major sins. The punishment to be dealt for this has accordingly been presented in rather dire terms.[196]

Due to Islam's regarding the human being to be so lofty, Allah's Messenger, upon him be peace and blessings, even used to exert utmost endeavour not to contend against his enemies. He made all kinds of accommodation in order to reach agreement with them; he would not be the side to start war and when the enemy waged war, he would descend upon them. When he was forced to fight, he applied insightful strategies in order for minimal loss of life. More often than not, he would compel his enemies to surrender without any bloodshed and would subsequently forgive them.

And so, when he conquered Makka without a single drop of bloodshed, all his enemies had surrendered however he forgave all of them and declared,

"Today is a Day of Mercy. You may go, you are free!" [197]

Subsequently, he inquired about the sons of his bitterest enemy, Abu Lahab, asking his uncle 'Abbas,

"O 'Abbas, where are your brother's two sons 'Utba and Mu'attib? I cannot see them." 'Abbas, may Allah be well pleased with him, replied,

"They withdrew to the side, together with other Qurayshi polytheists." He said,

"Bring them to me."

---

195. See, Bukhari, Diyat, 21.
196. See, Bukhari, Tib, 56; Muslim, Iman, 175.
197. See, Ibn Hisham, IV:32; Waqidi, II:835, III:352; Ibn Sa'd, II:142-143; 'Ali al-Muttaqi, *Kanz*, 30173.

'Abbas, may Allah be well pleased with him, rode off in search of Abu Lahab's sons. Upon finding them, he said,

"Allah's Messenger, upon him be peace and blessings, invites you." They hastened to ride with 'Abbas and came to the Prophet's presence. When he invited them to embrace Islam, they immediately accepted, pledging their allegiance to him. The Messenger of Allah, may Allah be well pleased with him, was most pleased with their entering Islam. Taking them each by the hand, he took them to Multazam[198] and made a long supplication for them. He then returned with a great joy visible on his face. 'Abbas, may Allah be well pleased with him, thus remarked,

"O Messenger of Allah, may Allah make you eternally joyful! I see great joy reflected in your face." The Prophet said,

"Indeed! I had beseeched my Lord for these two cousins of mine, and He gave them to me."

'Utba and Mu'attib, may Allah be well pleased with them both, never left the Prophet's side. They went with him to Hunayn, in Makka's surrounds, and took part in battle alongside him. Even when the battle turned against them during the Battle of Hunayn, they refused to leave the Prophet's side. Mu'attib, may Allah be well pleased with him, even lost an eye when defending Allah's Messenger.[199]

---

198. *Multazam*: The section of the Ka'ba wall lying between the Black Stone and the door of the Ka'ba. He stood in such a manner that his cheek, chest, arms and palms were against the wall of the Ka'ba, and entreated Allah, widely spreading out his arms and hands. (Abu Dawud, Manasik, 54:1899) In another Prophetic Tradition, he has stated: *"Between Hajar al-Aswad and Maqam al-Ibrahim is Multazam. The ill making supplication here will be healed."* (Haythami, III:246)
199. See, Ibn Sa'd, IV:60, Suyuti, al-Khasa'is al-Kubra, II:82; Halabi, Insan al-'Uyun, III:48.

WORLDLY TRANSACTIONS and MORALITY

The Messenger of Allah, may Allah bless him and grant him peace, granted amnesty to many leading Makkans who fled, like these two, invited them and forgave them all.[200]

Allah's Messenger, upon him be peace and blessings, did not wish harm even upon those who refused to believe in him and entreated Allah for their descendants to perceive the truth and believe in the One True God. As the saying goes, *"Where there is life, there is hope."* When you take the life of others, you remove any possibility of hope in their knowing and believing in Allah Almighty.

And at last, Allah Almighty brought life out of death and allowed the realisation of Prophet's prayer. By virtue of Divine mercy, Allah's Messenger, upon him be peace and blessings, pursued such an extraordinary statesmanship that the majority of his bitterest enemies became Muslim at will; similarly, the children of virtually all of them also believed and became individuals at the peak of humanity. When we look at the Prophetic Traditions and the narrators conveying the laws of Islam to us, we observe the fact that the forbears of most of them were polytheists. Even the children of individuals who harboured the fiercest hostility towards the Prophet later became great Muslim scholars.

c. Individuality of the Crime

One of the principles introduced by Islam is that a person cannot bear the burden of another's crime. Allah Almighty has frequently repeated this ruling:

"No soul, as bearer of burden, bears and is made to bear the burden of another."[201]

---

200. For instance, see Muwatta', Nikah, 44-45; Tirmidhi, Isti'zan, 34:2735; Hakim, III:269/5055, 271/5059; Waqidi, II:851-853.
201. An'am 6:164; Isra' 17:15; Fatir 35:18; Zumar 39:7; Najm 53:38.

Allah's Messenger, may Allah bless him and grant him peace, charged a delegation of ten people, with Madinan 'Asim ibn Thabit at their head, with teaching and gathering intelligence. The Lihyan tribe closely pursued this delegation with close to one hundred archers. Eight of these Companions were martyred, with Khubayb and Zayd ibn Dathina being taken prisoner. The Makkan polytheists took them and sold them in Makka. Khubayb was bought by the sons of Harith ibn 'Amir, whom he had killed in the Battle of Badr. Khubayb remained a prisoner with them until they agreed upon killing him.

During his time in captivity, **Khubayb** asked to borrow a razor from one of the daughters of Harith with which to shave himself. Giving the razor to her three-year-old son, she told him to give it to the prisoner. The woman relates what ensued as follows:

"He took a son of mine who had gone to him when I was inattentive. I found him sitting on his thigh and the razor was in his hand. I was so alarmed that Khubayb noticed it in my face and he asked,

'Are you afraid that I will kill him? I would never do such a thing.'"

The Makkan polytheists took Khubayb and Zayd to Tan'im, ten kilometres from Makka, and brutally killed them, such that the number of spear wounds could not be counted on their bodies. (Bukhari, Maghazi, 28, 10; Jihad, 170; Ibn Hajar, *al-Isaba*, I:418)

In other words, Islam penalises only the perpetrator and does not allow anyone other than the person committing the crime to come to grief. It prohibits going to extremes and exceeding the bounds when punishing the criminal. It is stated in a Qur'anic verse:

"Do not kill any soul, which Allah has made forbidden, except in just cause. If anyone has been killed wrongfully and intentionally, We have given his heir (as defender of his rights) **the authority** (to claim retaliation or damages or to forgive outright). **But let him

WORLDLY TRANSACTIONS and MORALITY

(the heir) **not exceed the legitimate bounds in** (retaliatory) **killing. Indeed he has been helped** (already and sufficiently by the provisions and procedures of the Law)." (Isra' 17:33)

"**If you have to respond to any wrong, respond** (only) **to the measure of the wrong done to you; but if you endure patiently, it is indeed better for the patient.**" (Nahl 16:126)

d. Islamic Jihad

Just as seeing jihad as being comprised merely of war is not reflective of the truth, it is also deficient with respect to the meaning and scope of jihad provided in the Qur'an and the Sunna. Denoting 'exerting an effort and endeavouring,' jihad can be actualised with all kinds of means such as the heart, tongue, the hand, wealth, life, culture, economy and arms. Islam demands human beings to engage in jihad more so with a sincere heart and soft words. Those who undertake this duty are advised in the Qur'an to use touching and eloquent expression. (قَوْلًا لَيِّنًا، قَوْلًا بَلِيغًا) It enjoins the believers to endeavour with their wealth and lives for hearts to be revived through union with Allah Almighty.

Islam deems peace as the norm or as the natural order. The greatest indicator of this is the following: The Qur'an names the **Treaty of Hudaybiya**, which imposed stringent conditions against the Muslims as a "**Manifest Victory**" (*Fath al-Mubin*) and this "**Victory**" has become eponym of one of the Qur'anic chapters.

The battles undertaken by the Prophet were all battles of defence. They were carried out for the purpose of either driving back assaults against the Muslims or to thwart the preparations for attack, which determined through intelligence gathering. Going to **Badr**, where the first major battle was held, the Prophet's intention was not to fight but to stop a caravan prospering with the property and belongings usurped from the Muslims and with whose profit an army would be equipped to fight against them. The caravan escaped by changing route; however, when the Makkan forces, having left Makka and travelling four hundred kilometres to the outskirts of Madina, rejected repeated offers of conciliation, battle was inevitable and victory was achieved. (Waqidi, I:61-65)

The **Battle of Uhud** and the **Battle of the Trench** were battles that were fought right at Madina's feet. The Makkan polytheists were aggressive and extremely hostile. They gathered forces left and right of the city in order to exterminate the Muslims. The Messenger of Allah, upon him be peace and blessings, however, fought battles in defence of Madina. Moreover, by having a trench dug around the city, he reduced loss of life to naught.

The **Battle of Mu'ta** and the expedition to **Tabuk** were conducted in response to the killing of an envoy and to stave off the enemy preparing for attack. Yet, there was no conflict at Tabuk and the forces returned after certain agreements were reached.

The **Conquest of Makka** was realised as a result of the Makkans' breach of the Treaty of Hudaybiya and also constitutes the restoration of the rights of the emigrant Muslims that were violated. This constitutes a peace movement unparalleled in history as well as a conquest of hearts for there was neither plunder, nor killing, nor exile, nor reprisal, nor blood feud in the conquered city. Far from it, all of these were forgiven unconditionally, despite the oppression, persecution and torture which had been perpetrated for more than a decade.

Similarly, the other battles of the Prophet were carried out in opposition to an attack or to thwart the enemy in preparation for war.

When Muslims are forced to fight the enemy despite all their efforts for conciliation, they are obligated to act within set legal guidelines. They cannot harm children, women, the elderly, religious leaders, civilian workers, places of worship, animals and trees. They are only able to use arms against combat troops. They cannot, however, torture them.

Whenever the Messenger of Allah, upon him be peace and blessings, was to dispatch a military force and appointed anyone as leader of the detachment, he would especially exhort him to fear Allah and to be good to the Muslims who were with him, and would then declare:

"Fight in the name and in the way of Allah. Fight against those who reject Him. Do not embezzle the spoils. Do not break your pledge. Do not **oppress**. Do not mutilate. Do not kill children." (Muslim, Jihad, 3; Ahmad, V:352, 358)

In other narrations, Allah's Messenger, may Allah bless him and grant him peace, states:

"...Do not kill children or people who devote themselves to worship in churches! Do not destroy churches or cut down trees. Do not destroy houses."[202][203][204]

"A woman was once found slain in one of the expeditions of the Prophet, may Allah bless him and grant him peace, and the Messenger of Allah, may Allah bless him and grant him peace, at once forbade of killing women and children." (Bukhari, Jihad, 148; Muslim, Jihad, 24, 25)

At the Battle of Hunayn, the Banu Sulaym formed the vanguard and were led by **Khalid ibn Walid**. During the expedition, he encountered the body of a woman who had been killed. He said,

"This is not one with whom fighting should have taken place." So he sent a man and said,

---

202. See, 'Abd al-Razzaq, *Musannaf*, V:220.
203. See, Ahmad, I:300; Tabarani, *Mu'jam al-Kabir*, XI, 224:11562.
204. See, Tabarani, *Mu'jam al-Awsat*, I, 48:135.

"Tell Khalid not to kill a woman, child, the elderly or a hired servant."[205]

When the Prophet was informed that some children had been killed also he was deeply grieved and, showing marked displeasure, said,

"Why are some today so determined on killing that they even kill children?" One of those present asked,

"O Messenger of Allah, are they not the children of polytheists?" Upon this, the Prophet said,

"Are not the best of you the children of polytheists?" He then continued,

"Take heed! Do not kill children! Do not kill children! Every child is born with a natural disposition [to the true religion] and remains so until their tongue gives them power of expression. Then their parents make Jews or Christians of them." (Ahmad, III:435)

Taken captive by the Turks in the **Battle of Mohács** (1528), **Bartolomej Georgijević** detailed in his work on the customs and traditions of the Turks:

"There is such a firm discipline in the Ottoman army during war that no soldier can dare to do any injustice. One who perpetrates injustice is punished without pity. There are sentinel and those posted to establish order... Even a single apple is not picked from a tree along the routes without the permission of their owners." (Onur Bilge Kula, *Alman Kültüründe Türk İmgesi*, Ankara 1993, 164)

The lands in the surrounds of Gebze (situated 30 miles east of Istanbul on the northern shore of the Sea of Marmara) through which **Sultan Yavuz Selim**'s army travelled on their expedition to Egypt,

---

205. Abu Dawud, Jihad, 111; Ibn Maja, Jihad, 30; Waqidi, III:912.

WORLDLY TRANSACTIONS and MORALITY

were abounding in vineyards and orchards. Sultan Yavuz Selim was lost in thought:

"I wonder if my troops have taken grapes or apples without the permission of their owners?" Then calling the Commander of the Janissary corps, he commanded,

"It is my decree that the packsacks of all my Janissaries, cavalry and vanguard troops are searched. If there are any among them in whose packsack an apple or bunch of grapes is found, bring them to me at once!"

Taking immediate action, the Janissary Commander had all the packsacks thoroughly searched. Subsequently coming before the Sultan, he said,

"My lord, we did not find a trace of apples or any other fruit."

The Sultan was most pleased with this news. A great burden was lifted from her shoulders. Raising his hands, he entreated Allah saying,

"O Allah, endless praise and thanks be to You! You have favoured me with an army that does not consume from the unlawful." Then addressing his Commander, he said,

"Had my troops plucked fruit unlawfully, I would have abandoned this campaign as conquest is not possible with an army that eats the unlawful."

As a result of such spiritual standing, manifestations of Divine aid and grace were constantly a friend to him.[206]

As is evident, Islam prefers peace first and foremost, and when war becomes inevitable, it commands measure, justice and humane-

---

206. Osman Nuri Topbaş, *Âbide Şahsiyetleri ve Müesseseleriyle Osmanlı*, 166-167.

ness and not exceeding the legitimate bounds. For Allah, exalted and glorified be He, declares:

"**Fight in Allah's cause** (in order to exalt His Name) **against those who fight against you, but do not exceed the bounds** (set by Allah)**, for surely Allah loves not those who exceed the bounds.**"
(Baqara 2:190; Ma'ida 5:2)

If Islam does not consent to the killing of innocent people and those not actively participating in combat even during war, how can it allow the killing of innocent people outside warfare?

War in Islam like the Scalpel in the Hands of the Surgeon

It is possible to say that Islam is, in its entirety, a struggle against terror. In Islam, going to war to shed blood and seize land is forbidden. The sword can only be used as a means to removing oppression and to facilitate the guidance of the people. A sword that does not serve this purpose is only a scrap of metal.

In other words, jihad is like the scalpel in the hands of the surgeon. It is used to stop those who create mischief and corruption and who destroy people for their own vested interests. In the same way that a limb with gangrene is amputated for the soundness of the entire body, evil that is beyond rehabilitation are also removed from society for the peace and security of all humanity.

Allah Almighty declares:

"And when they went forth against Goliath and his forces, they prayed: 'Our Lord, pour out upon us steadfastness, and set our feet firm, and help us to victory over the disbelieving people.' So they routed them by Allah's leave, and David killed Goliath, and Allah granted him kingdom and Wisdom, and taught him of that which He willed. Were it not that Allah repelled people, some by

WORLDLY TRANSACTIONS and MORALITY

means of others, the earth would surely be corrupted; but Allah is gracious for all the worlds." (Baqara 2:250-251)

"If only there had been among the generations before you (of whom some We destroyed) **people with lasting qualities** (such as faith, knowledge, virtue, and good deeds, whose goal was what is lasting with Allah, the eternal life of the Hereafter, and) **who would warn against disorder and corruption on earth! Among them only a few, included among those whom We saved, did this. But those who did wrong** (against Allah by associating partners with Him, and against people by violating their rights) **were lost in the pursuit of pleasures without scruples, and were criminals committed to accumulating sins. And it has never been the way of your Lord to destroy the townships unjustly while their people were righteous, dedicated to continuous self-reform and setting things right in the society."** (Hud 11:116-117)

No Compulsion in Religion

Islam wills that truths is conveyed and communicated to the people; however, under no circumstances does it force them to accept these.[207] For Allah, glorified be He, wills that His servants, whom He has sent to the world to be tested, are free. Those accepting Islam must accept it with their own free will and those rejecting it must reject it with their own free will for them to be either rewarded or punished in the Hereafter.[208] Such being the case, fighting against powers that prevent the communication of the message of Islam to human beings and prevent their investigating it with their independent will, might sometimes be required, as they impose restrictions on the freedom of people who do not believe and force them to stay away from Islam.

---

207. See, Baqara 2:256; Yunus 10:99; Abu Dawud, Jihad, 116:2682.
208. See, Anfal 8:42; Kahf 18:29; Zumar 39:7; Jathiya 45:15.

Belief is a blessing that can only be attained with free will. It is not possible to make people believe with force and coercion. Those who are thus compelled can only be hypocrites. Islam, however, deems hypocrisy as worse than unbelief. For this reason, Muslims throughout history have not forced anyone to enter Islam and have even left the captives in their possession at liberty in this regard. **Ziyad ibn Jaz'**, present during the conquest of Egypt, relates:

"...Then [after the battle] we assembled all those captives who were still in our care, and the Christians among them were grouped together. Then we began to bring forward every single man from among them and we gave him the choice between Islam and Christianity. When he chose Islam, we all shouted, "Allah is Great," even louder than we had done during conquest, and we gathered him within our ranks. (We now shared the same rights and responsibilities.) When he opted for Christianity, the Christians would pull him back into their midst, while we imposed the poll-tax (jizya) on him. However, we experienced great anguish at this, as if one of us had joined their ranks..." (Tabari, *Tarikh*, I:512)

e. Humane Treatment of Prisoners of War

The Messenger of Allah, upon him be peace and blessings, through various instruction, exhortation and practices, demanded that captives be treated well and prohibited their torture and torment. He indicated that it was not proper to use force against captives even for the purpose of obtaining information from them.[209] Muslim jurists too affirm the immorality of tormenting captives in such ways as depriving them of food and water. (Kasani, *Badai' al-Sanai'*, 1406, Dar al-Kutub al-'Ilmiyya, VII:120)

---

209. See, Abu Dawud, Jihad, 115; Ibn Hisham, II:255; Waqidi, II:514.

WORLDLY TRANSACTIONS and MORALITY

Mus'ab ibn 'Umayr's brother **Abu 'Aziz** was the standard-bearer of the Makkan polytheists at Badr. He was taken captive and relates the compassion and mercy the Muslims showed to him as follows:

"Having been taken captive during the Battle of Badr, I was handed over to a group of the Ansar. Upon returning from Badr, whenever I sat with my captors for lunch or dinner, they would offer me the bread and themselves have dried dates, in obedience to the Prophet's recommendation to treat us well (with bread being the more luxurious item of food than dates). Whenever any of them obtained a piece of bread, he would immediately offer it to me. When I politely refused to have it, thus returning it to (one of) them, they would return it to me insisting that I eat it and on not account take it back." (Ibn Hisham, II:288; Haythami, VI:86)

Also from among the captives, **Abu al-'As ibn Rabi'** and **Walid ibn Walid**, too, reported to have been treated in the same way. According to an account of one of the Qurayshi captives **Yazid**, on the way to Madina, captives were mounted on the riding beasts while the Muslims walked. (Waqidi, I:119)

Allah's Messenger, upon him be peace and blessings, did not hold all prisoners taken captive during the Battle of Badr together in one place Instead, he divided them up among his Companions one-by-one and advised them to host them as guests in their homes and treat them with warmth and generosity. (Ibn Hisham, II:288)

Following consultation in this regard, these captives were released in return for ransom. The ransom for those who were literate among them was to teach ten Madinan children how to read and write. Those unable to do so were released unconditionally. (Ahmad, I:247; Waqidi, I:129; Ibn Sa'd, II:22)

During the **Battle of Hunayn**, many prisoners were taken from the Hawazin tribe. Allah's Messenger, may Allah bless him and grant him peace, commanded **Busr ibn Sufyan** to procure clothing for the prisoners. Busr subsequently clothed all the captives with the garments he purchased. Out of respect for his foster-aunts, the Prophet first released the prisoners falling to his share as well as to the share of the descendants of 'Abd al-Muttalib. Upon this, the Companions too released their share without ransom. To those Muslims who declined to forego their shares, Allah's Messenger, upon him be peace and blessings, vowed personally to pay their ransom. In this way, six thousand prisoners were released unconditionally. Moreover, of the war spoils obtained, 24,000 camels, 40,000 sheep and 4,000 *uqiyya* of silver (approximately 500 kilograms) were returned. (Ibn Hisham, IV:135; Waqidi, III:943, 950-954)

Allah's Messenger, upon him be peace and blessings, similarly released without ransom a great number captives taken during other battles.[210]

The Prophet took advantage of every opportunity to release prisoners of war. During the month of Ramadan, for instance, he would release all captives and would meet the needs of all those who asked from him. (Ibn Sa'd, I:377)

Abu Bakr, may Allah be well pleased with him, spent most of his wealth in the way of emancipating slaves and captives. Displeased with his son's using his wealth in this way, his father Abu Quhafa said to him one day,

"Son, I see you constantly freeing weak and powerless slaves. Since this is what you seek to do, why don't you free some strong slaves among them so that they can defend and protect you?"

Abu Bakr, may Allah be well pleased with him, most nobly replied,

---

210. See, Muslim, Jihad, 132, 133; Abu Dawud, Itk, 2:3931; Ibn Hisham, IV:32; Waqidi, II:559, 560, 835; Ibn Sa'd, II:88, 142-143.

"Father, my sole aim in doing this is to earn the good pleasure of Allah. In setting them free, I seek only the reward before Allah."

The following Qur'anic verses were revealed in praise of Abu Bakr's generosity:

"Then, as for him who gives (out of his wealth for Allah's good pleasure)**, and keeps from disobedience to Him in reverence for Him and piety, And affirms the best** (in creed, action, and the reward to be given)**, We will make easy for him the path to the state of ease** (salvation after an easy reckoning)**,"** (Layl 92:5-7)[211]

f. Working for the Welfare of all Humanity

Islam is the religion of peace and salvation that Allah has sent to all humanity. And the Messenger of Allah, upon him be peace and blessings, is the Prophet of Mercy that the Almighty has bestowed upon all the worlds.

Allah Almighty declares:

"We have not sent you (O Muhammad) but as an unequalled mercy for all the worlds." (Anbiya 21:107)

Ibn 'Abbas, may Allah be well pleased with him, noted the following in relation to this verse:

"Whoever believes in Allah and the Last Day, mercy will be decreed for him in this world and in the Hereafter; whoever does not believe in Allah and His Messenger, will be protected from the Divine punishments that were dealt to former civilisations, such as earthquakes, faces becoming transformed and stones raining down from the skies. This is the mercy in the world that they will attain by virtue of Allah's Messenger." (Bayhaqi, *Dala'il al-Nubuwwa*, V:486; Haythami, VII:69)

---

211. Ibn Hisham, Sirat al-Nabi, I:341; Tabari, Jami' al-Bayan, XXX:279 [Layl 92:5-7]; Suyuti, *Lubab al-Nuqul*, 257-258.

The Messenger of Allah, may Allah bless him and grant him peace, beseeched his Lord to protect his community from ruin through wide-scale famine, drowning and to be secure from mass destruction.[212] From the time he was sent as a Prophet, all human beings are his community.[213] On account of this, the Messenger of Allah, upon him be peace and blessings, protects all humanity from cataclysmic disasters.

In one of his Traditions, the Prophet states:

"*The most beloved of people to Allah is the one who brings most benefit to the people.*" (Hathami, VIII:191)

Hence, Muslims strive for the welfare of all humanity. They work for the good of all human beings, not differentiating between religions, and assist the downtrodden, acting according to the principle of **loving the created simply because of the Creator.** Due to their love of Allah, they love all the human beings that He has created. They interfere in the affairs of no one, whatever their belief, provided they do not commit injustice and restrict other's freedom of thought.

Upon an examination of history, we see that the civilisation of Islam never attempted to obliterate other civilisations. To the contrary, it took on the elements that were in line with its own values and developed them. It protected those under its administration. Jewish, Christian, Buddhist, Hindu and Zoroastrian cultures were protected in the Madinan State established by the Prophet, during the era of the Four Righteous Caliphs, under Umayyad and Abbasid rule, and in Andalusian, Indian and Ottoman societies. If Islam had worked solely for the welfare of its own followers, than at the very least, some of these civilisations in question would have been erased from the annals of history.

---

212. See, Muslim, Fitan, 19-20; Tirmidhi, Fitan, 14:2177; Abu Dawud, Fitan, 1:4252.
213. See, Haythami, I:174.

WORLDLY TRANSACTIONS and MORALITY

Islam's acceptance of others and its distinguished horizon of understanding was experienced by many a race, religion and nation in the African, Asian and European continents.

There are many examples which demonstrate that Islam embraces all humanity. One such example is the following: **Caliph 'Ali**, may Allah be well pleased with him, wrote to Malik ibn Harith, whom he appointed as Governor of Egypt, instructing him as follows:

"Habituate your heart to mercy for the people and to affection and kindness towards them. Do not stand over them and regard them like a beast over a herd, since they are, without exception, of two kinds, either your brother in religion or your like in creation. Human beings can err and make mistakes. They may act wrongly, wilfully or by neglect. So, extend to them your forgiveness and pardon, in the same way as you would like Allah to extend His forgiveness and pardon to you... Do not set yourself against Allah, for neither do you possess the strength to shield yourself against His displeasure, nor can you do without His mercy and forgiveness. Do not regret any act of forgiveness, nor rejoice over any punishment that you may mete out to any one..."[214]

In Islam, the property, life and honour of the people, including those of the unbelievers, are forbidden.

Even cursing people, let alone killing them, is something that is denounced in Islam.[215]

The Messenger of Allah, upon him be peace and blessings, always advised tenderness and compassion and forever condemned violence, roughness and despotism. He said:

---

214. Muhyiddin Seydi Çelebi, Buhârî'de Yönetim Esasları, Istanbul 2000, 47.
215. See, Muslim, Birr, 84-86; Abu Dawud, Adab, 45.

"Allah has made me a generous and noble servant, and He did not make me an obstinate tyrant." (Abu Dawud, At'ima, 17:3773)

"Allah did not send me to be harsh, or to cause harm, but He sent me to teach and make things easy." (Ahmad, III:328)

Indeed, the Messenger of Allah, upon him be peace and blessings, was sent to perfect good character and to confer goodness and beauty upon all humanity.

This sublime character that he displayed as a statesman towards a Jewish subject who set to trap him, is filled with a great many lessons:

A group of Jews visited the Messenger of Allah, may Allah bless him and grant him peace, and said,

"*as-Samu 'alaykum*" (death be upon you, instead of *as-salamu 'alaykum*, or peace be upon you).

Understanding their meaning, **'A'isha**, may Allah be well pleased with her, retorted from behind a screen,

"And on you and may Allah curse you and be angry with you!"

The Messenger of Allah, may Allah bless him and grant him peace, who was sent to perfect good character, intervened and said,

"Gently, 'A'isha. You must be kind and beware of harshness and coarseness."

She said,

"Messenger of Allah, did you not hear what they said?" The Messenger of Allah, may Allah bless him and grant him peace, said,

"Did you not hear what I said? I answered the same to them, and what I said about them will be answered and what they said about me will not be answered." (Bukhari, Adab, 38)

WORLDLY TRANSACTIONS and MORALITY

According to another narration, the Prophet also said to 'A'isha,

"Gently, 'A'isha. Allah loves kindness in all things." (Bukhari, Isti'zan, 22)

Anas ibn Malik, may Allah be well pleased with him, said:

"The Prophet, may Allah bless him and grant him peace, did not use abusive or obscene language nor did he curse people. If he wanted to blame one of us, he would say,

'What is wrong with him! May his brow be dusty!'" (Bukhari, Adab, 38, 44)

Constituting a supplication, this Prophetic expression means, 'May your forehead be dusted with the prostration of Prayer.'

The following incident also demonstrates that there was no room for harshness, incivility and offence in the life of the Prophet:

A man (one of the hypocrites) asked permission to visit the Prophet, may Allah bless him and grant him peace. When he saw him from afar he said (with a view to protecting the people from his evil),

"An evil brother of his tribe! An evil brother of his tribe!"

When the man sat, the Prophet, may Allah bless him and grant him peace, was cheerful with him to his face and expansive to him. When the man left, **'A'isha** said to him,

"Messenger of Allah, when you saw the man, you said such-and-such about him. Then you were cheerful to him and expansive to him."

The Messenger of Allah, may Allah bless him and grant him peace, said,

"A'isha, when was it my habit to speak coarsely? The person with the worse position with Allah on the Day of Rising is the one whom people leave because of his evil." (Bukhari, Adab, 38)

The wickedness of the man mentioned here later increased and eventually, during the Caliphate of Abu Bakr, may Allah be well pleased with him, he was taken captive while fighting against the Muslims. It was then understood that the Prophet's remark concerning him was a miracle pertaining to the future.[216]

Such being the case, it is not possible for Muslims to participate in an act of terror due to their faith. If some show terrorist activities as though they had something to do with Islam, this claim is either a treachery purposefully perpetrated to denigrate Islam, or is a great negligence and ignorance.

---

216. Imam Nawawi, *al-Minhaj fi Sharh Sahih Muslim*, Beirut 1392, XVI:144.

EPILOGUE

By virtue of their predisposition to truth and reality, the human being does approve of the obscure and unknown. Constantly curious of the truth, they strive to research the truth and are in pursuit of it, for the things that they do not or cannot know render them spiritually bereft and suffering.

The greatest mystery most preoccupying human perception throughout history has been the unknowns relating to '**death**' and the '**realm beyond death**'.

Indeed, human beings, whatever their living conditions, are in a shared agony before death. The eventual fading of all the winding paths of life in the horizon of death causes hearts profound anguish.

Greater even than the miracle '**life**' and enveloping human beings and dragging them into its fiery vortex more ferociously, '**death**' is the most formidable truth to befall all souls – without exception – in this world; it is for this reason that enabling its unknowns to become known precedes all other human objectives.

For life is a truth as exalted as not to be contained with the distance between the cradle and the grave. If, in response to the question **"What is life?"** which occurs to human consciousness, is to rise merely the humidity of the soil and the hardness of the tombstone as an answer, what can there be that is more grievous than this?

Only the power of revelation can untie the knot of death and life beyond it, which cannot be fathomed purely with the intellect and human cognition.

What is life? Why was this universe created? What is the reason for the journey to this world and then to the grave? What will happen after death? The only religion providing satisfactory answers to all these questions is Islam. The sole religion enabling human beings to attain peace of mind by illuminating the points of darkness of death and life after death is Islam.

The purpose of life is to be able to attain eternal felicity by living in the spiritual blessing and tranquillity of the truths of the Qur'an and the Sunna. The world is the place of sowing, while the Hereafter is the abode of reaping what one sows. The human being is a traveller to eternity and the world is a guesthouse. That is to say, the world is a fleeting abode of trial in the way of earning eternal happiness. The true life is, with its Paradise and Hellfire, the eternal life of the Hereafter.

While humanity ought to be obliged to all the Prophets and especially the Prophet Muhammad, upon him be peace and blessings, who conveyed this news of the future, it is most unfortunate that it was received with ridicule, insult and indifference by many heedless individuals. The polytheists and unbelievers, who pursued a life contradicting the wisdom and purpose of their creation, first responded to the Prophet's news of the Hereafter that he conveyed through revelation with astonishment and confusion; subsequently, they rejected this invitation to eternal salvation which was at variance with their carnality with extreme obstinacy and aversion.

Through the way of life it introduced, Islam put an end to the carnal excesses of the polytheists and made mention of truth, justice, Judgement, resurrection and being called to account and stipulated that evil and injustice would not go unpunished.

EPILOGUE

Attempts have been made in every age to silence, suppress or imprison to one's subconscious, via various falsehoods, the questions relating to death and beyond – which have settled in minds like a poisonous snake and have made a person anxious each time it stirred.

Assuredly, this state is the manifestation of a 'psychology of evasion' which the carnal self resorts to avoid being crushed beneath the spiritual weight of those truths for which it does not want to answer. However, no truth can be eliminated by fleeing from or neglecting it. On the contrary, one who amuses themselves with such empty solace and who assumes their wretchedness to be happiness fools only themselves. They cannot escape being caught unprepared for death, taken unawares by Archangel Azrail and facing – even if their carnal self does not desire it – the formidable surprises of eternal life...

As there is no more important event for the living than death, it is essential that the majesty pertaining to tidings thereof are duly comprehended. And so, the Qur'an refers to the Hereafter, unanimously communicated by all Divine religions, as the **"Awesome Tidings"** (*Naba al-'Azim*) and has expounded it with multifarious proofs, intellectual, emotional and moral.

Those paying heed to the revelation and duly perceiving tidings of the Hereafter have avoided being deceived by fleeting bounties and have turned away from a false future to a true and eternal one. They have come to perceive that the skies, decorated with chandeliers of stars and the earth decked with assorted adornment and magnificence does not at all give the impression that it is coincidental and without purpose. Far from it, it declares with its tongue of disposition to those with intelligence that much mystery and wisdom is to be found in its every particle.

This universe, which transcends human perception and appreciation and which is furnished with great delicacy and care, constitutes a showcase of manifestations of Divine power and grandeur, with its trees and plants, animals, humans and all its inanimate beings.

A person who beholds themselves, life, the universe and events in the light of revelation with an eye to learn lessons and with wisdom, immediately understands that speaking of an impossibility of the Hereafter before the Divine power and dominion apparent in the creation of all these beings, the continuation of their existence and their being doomed to transience, is an enormously ludicrous and fanciful claim.

It must not be forgotten that a life lived without taking lesson from death is no different to a dark, ominous night. The sun of eternal happiness rises at the end of a life lived in the light of Divine truths and in servanthood to Allah. For this reason, the religion of Islam has advised the constant remembrance of and preparation for death and, as such, its beautification via the removal of its formidable face. In the words of **Mawlana Jalal al-Din al-Rumi**, Islam has conveyed the paths of meeting death with the jubilation of, as it were, a "*shab-i 'arus*", or a "**wedding night**".

Happy are the believers who are able in their inner worlds to solve the mysteries of **death** and the **afterlife** with the light of revelation and who live in the endeavour of properly preparing for death and transforming their Hereafter to an eternal bliss...

May Allah Almighty render us those who attain His good pleasure and approval by learning and practising Islam in the best possible way and who thus acquire tranquillity of heart in this world and neverending felicity in the Hereafter...

Amin...